SACRAMENTAL WHINE: VOLUME III

CHRONICLING THE INDEPENDENT SACRAMENTAL MOVEMENT

DAVID OLIVER KLING

D1293137

CONTENTS

Forward

Patriarch Shaun McCann

History is the alchemical lab that makes gold out of otherwise lead-like times. The heavy poisonous weight of difficulty both creates the raw material for and the circumstance of, transformation.

The High Middle Ages, representing a then-pinnacle of new challenges and conflicts, saw stretched out between its pinions of persecution and crusade, the birth of the mendicant Orders, the flowering of independent spiritual trajectories such as the Cathars, the heavenward architectural aspirations of the Gothic Cathedrals and the birth of the modern University system as we would recognize it now.

This itself echoes other such dichotomies from centuries prior- the consolidation of the councils of Constantinople with the rise of the Syrian Orthodox Church through the consecrated hands of Jacob Barradaeus - an example that is close to home for any Independent Sacramental cleric- Syrian orders forming a bedrock of episcopal transmission of Holy Orders to the Independent Sacramental Movement itself on the one hand, and the fact that Barradaeus was a lone wanderer and the first Episcopus Vagans of significant note and stature.

Whether history repeats or merely rhymes, the Independent Sacramental Movement finds itself as one such modern ounce of gold amidst pounds of so much modern difficulty, a melodic counterpoint to the dark notes and low frequencies of war, poverty, disease, fundamentalism that have been the sonorous waypoints of the 19th, 20th and 21st centuries, that have shaken the ground underneath our feet, our institutions, and societies.

As political, social, and spiritual bonds fray, the world becomes smaller and moves more quickly owing to a constant news cycle, the instant reporting that buoys it, social media and antisocial conduct, and a complete toolkit for dissemination of every fact, every opinion, every editorial, every nonsensical bit of information, valuable or not, in one's own pocket.

Additionally, in the race for bigger, faster, stronger, cheaper everything, this has also allowed our challenges, our wounds, our stressors, our damages, collectively and individually to move parallel to advances with greater pace than most of our lagging traditional tools to respond and reconcile them.

The slow purpose-built foundations of institutional Christianity have enabled it, for good and for ill, to weather change, and remain unmoved by the tides of most events, but its deep tangled roots have also hindered it from responding to a pace of change that is almost imperceptibly quick. Institutions respond institutionally, not individually, and our individual struggles have rapidly been raised to the level of the collective while remaining individual in context, need and solution.

The ISM did not set out to be a counterpoint or antidote to this stormy present and its uncertain future, but only to the dogmas of the so-called quiet past, and in doing so, it may have unintentionally found itself on the vanguard of a new spiritual impulse that in fact does so or at least, can serve to do.

In order for it to do so, it must now make the implicit explicit and the unconscious conscious. As the Gospel of Thomas teaches, if you bring forth what is within you, what you have will save you. If you do not have that within you, what you do not have within you will kill you.

Many institutions have been created by community or its impulse and the value of institutions is such that they can embody the ideals and strength of a community or those impulses with one clear voice and act with unified effort, but institutions more often than not address individuals accidentally, rather than intentionally.

The Independent Sacramental Movement has been built by the tools of the Churches from which it has diverged, yet it is possessed of a freedom, mobility and responsiveness that its ancestor and predecessor communities have long since lost. This in turn empowers it to address a need that is not acknowledged by those same predecessors, assuming it is seen at all. Taken in total, it now has the fortune to learn from those histories and solutions while not being tied to its problems.

Simply put, it has the ability to meet individuals where they are, their point and context of greatest need, not with structures, rules, and purity tests, but with flexibility, guide-rails, and sincerity; the organic power of community applied with the voice and narrative of an institution to the needs and journey of the individual. The Independent Sacramental Movement must scale up its service and its character and scale down its focus, rather than the converse demonstrated by the history of those who have worked the vineyard before them.

Yet, too often it seems, small independent churches have sought to replicate the past rather than learn from it; to be a version of the Churches that gave them birth instead of being the next generation of its mission.

We need not reach for a new analogy or allegory to understand this temptation- Christ himself spoke of it in the Parable of the Talents. Rather than building on, multiplying and applying these talents in a way that can be spread more fairly, more widely, more individually, and more purposefully, all too often we bury what talent we have just as we have it, out of fear it might be lost or that we will fail to preserve it.

It is exactly this fear which produces exactly this result.

So, what does the opposite of this fear and the result we get from it look like?

It looks like a movement that is unashamed to be who it is, armed with the knowledge of what it has and most importantly oriented by the compass of why it exists.

The key to much of this, of course, lies in the name itself- The Independent Sacramental Movement.

Each of these words carries a host of connotations and context concentrated in them – and often enough, each group or cleric that wears the label places a different weight on one of them over the others.

For some, it is the independent that carries the weight and gets the emphasis- usually for all the wrong reasons. Instead of indicating that they are free of the encumbrance of so many centuries of things like Western legalism or Eastern ethnocentricity, to name but a few examples- it exists as a quicker way to say, 'You're not the boss of me'. And why? To whom are we speaking, and are we sure they are even listening? If the answer is Rome, Constantinople or Canterbury – I assure you, they are not.

Extracted and contextualized beyond simply a case of obedience to Rome or to concepts like Canonicity, we need to remember that we serve people first. Which people? Surely it is not those of our jurisdictions alone, because that would not add up too much. Embracing a wider view of who we serve allows us to organically inoculate ourselves against various strains of tribalism, territorialism, as well as tyranny by an aloof hierarchy. None of these things have served our ancestor, predecessor, or parent traditions, who are much larger, much older, and much more established than we are. It looks bad on them, but it looks ridiculous on us.

Others have shifted their weight on to the foot of the word movement, refracting the light it offers in such a way as to obscure the lesson of its meaning. A movement is something that happens naturally, organically, in concert, facing the same direction with the same goals. None of this is true when we have defined ourselves in such a way as to define people out. Purity is almost always a lie as Dr. William Behun has noted. Our efforts are far more efficiently placed when we apply that zeal to the quality of our ministry, and not who is worth ministering to or for.

As a result of this dance between the bookends, the word Sacramental, oddly enough, is the one that gets neglected – but not in the way one might think.

All clergy of the ISM, the communities and laity they serve are aware of the basic sacramental reality – it is after all what makes them clergy at all. The word independence doesn't do that, the word movement as such, does not do that either.

Sacramentality is the ladder by which they arrive at their ministry, but not always the platform from which they minister.

Earlier I made reference to the approach that the ISM is ideally positioned to occupy and minister from – that of the organic power of community applied with the voice and narrative of an institution to the needs and journey of the individual.

In its quest for continued relevance and credibility, the ISM hasn't just historically sought to replicate its progenitors in an organizational way but also in a sacramental and pastoral fashion as well. As it follows the steps traced by them, it also walks into versions of the same problems and a few unique ones – which while they may or can be shrugged off by our predecessors – are potentially damaging - organizationally, pastorally and spiritually to the Independent Sacramental movement.

Seeking to stand as tall and reach as far, ISM Churches are plagued by numerous self-inflicted wounds and unforced errors to achieve but a pittance of the same effect as their mainstream counterparts.

When a church's public material says more about its pedigree, its lineage or canon law, than it does about where to receive communion, have your troubles heard or where to get a coffee with like-minded and inclusive people - you've missed the sacramental reality.

In the ordination to the Holy Priesthood – the deacon to be ordained is instructed to imitate the mysteries they celebrate – they are not instructed to merely imitate the ones who celebrate them. The key is in the mystery, not in the minister.

Denis McNamara in his work Catholic Church Architecture and the Spirit of the Liturgy (2009) writes, *"And so the church we build today is indeed an important theological thing. In its sacramental reality, it does three things: recalls and fulfills the temple; tells of our current condition as earthly fallen beings living with grace available in the time of image; and gives a foretaste of our heavenly future. It is concurrently a place of anamnesis, imminent experience of God's presence, and anticipated eschatology. Like the liturgy, it contracts time by pulling the past forward and pulling the future backward, all for our sanctification now"*

Again - the Liturgy "contracts time by pulling the past forward and pulling the future backward, all for our sanctification now".

This is what we are to imitate, this is what we are to replicate, this is what we are to emulate. The Independent Sacramental Movement has it within itself and all the attendant conditions and strengths to do this. We must let the Divine speak for itself in the words of mystery and silence and not through our own mouths in the form of every twenty-dollar word we know strung in a row like gaudy Christmas lights. Make straight the way of experience but not your experience – unless asked. Open a path for them to have their experience, not yours.

This isn't just about creating a space where the Divine can be heard, this is also about how and to whom we are speaking, who our audience is and who is listening. Reserve the theological terms for topical discussion, and Monday night classes. People are theologically smarter and more literate than they have ever been and want their spiritual journey to matter as much to another as they take it themselves, but in order to want to engage more, it has to be relevant first. They'll understand you when you talk about transformation, but perhaps less readily when you say Metanoia first. Your vocabulary isn't what signifies your ordination.

This is a lesson I've had to learn and re-learn across two decades of ministry as a priest serving in a community that embraces Gnostic thought and scripture. Many of the foundational concepts are unfamiliar to most ears, yet deeply indicative of the human spiritual journey. There will be time for precision and exploration, I promise.

Additionally, seeded throughout the context of the difficulties I outlined at the outset of this piece, is one more additional obstacle – the Church as a metaphysical reality has not only changed with time, the physical, social and spiritual realm in which it works has changed.

Played out since the advent of the Roman Catholic Church's Second Vatican Council but present well before it, is the secularization, education and increasing mobility of the laity. The laity has undergone a radical change. This is a good thing even though it may narrow the scope of what we can do.

In both the distant mists of time and within near living memory, the Priest has embodied many roles and facets in their work – part social worker, part schoolteacher, part psychologist, part counsellor and part Hierophant. As society has undergone shifts in status, education, access and need – almost all of these roles have been secularized, formalized and professionalized into the distinct and licensed professions we know them to be now.

All of them except one.

The English word priest has some of its roots in two terms- the Latin Sacerdos and the Greek Presbyteros. The former refers to that of one who offers sacrifice, a priest in the ritual sense, and the latter means quite directly – Elder.

In an effort to keep pace with the times, retain a fading social status, and inch further along the twin paths of relevance and viability, ISM Clergy have attempted to claim and reclaim these facets for which the majority of us have neither the training or the resources to do so. And it risks as much harm as good.

Let me be clear - I am not suggesting that ISM Clergy should avoid opportunities for secular education, training, or experience- far from it, take every opportunity you can get- these skills have a real need in the world, and there are real obstacles towards people receiving them from the now accepted venues- but rather that in chasing four rabbits, they catch none, and people get less than the help they need, with the added bonus of wasted time at best, and permanent damage at worst.

A priest should be equipped with the training and skills to recognize when someone in their charge needs more assistance than they can provide and enough knowledge, patience and pastoral care skills to help accompany them and navigate the world of seeking that help.

These facets and roles are somewhat covered and baked into the concept of the Elder or Presbyteros as we know it, even if we cannot fulfill it in the same way as our predecessors - but Sacerdos has no true secular counterpart. We should embrace that. Again- the key is in the mystery not the minister. Let the Divine speak for itself in the mysteries you celebrate – be it at the bedside of one who is ill, the new life of one who is born or an adult that comes to the spiritual life anew, or those who embark upon a lifelong journey of companionship through marriage.

I opened this exploration by highlighting how the alchemy of difficult history seems to produce both the opportunities and tools for transformation and transmutation. We are living in one such difficult time - a time in which people continue to seek meaning and the comfort of the spiritually familiar without all the familiar problems that have come with it. The ISM, being focused first and foremost upon the sacramental reality – has a set of rites and tools before it that not only transcend the times in which we live but touch upon something that few things in the secular world can- that of the Timeless.

Yet unlike those who have gone before us, we have access to these things free of social or political assumptions and biases, or denominational accretions through centuries of reactionary rules.

So, having outlined what I see as some of the strengths of the Independent Sacramental Movement as well as its historical weak spots, this brings us squarely to - why this book and the catalogue of insightful interviews upon which it is based?

Alchemy is a process of many stages - and this is equally true when applied to the Independent Sacramental Movement. The difficulty of history has produced the conditions, the material and the equipment in order to make possible the spiritual gold of a fulfilling path for those seek it. Whether it is a seeker whose path has been unfulfilling, or worse, damaged, by our predecessor communities or even other independent communities, or an opportunity for vocation and service for someone whose life and experience doesn't neatly fit within the well-worn grooves and pitfalls of larger, older Churches – the ISM has an opportunity to address the gaps, and reach the places and people that have no place to go.

We have all the things we need, but initiating, stewarding and refining the process is yet to come in some cases, unfinished in others and can always use more refinement in most.

This is why the alchemy of Sacramental Whine and the ministry of Bishop Kling is needed and timely – it has opened a path to honest dialogue, needed questions, and self-examination as well as the ability to see the approaches, successes and failures our of sisters and brothers at the altar in other churches and learn from them.

In order to get where we are going, we must start where we are at, and this cannot be done without dialogue, questioning or self-examination. It also cannot be done without humble service, and the posture, questions and perspective of David Oliver Kling is service. We wouldn't follow a guide who isn't on the path, and we can no wise expect others to do the same for us unless we are walking and living it – Bishop Kling has exemplified many ways in which we can do that, especially by not placing himself as the focus of the work.

In time, as we refine ourselves, our intention and our materials, through the process begun by these books and the podcast of the same name, the work we do in the world, with and for each other, will likewise be refined and enough gold produced, not to adorn our physical sanctuaries, vesture and altars- but the hearts of those who seek life more abundantly.

+ Most Rev. Shaun McCann, Ep.Gn.
Patriarch of the Apostolic Johannite Church

DEDICATION

BISHOP THOMAS T. BRYANT

When I think of my Ecclesial colleague and dear friend, Bishop Joseph Kenneth Grieboski I am uncharacteristically at a loss for words. Needless to say, I relied upon his knowledge, broad ecumenical and interfaith connections, and "feel" of how faith, life and real-world problems intersect. Since the 24th of February 2021, when I learned of his death my sadness and ecclesiastical loneliness has been intense. I have found that I am less certain in my decisions not having Joe to call, wrestle through the issues, and receive one of his typical long, but extremely valuable e-mails summarizing the pertinent factors. I also found that I don't laugh as much at Diocesan gatherings. His wit was delightful as it could be properly penetrating. Joe always spoke the truth, but always in love.

I think of an event that happened several months prior to my birth. Then President John F. Kennedy (one, by the way, of which I see similarities in style, thinking and values with Bishop Joe) called a meeting on April 29, 1962. It was a roomful of Nobel Prize winners who had been called to the White House for honoring. President Kennedy, while recognizing the intelligence and wisdom of those gathered, chose to illuminate another. Kennedy said:

> "I think this is the most extraordinary collection of talent, of human knowledge, that has ever been gathered together at the White House, with the possible exception of when Thomas Jefferson dined alone. Someone once said that Thomas Jefferson was a gentleman of 32 who could calculate an eclipse, survey an estate, tie an artery,

plan an edifice, try a cause, break a horse, and dance the minuet."

While I never saw Joe dance, I have no doubt when he did he not only swept his beloved Tracy off her feet, he would have all of us watching and thinking "this is beautiful." I truly miss my beautiful friend but know his legacy will continue and this fitting dedication will continue to spread the love for the Catholic Faith to which Bishop Joseph Grieboski committed his life.

The Rt. Rev. Dr. Thomas T. Bryant
Eastern USA Diocese, Independent Old Catholic Church

INTRODUCTION

BISHOP DAVID OLIVER KLING

As I write this introduction, my daughter, Vivianne Leona Kling, is four and a half years old. It brings her joy to watch "her shows" on YouTube through our television. One show is a short, animated video about an Elasmosaurus, which was an aquatic dinosaur. In the video the Elasmosaurus sings, "The Ocean, Ocean where I live; the Ocean, Ocean where I love." As I sit down to write this introduction, I have that chorus from the song stuck in my head and it reminds me of my work within the Independent Sacramental Movement or ISM. The Independent Sacramental Movement is my ocean. It is where I live, and it is where and what I love.

The Independent Sacramental Movement is a majestic and wonderful ocean, but like the physical oceans in our world, there are deep shadows in the depths of the ocean. I think it is important to point out those shadows when we see them and shed light on them. Illuminate those problem areas within the Independent Sacramental Movement. The podcast, Sacramental Whine: An Independent Sacramental Movement Podcast, has always tried to shed light on the problem areas within our ocean of a Movement. We need to police our own.

In the past few years, I have discovered at least two bishops consecrated over the Internet. The first claimed the consecration as a long distance "reiki-like" attunement and ordination and the second consecration held justification based on it being illicit but valid. Ordination or consecration done over the Internet is invalid, regardless of any claims or justifications. I am still sad that these practices continue to take place, often at the hands of good people, thinking they are following the dictates of the Holy Spirit. When we discover these shenanigans are occurring, we should collectively, as a community, call them out and say, "No!" Sacraments require matter, form, and intention. It is not a two out of three works fine, as sacraments require all three to maintain the efficacy of the sacraments.

Yes, I am critical of bishops who conduct online ordinations and consecrations. I will always be critical of this practice and do not accept any of the arguments used to justify these practices. I was looking through some essays that I had written in the past and found one from 2004 titles, *"A Look at Ordination and Consecration,"* the essay is a look the sacrament of Holy Orders from a Gnostic and esoteric point of view which is my background, especially back then.

A Look at Ordination and Consecration
[An Essay From 2004]

There are many different forms of ordination. The type of ordination that I wish to address in this entry is the type of ordination that is transmitted through apostolic succession by a bishop - in my case within the Sacramental Christian Movement (also known as the Independent Sacramental Movement), in my case of the Gnostic variety.

This is a specific type of ordination and involves a laying on of hands by a bishop and an energy transfer by passing on a lineage of apostolic succession. This succession (allegedly) originated with Jesus Christ and was passed onto his disciples and - via a succession of bishops through the centuries - to eventually reside within the bishop conducting an ordination or consecration in our modern times. This sort of ordination/consecration is special because it contains this energy transfer and that energy transfer does have an effect upon the person being ordained/consecrated.

In a theological sense this energy transfer places an "indelible" characteristic upon the soul or spirit of the individual being ordained, that is a characteristic that cannot be removed. This alteration, conducted sacramentally, is similar to the sacraments of baptism and confirmation because it changes who you become after the ordination takes place. For those individuals who subscribe to the idea of reincarnation I would even hypothesize that the indelible characteristic of ordination is passed onto subsequent incarnations, and because of this a level of responsibility needs to be acknowledged by the potential ordinand. Things to consider:

- Do I accept this ordination/consecration forever in this lifetime?
- Do I accept this ordination/consecration forever for all subsequent lifetimes?

You might find yourself, in the future, in a position where you might no longer subscribe to a desire for priestly or apostolic ministry but the status of your spirit or soul is not changed by your willingness to "leave" a sacramentally ordained or consecrated life. It will still be there no matter what your future disposition becomes. This is something very important to consider, and to evaluate in your life.

Something else to consider is the person who is ordaining or consecrating you. The originator of the priesthood/episcopacy is Jesus Christ, however, when an ordination or consecration is conducted those individuals within the succession are also passing something of themselves on to the new ordinand, and this is an important consideration.

Things to consider:

- Is the person who is about to ordain/consecrate me a person with whom I would normally be "in communion" with?
- How do I view the person ordaining/consecrating me? Do I respect him or her?
- Would I ordain/consecrate the person who is ordaining/consecrating me if the situation where reversed?

These are important questions to ask yourself because an ordination/consecration is a very powerful energy exchange and the energy passed onto the new deacon, priest or bishop will affect each of us in different ways.

Again, something else to consider is how you plan on coping with the changes that will take place after an ordination or consecration. Instead of looking at this energy exchange as, "I'm a new priest" or "I'm a new bishop", think of it as you now being a priestly initiate or episcopal initiate into the sacred mysteries of the priesthood and episcopate. The essence of the priesthood and episcopate is mystical in nature and NOT administrative or jurisdictional -- these are constructs resulting from the priesthood and episcopacy and not directly linked to the mystery of the sacrament. The mystery of the sacrament is about the sacraments themselves and not about anything else. All too often I have seen bishops within the Sacramental Movement focus their attention on the jurisdictional or administrative side of episcopacy. This is not what the sacramental initiation of consecration is about -- it is about the fullness of priestly initiation and the fullness of the sacraments.

Things to consider before ordination and consecration:
- What was my life like before ordination/consecration?
- Am I equipped to deal with a major change in my life?
- Am I ready to deal with the added responsibility that this change will bring upon me?

Things to consider after ordination and consecration:
- How has my life changed since ordination/consecration?
- Do I find myself depressed? What will I do about this depression?
- What is my support network, do they understand ordination/consecration? Do they support my decision? What sort of support do I have from other priests and/or bishops?

Having a support network is important for a new priestly or episcopal initiate. It is important because the effect that it has on an individual is specific and peculiar to each individual. Having had experience with energy transfer and initiations I was somewhat prepared for my episcopal consecration and was able to channel the effect in a positive manner: I left full time employment and went back to school full time, radically changed my lifestyle (had to slim things down) and had to deal with the changes that result from becoming a full time student again. I had a supportive network for my life changes, but not necessarily a supportive network for my decision to get consecrated (although it has gotten much better). The effect of my consecration could have been horrific since I was dealing with the recent death of my father a month prior to my consecration and dealing with the depression resulting from that loss. However, being aware of the effects of consecration helped me ride the storm of emotions I was feeling at the time -- both from dealing with death and also from dealing with the death of myself as the old me was replaced by a new "me."

As a final note I want to also point out that consecration is not about wearing purple, wearing a mitre, or other episcopal regalia. All these items are externals and not absolutely necessary for administering the sacraments. Please ask yourself, "Do I fantasize more about wearing a mitre than imagining myself as a apostolic representative of Christ?" The deep responsibility of ordination and consecration far outweighs any sort of external or "episcopal privilege."

One more point to consider. In the Sacramental Christian Movement (also known as the Independent Sacramental Movement) the idea of jurisdiction is a construction of our modern sensibilities. It is simply absurd to think "if I create it they will come." Jurisdictions (i.e., new "denominations") are created almost every day, and they also die every day. What exists is the episcopacy, the priesthood, and the deaconate. Until there is a renaissance within the sacramental movement and circumstances radically change the situation will be as it is now, which is very fluid. If a priest doesn't like his bishop he or she will simply go someplace else. If a bishop is unhappy with his or her fellow bishops he or she will create his or her own jurisdiction. This is the nature of this movement. It is unfortunate that this is this way, but it is simply the nature of the movement. This is why I view consecration and ordination as an initiatory experience and not simply as admission into a jurisdiction clergy roles. The apostolic succession sees through any jurisdictional lines and does not recognize "clergy roles" or "jurisdictional canon law". It acknowledges only correct "matter and form."

<hr />

That essay is almost twenty years old, but I think it still holds up. I think online ordinations and consecrations are something we should avoid.

Other areas within the Independent Sacramental Movement require our attention too, such as proper priestly formation and even building up a sense of ecumenical community that spans jurisdictional lines. A couple of years ago, several bishops got together and created the United Conference of Apostolic Sacramental Bishops (UCASB); however, this project failed to succeed. There have been several attempts over the years for bishops and jurisdictions to seek cooperation and mutual support, but all have failed. The Independent Sacramental Movement is often a chaotic bunch of people, with several jurisdictions trying to "reinvent the wheel," and find their voice in an already boisterous ocean of personalities and voices.

In the Independent Sacramental Movement collaboration can be challenging, but I hope that some fruit will eventually emerge from the ashes of the UCASB.

This book, Volume III, speaks to the memory of Bishop Joseph Grieboski. I am sad that he passed away and hope that his memory will continue and that the passage of time will not forget him. He was someone that I did not know well, but whose growing friendship I valued. If more people within the Independent Sacramental Movement would take a moment to "be more like Joe," the waters of the ISM would be a more harmonious and tranquil place.

Rt. Rev. David Oliver Kling, M.Div
Co-Presiding Bishop, Ancient Apostolic Church of Alexandria
Affiliated Bishop, The Ascension Alliance

CHAPTER ONE

— ⁑ —

"BE WHO YOU ARE"

FATHER JOSEPH K. GRIEBOSKI

"Truly, I say to you, today you will be with me in Paradise."
- Luke 23:43

Joseph K. Grieboski
December 27, 1974 – February 24, 2021

This interview was conducted in August of 2020 and made public on August 15th. In October of 2020 Father Joseph Grieboski was consecrated a bishop and sadly he passed away in early 2021. This volume of *Sacramental Whine: Chronicling the Independent Sacramental Movement* is dedicated to his memory.

Requiescat in Pace.

The Most Reverend Joseph Kenneth Grieboski, 46, of Alexandria, Virginia, passed away in his home on February 24, 2021, after a brief illness. Joseph was born in Scranton, Pennsylvania on December 27, 1974, and adopted by Joseph Bernard and Patricia Ann Grieboski on March 6, 1975. A graduate of Our Lady of Peace and Scranton Preparatory School, Joe traveled the world and pursued interests in religious and political affairs, especially religious freedom, and human rights, even in his early years. In 1992, Joe began his studies at Georgetown University in Washington, DC. He graduated with honors in 1996 with a Bachelor of Science in Foreign Service after spending a year at the Hebrew University of Jerusalem, Israel. He continued his studies at Georgetown and earned a Master of Arts in National Security Studies in 2000. He received a Doctor of Divinity degree from Agape Seminary in 2020 and received an honorary Doctorate of Humane Letters from Marywood University in Scranton, Pennsylvania in 2008. Ordained a bishop in the Independent Old Catholic Church in October 2020, Bishop Grieboski is survived by his beloved wife, Tracy Casey Grieboski.

Together with Tracy, he worked tirelessly to improve human rights and health around the world and domestically and was a true servant of God. His laugh was boundlessly contagious, and he was every stranger's, and every animal's best friend. He loved fiercely, and his and Tracy's love, partnership, and admiration for one another inspired many. Joe leaves behind countless adored friends and colleagues around the world and will be desperately missed. Grieboski founded The Institute on Religion and Public Policy, a well-respected and world-renowned non-governmental organization at the forefront of religious freedom advocacy, as well as Grieboski Global Strategies, a human rights focused consulting firm. Most recently, he was serving as the Head of the Global Bank North American Representative Office, an extension of both his ministry and legacy. He served as Secretary for Ecumenical, Interfaith, and Global Engagement of the Independent Old Catholic Church, making him the point person for the Church's religious, political, and diplomatic engagement. He served as the Chair of the Faith-based Council of National Stop the Violence Alliance, was a Senior Fellow at The Dietrich Bonhoeffer Institute, Co-Chair of the Coalition for a Hate-Free Internet, Secretary of the Board of Directors of the Interfaith Alliance and served on the board of many other organizations and foundations working towards establishing peace and furthering human rights.

Joseph was the Former Chair of the US State Department Strategic Dialogue with Civil Society Working Group on Religion and Foreign Policy Subgroup on International Development and Humanitarian Assistance under Secretary of State Hillary Clinton, and in April 2010 he was inducted into the International Board of Sponsors of the Martin Luther King Jr. International Chapel at Morehouse College - Martin Luther King's alma mater. The award honors those who have made significant contributions to the civil and human rights nonviolence movement in the tradition of the Reverend Dr. Martin Luther King. He dedicated his life to the service of God and the betterment of humankind.

KLING: My first question is what is your elevator speech? How would you describe the Independent Sacramental Movement to somebody who has no idea what it is?

GRIEBOSKI: That's a great question. The best way to answer it is Catholicism existed before Christianity did and the Independent Sacramental Movement recognizes that the churches created by the apostles were carried on before the middle-ages. The Sacramental Movement isn't against the beginning or where we are now, it is trying to skip the middle. It's getting rid of all the politics that existed under the middle-ages and where Kings and popes fought. It's getting back to what we actually believe. Getting back to what Jesus taught and how we can live that life and expand that spirituality.

KLING: A follow-up on that. Would you consider that more of a reconstruction process?

GRIEBOSKI: The Independent Sacramental Movement isn't, as far as I'm concerned, Protestant or Reformed. It's not trying to recreate something and it's not trying to replace Rome. This is what Christ and the apostles taught. This is where we are now. That's not to say that the stuff that Rome did over the years, isn't bad. In fact, we use and adopt it. It's all a part of the collective magisterium of true orthodox Christianity. We're not recreating or reconstructing something. When you make a steak, you sometimes have to cut off the fat in order to put it on the grill. That's where we are in terms of this version of Catholicism and Christianity. We're cutting off the fat and making sure that we have the prime meat.

KLING: I like that. We've cut the fat off.

GRIEBOSKI: Yeah, we've cut off the fat.

KLING: Until recently, I was not aware of the Independent Old Catholic Church. Can you talk about the Independent Old Catholic Church and your studies at Agape Seminary? I'm interested in why you chose to be a priest in the Independent Sacramental Movement. With your resume I suspect you would have been welcomed anywhere. What drew you to the Independent Sacramental Movement in general and the Independent Old Catholic Church in particular?

GRIEBOSKI: Oliver, let me answer your second question first. I was very Roman for a very long time. I was adopted through a Catholic adoption agency. I was named in a Polish Roman Catholic parish, Our lady of Częstochowa. I was an altar boy to Bishop John O'Connor when he was in Scranton before he became Cardinal O'Connor in New York. John Paul II and I knew each other exceedingly well and spoke quarterly, if not monthly, depending on the time period. As I aged, I had a calling, I always had a calling. I always knew I wanted to be a priest. People would ask me, "Why didn't you become a priest?" And my answer was, "It had nothing to do with celibacy. It had everything to do with obedience." I know how dumb I am. I don't want to work for someone dumber than I am.

I also know that I'm just going to be sent to preach to the squirls in Montana at some point. But that being said, as I continued my life, and I had my professional successes I never lost the desire for priestly ministry. I knew there was never going to be a place for me in Rome, the fight over ordaining married men in the Amazon that just happened. Rome's just not in a position to be able to want people who want to be married and want to minister. I went searching and I came across the Independent Old Catholic Church.

I reached out to them. I hadn't gone to church in a while because I felt a fundamental separation between Rome and me. I can't blame Rome, Rome doesn't shift, nor should it. That's why it's the Roman Catholic Church. But I had shifted, and I found that I wasn't where Rome was, and I didn't want to be where Rome was, and I went searching and I came across the Independent Old Catholic Church. I emailed the primate. I told them my desire, and he called me, and he said, "Do you have a date by which you want to be ordained?" I said, "Well, you know, my mother passed on this date in this year. I'd really like to be able to say a Memorial mass for her." He dropped it, that was it and said, "We need to talk to the dean of the seminary. He'll figure out whether or not you deserve to go to seminary."

My very first call with now, Bishop Tom Bryant, he says to me, "I understand your mom's memorial is this date, and that you'd like to say mass for her." I said, "Yes." He responded, "Okay, let's make that happen." I said, "I don't understand," and he goes on, "We're going to get you ordained so that you can say that mass." And I said, "I don't understand." And he goes, "This is what Jesus does. Jesus takes care of his own. You want to celebrate her life in a priestly way? Why would God ever say no to that?" Oliver, I found a family that I could never have found in Rome because Rome is always about rules. It's not about compassion, but I found rules and compassion. I found Mater et magistra outside of Rome.

KLING: Can you talk a little bit more about your studies at the seminary there?

GRIEBOSKI: Agape is a fully online seminary. They don't require any in-person study. It focuses very heavily on the writings of Father Richard McBrien. What I like about Agape is that it's a place for Lutherans, Methodists, Anglicans, and Independent Catholics. The seminary has studies for all of those and how those communities fit within the Old Catholic -Independent Sacramental Movement. What's great about the seminary is the diversity. I'm High Church Roman when I say mass, my Bishop comes from a Methodist and Lutheran background, and he's more Middle Church. One of our priests in New England comes from the Orthodox Church, and he's even Higher Church than I am. We have another priest who comes from a Low Episcopalian methodology. Within our canonicity, we talk about the necessities within a liturgy to be considered a valid liturgy, and we all recognize that the true presence is in the Eucharist. It's a wonderful panoply of approaches to the liturgy without rules requiring how it's done.

KLING: So, there's freedom?

GRIEBOSKI: Exactly. There's liberty, and you talked in the introduction about my background in religious liberty. One of the things that I love about the IOCC is that while they give us standards, as I mentioned, such as, these are the things that need to happen to be considered a legitimate Eucharist. There are no rules by which you have to do this to do this, to this, to this, etc. Just make sure this is all in there, and it doesn't have to be in the order we say. Just make sure these things are there. There's a faith in the liberty of expression to worship.

KLING: It sounds like there is accountability, but accountability with liberty and freedom.

GRIEBOSKI: Exactly! There must be accountability. I mean we are a liturgical church. We are a Catholic church. There is a magisterium and there must be accountability, but the wonderful thing is that it's within how we celebrate, not just the Eucharist, but all the sacraments.

KLING: In my own jurisdiction, the Community of Saint George, which is a part of the Young Rite which is a part of the Liberal Catholic Church tradition, we have a standard liturgy. That's essentially the Liberal Catholic Church liturgy, but with a few differences. That is our standard liturgy, which we expect everybody to know, and to be aware of and to be able to use and be able to say mass in that manner; however, we also allow for experimental liturgies. The only criteria is that it be approved by one of our bishops because we need to make sure it still has the proper matter form and the proper intention.

GRIEBOSKI: Absolutely. And again, I'm not saying that within the IOCC, everybody's doing whatever they want to do, as I said, under canon law, we have a prescription by which the Eucharist needs to be done. These things are canonically set, but as you said, we allow for expression within those limits. Here's the prescription for this, here's this, here's, this, here's this, but in between those we're allowed to have expressions of true faith. That's the wonderful thing about the Independent Sacramental Movement is that we recognize tradition, we recognize the methodologies of theology, we recognize what order is required, but we also have freedom to expand when possible, without breaking the necessary rules.

KLING: Thank you for sharing that, what I am really interested in learning is why you picked the Independent Sacramental Movement, and you answered that, and to summarize, you come from a high church Catholic background. If you're looking at ministry in that context, there are not a whole lot of options out there. There is the Orthodox Church, but for most people, that's not an option. For those of us here in the USA the Episcopal Church would seem to be the likely alternative, but that's a daunting option. I know somebody who struggled with being ordained a deacon for seven years before the bishop would finally ordain him, and it seems like an elitist club that is very difficult to get into, to join the Episcopal Church priesthood.

GRIEBOSKI: I'll tell you a story. We incardinated a new priest into our diocese in October of last year, and we did it at the National Cathedral. The National Cathedral has been wonderful to us, The Episcopal Church is a very good friend to our denomination, and here within the DC region we have wonderful relationships after the incardination. We went to a Washington DC, iconic establishment known as Martin's Tavern. So, you've got three priests sitting around a table, and each of us has had a drink and somebody leans over and says, "So, you guys Catholic? You Protestant? What are you?" Our bishop said, "No, we're Old Catholic." And he said, "Explain that." Our bishop did some explaining, and the man says, What's the difference between you and Episcopalians?" The bishop summed up the historical differences, but the bishop offered one thing that sets up apart. To answer your question of why did I go with the Independent Sacramental Movement rather than the Episcopal Church? Because we believe in the true presence and I can never get away from that. It doesn't matter what denomination or movement. I will never get away from the reality that if I receive communion, it must be because it is the true presence, and the wonderful thing about the Independent Sacramental Movement is that we have not moved down that Protestant question of, well it's consubstantiation, or it's a representation. No, this is the true Body and Blood of our Lord Jesus Christ.

KLING: Yeah. That's a good point, and if you look at the history of the Anglican Church, since its foundation to our modern times they have gone through periods of Low Church, High Church, Low Church, High Church. They have been all over the place, and I think that was one of the reasons why Rome declared Anglican holy orders invalid at one point, and the Old Catholic Church of Utrecht up until I think the 1930s did not consider Anglican orders valid either.

GRIEBOSKI: That's right. Even the Church of Utrecht, which all the Independent Sacramental Movements jurisdictions are children of in a certain sense. They had questions about that because of the question of the true presence. What I find interesting now is Rome's argument with the Anglicans is all about the ordination of women. it's less about the presence of Christ in the Eucharist than it is about whether or not a woman can wear a collar.

KLING: Right! Looking over your resume, which is very impressive and very interesting, brings me to my next question. I'm sure you have a lot of fascinating stories that you could tell. Can you summarize your work in religious freedom and advocacy and share how it informs your work as a priest, or talk about how your work as a priest informs your religious freedom advocacy work?

GRIEBOSKI: When I was doing my religious freedom work as an avid Roman Catholic, people would always say to me, "How can you advocate for Muslims, Jews, Jehovah's Witnesses, Mormons, Scientologists, all the rest?" I would respond, "Look, we live in a supermarket. If I believe my faith, if I believe what I'm taught, that we are given free will, then we have to choose and where religious freedom becomes the question is in places like Greece or Russia or India, where religious nationalism comes into place. If your religion is really doing what it's supposed to be doing, you don't need the government to protect you." My faith has always driven my religious freedom because I believe that God gives us free will to choose what we believe.

I'm not a fan of the concept of evangelization. I think evangelization causes a problem, especially within a societal context or when we send people abroad because we don't teach cultural or societal realities. It places them into physical harm and potential physical problems, legal problems, and religious freedom needs to be understood within the larger context, not just theologically, but legally. Religious freedom needs to be understood within a human rights framework, about how best expressions of faith do not necessarily mean breaking laws or advancing ideas, or advancing revolution, but how best do we use the concept of what we believe to free the human soul?

KLING: I'm interested in your work with the interfaith Alliance. Can you talk a little bit more about that?

GRIEBOSKI: The Interfaith Alliance was founded about 25 years ago to be a domestic interfaith religious freedom organization and what the Interfaith Alliance does so effectively is recognizes that religious freedom issues are not just about institutional versus individual. It's also about social justice issues in a larger context that includes societal issues. When we talk about religious freedom, if a gay couple is not allowed to get married because the County Clerk doesn't believe in it, those are her issues. That's not a protection of the County Clerk's religious freedom, it's a violation of the religious freedom of the couple. The abortion question, I can't tell you the number of people who say, "Abortion is a violation of my religious freedom." Okay, that's great, but that's not how religious freedom works.

One of the wonderful things about how the Interfaith Alliance works is that it builds coalitions. It works with social justice movements. It advances the rights of individuals and communities to respect, protect, and promote their beliefs without external, both governmental and societal prosecution. When I say prosecution, I don't necessarily mean legal. I mean social media. I mean societal. I mean in the world. In the political world in which we live today groups are persecuted everywhere. The Interfaith Alliance does a wonderful job of providing an umbrella to protect those communities that are facing persecution, but also advancing a larger goal of religious freedom which means religious freedom for everyone. In this larger sense, it also means protecting the first amendment.

KLING: A follow-up question. Dealing with all the different things that you're involved with, the Independent Sacramental Movement is extremely diverse, and there are a lot of people that unfortunately, did not have the opportunity to get educated and become up to date on everything that's going on in the world. I'm looking at the different things that you've done in the different organizations that you've worked with and I'm especially interested in your work with various Islamic organizations that protect the rights of Muslims. I currently work with Muslims for Progressive Values. What is one thing that you think people in the Independent Sacramental Movement should be aware of that's going on globally that doesn't necessarily have to do with the Independent Sacramental Movement but has to do with the world and what's going on now. What is something that they should be aware of that they may not be?

GRIEBOSKI: Your question may potentially be my PhD thesis! There is a rise of nationalism. Some of it hides behind religion. Some of it hides behind ideology and some of it hides behind race. One of the things that anyone within the Independent Sacramental Movement needs to watch globally is where is religion being used as an excuse or a cover for fascism, for authoritarianism, or for dictatorship. I will happily out Viktor Orbán, the Prime Minister of Hungary. I've known Viktor for a decade. He hides behind the idea of being a populist, but he uses religion as a cover for authoritarian activities. Ten years ago, they deregistered all of the religions in Hungary except for fourteen of them. Then if any other religion wanted to be back on the list of accepted groups you had to have the approval of the Minister of Justice and two-thirds of a vote of parliament.

Our Christian friends on the Right love him because of his abortion position, and because he fundamentally dislikes Muslims. He's built fences all around hungry. So, the Syrian refugees or Turkish refugees cannot come into Hungary. We need to recognize that Christianity and its intersection with politics is the problem. If you are going to intersect Christianity with politics, it's not supposed to be about ideology. It's supposed to be what Jesus said. If your intersection, as a Christian with politics is going to happen, it needs to be based on the Sermon on the Mount. It needs to be based on the Passion and it needs to be based on the resurrection. Those are the only ways and what Jesus told us was only two rules that God cared about; love God with your whole heart, mind and soul, and love your neighbour as yourself.

If you don't do that as a Christian in politics, then you're not actually a Christian. These are the things that I hope people understand, that this isn't technically about politics. This is about Christianity. If you're going to be involved in political activity or in politics, make sure that if you claim to be a Christian, you're doing it from the base that Christ said we should come.

KLING: Well said, thank you for that. I hope people understand what you are stating because that's a good message. I work as a hospice chaplain and occasionally I conduct worship services at nursing homes. I usually preached on those two things; love God with your whole heart, your mind, and your soul, and love your neighbor as yourself. The elderly people in the nursing homes are often in wheelchairs and sometimes they like to fight with each other and bicker with one another. They need to hear that message just as much as everybody else does, which I don't think gets preached enough.

GRIEBOSKI: It's funny, you mentioned that. As a hospice chaplain, you understand this better than anyone. The Fourth Commandment, "Honor, thy father and mother." It doesn't mean that kids need to listen to what their parents tell them. It was biblical social security. Take care of them, take care of your parents. Don't leave them by the side of the road. This is one of the social justice issues I have fundamental problems with is that people claim to be Christian yet dump their parents into long-term facilities, and then never see them. I mean, honor thy father and mother means to make sure they're okay, take care of them until God has said, "I want to bring them home."

KLING: That's Right! My next question deals your greatest challenge. What has been your greatest challenge in ministry and or your work in general?

GRIEBOSKI: My greatest challenge in ministry is coming from a small church. It's getting people to understand who and what we are and explaining this, and I'm sure you know this within the Independent Sacramental Movement. When you say Old Catholic Church, people are like, "Oh, so you only do things with the Latin mass and you don't believe in this you don't believe in that." There is intellectual confusion. Then there's actual reality. We're all Pauline, bivocational. We all have other jobs that we do while trying to minister. One of the greatest challenges that I have faced within my ministry is understanding.

Helping people come to the idea that Catholic doesn't always mean Rome and that I can like and appreciate Pope Francis and what he does and what he says, but I also don't have to listen to him. I don't have to take orders from him. The other side of that coin is that because we are bivocational is creating sacred space for people to worship, it becomes much more difficult. That's not just part of the ministry issue, now that we've got COVID and quarantine, that adds to it.

In terms of my larger professional challenges, no one wants to listen to anyone talk about religious freedom. I was one of the authors of the International Religious Freedom act in 1998, and when we created the law there was a lot of people who rightfully said, "Isn't this just a propagation of evangelical proselytization?" Back then I argued, "This is the rights of everybody. We're protecting everybody." Fast forward, now we're living in a world where Mike Pompeo has basically said, it's about Evangelicals.

Governments are putting in money, but it says everything when the next government to host the next International Meeting on Religious Freedom is Poland, which has problems with racial issues, with LGTBQ issues, with women's rights issues. When religious freedom is taken out of context, rather than placed as a central part in a larger context of democracy and human rights that is a major fundamental problem for me while I promote religious freedom. I don't do it outside of context.

KLING: My final question is what has been your greatest blessing?

GRIEBOSKI: My wife, and I know that sounds like what everybody should say. I have had a lot of blessings. I was adopted by two of the most amazing people who have ever lived, and they gave me the grounding and the worldview and freedom to be who I am. Honestly, my greatest blessing is my wife. She gives me the freedom and the Liberty to go fight the fights you need to fight. If there's a dragon, go get it Saint George. If there's a windmill, I got a donkey for you. My wife has been a wonderful blessing and a tremendous asset in the fight to fight the good fight. If there's one thing I can say to people, always fight the good fight. Whether you think you're going to win or not.

KLING: How would you define that good fight?

GRIEBOSKI: If you believe in something, stand up for it. If you don't believe in something, stand up against it. We, as Christians are called to be active, we're not called to be passive. The worst thing to ever happen to Christianity was Theodosius making it the state religion so that everybody can come out and say, "You're just a Christian." The reality is we as Christians are called by Christ to do good, and Paul tells us, "You will be judged by your actions." That is where we need to stand up for what's right, stand up against what's not right, and be who you are, we are called to be who we are in Christ and through Christ. If we can't do that, then we need greater support from Christ through Christ in Christ. The fact is we are called to do that, it is our reality. I had a wonderful friend many years ago who said to me, "I really believe that when our judgment day comes, God's not going to ask us, how many converts did you make? How many masses did you go to? God's going to look at me and say, did you learn how to love?" That's ultimately what this means, standing up for what's right. It is standing up for love.

"Cheap grace is the grace we bestow on ourselves. Cheap grace is the preaching of forgiveness without requiring repentance, baptism without church discipline, Communion without confession... Cheap grace is grace without discipleship, grace without the cross, grace without Jesus Christ, living and incarnate."
- Dietrich Bonhoeffer

Concluding Thoughts

This volume is dedicated to the memory of Bishop Joseph Grieboski. When I first reached out to him for an interview, I asked him to send me his bio. When I received it, I looked it over and thought, "There is no way this is real." I started to investigate his biographical claims and discovered, "This guy is the real deal." I did not get to know Joseph as well as I would have liked before he died, but the interactions I did have with him are memories that I cherish.

His closing words stick out to me, "If you believe in something, stand up for it. If you don't believe in something, stand up against it." This book series, and the podcast that spawned it, are a result of me believing in the Independent Sacramental Movement and believing that more people need to hear about I term, "The best kept secret within Christianity." It took me some time to conclude that I needed to start a podcast. Authenticity sometimes takes time to fully manifest, to fully understand "what is important to me, and what should I do now?" Joe could have found a home in any number of mainstream big-box denominations; however, he chose the path of authenticity and embraced the Independent Sacramental Movement.

Bishop Joseph Grieboski believed in many things and he continuously took stands for what he believed in and what he thought was important. Each of us should strive to be a little bit like Joe! The world was a better place with him in it, and now it our task to do our best to honor his memory by trying to make the world a better place too. May he rest in peace and let us remember him!

For Reflection, Contemplation and Prayer:

- What are some things that you feel strongly about? Strong enough to publically take a stand?

- How do you balance theological doctrines and rules with compassion?

- In the Independent Sacramental Movement liberty seems to be valued more than anything else; however, accountability is seen as important to many. Do you value accountability, and do you think it is necessary within the Independent Sacramental Movement?

CHAPTER TWO

—·—

"METANOIA REACTIONS"

FATHER MICHAELANGELO D'ARRIGO

"The Lord is my strength and my song, and he has become my salvation; this is my God, and I will praise him, my father's God, and I will exalt him."
- Exodus 15:2

_____

The Reverend Canon Michaelangelo D'Arrigo lives in the Metropolitan Atlanta, Georgia, area with his wife, Claudia, a Therapeutic Massage Therapist, son, D'Mitri, a high schooler, two doggies, and a cat. Before ordination, he worked as a professional musician, and as a substance abuse counselor

He was ordained to the Anglican Priesthood in 2006 and spent two years in parish ministry, specializing in Pastoral Counseling and Liturgical Writing. He then worked as a missionary to the homeless community in the Little Five Points neighborhood of Atlanta, Georgia, for three years.

After his mission work ended, Michaelangelo spent the next two years working with non-denominational churches in the Metropolitan Atlanta area, specializing in Pastoral Counseling, and Music Ministry.

In 2012, after a brief stint back in a parish setting, the Holy Spirit led him to start Metanoia Ministries. This church was established to serve everyone; gay, straight, trans, disenfranchised, seekers, those abused by other churches, and everyone in between. His mission continues to be to spread the Good News to all. To counsel as needed, to teach, to provide folks the tools they need to work through their salvation.

Metanoia later transformed into what is now Agape Fellowship of Greater Atlanta. They are exploring what it means to be the church in our ever-evolving cultural landscape.

Michaelangelo is an Elder/Priest in the Convergent Christian Communion and a Canon to the presiding bishop.

KLING: What is your elevator speech? How would you describe the Independent Sacramental Movement to someone who does not know what it is?

D'ARRIGO: People ask me this regularly. The easiest answer that I give is to imagine the richness, the history, the tradition, and the liturgical sacramental sense of the Catholic Church and remove the Pope.

That's the easy answer. When I have time to have a longer conversation, it's more about it's independent, it's without borders. It is a more convergent form of Catholicity, meaning that, although we are fully Catholic by sacrament, by liturgy, by apostolic succession, we are also open to the progressive expression of faith. When you come and worship with my church, with my people, our people, you may experience the Holy Spirit in a similar way that you would at a charismatic church or at a Pentecostal church, but where the form, the liturgy, and the body of worship will feel entirely Catholic in its order in its pacing.

Our worship experience will be what we strive for, which is a first century followers of the Way, a Christian prototype church. We are open to the movement of the Spirit. We are open to the pacing that the movement of the Spirit may create and to the various ways that participants, both lay and clergy, may experience the Spirit in the moment. We are more open to off-script behavior than in a traditional Roman Catholic environment, and then from there, the usual response is why don't you come worship with us and have an experience of what that feels like? Does that answer your question?

KLING: Yes, thank you, but why the Independent Sacramental Movement? Why a small micro-denomination and why the Convergent Christian Communion?

D'ARRIGO: That could be a long story, but I will give you the extremely short version. I come from a traditional Anglican background, and though I was raised in a Sicilian, Roman Catholic family when I was a teenager and discovered that I was going to be Christian, and no longer call myself a Hindu or something else,

I fell in love with the worship of the Episcopal Church. When I moved to Atlanta, Georgia, in December 1998, I needed an Episcopal Church that I could walk to because this silly man from New York City thought he wouldn't need a car in Atlanta, which, of course, was wrong.

I discovered a small Anglo-Catholic parish in the diocese of Atlanta known as The Church of Our Savior and the rector at the time was a guy named Father Warren Tanghe. Father Tanghe, amongst many things, helped create Forward in Faith North America. He came from a traditional Episcopal background.

We used something similar to the Rite One Mass; however, he wrote the liturgy for our mass, which is probably why I love writing liturgies. It's his fault. When I went through the ordination process, which I did kicking and screaming because I didn't think a substance abuse counselor with a background in rock music was necessarily the best fit for the priesthood, it ended up that there were a series of things that made me uncomfortable about going through the Episcopal diocese. I went through what then was the Anglican Diocese of Rwanda in which later became the Anglican Mission in America, which if you know about them, they're extremely hardcore African conservative Anglicans. I was proud of that entire decision, and I'm happy with the amazing formation that I received from them. It quickly became obvious to me when I got involved in what was Independent Anglicanism and that I didn't fit.

I have this quirky notion that the Church is the hands and feet of Christ on this Earth. I have this quirky notion that Jesus didn't turn anyone away, and that he approached the unapproachable and talked to them first. That Paul talked to Gentiles instead of just Jews and when I got into the natural environment of that end of the Anglican Communion, I was greeted by people that were happy to worship, and were happy to tithe, and happy to give to the church, but were not very happy to give to the poor or the widows or the orphans. They didn't want to take care of people outside of their own community, unless they could push their brand of Christianity on those people, and unless those people changed. That's not the gospel message to me. Actually. I think Christianity is like Alcoholics Anonymous, which at its best is attempted through attraction rather than promotion. You will see what I have and want it for yourself. I'm pretty sure Paul taught that.

When I got into very traditional Anglican churches, I found myself at odds with the membership and with the boards because I wanted to help people. They wanted to help the Church. When I realized that this shouldn't be a conflict, it was. Slowly but surely, I found myself becoming this constant, independent Anglo-Catholic Renegade.

Then I learned about the Independent Catholic Movement and this notion that one could be a Catholic priest independently of a larger body and be sacramental and be apostolic and truly serve creation. It wasn't about a paycheck anymore, and it wasn't about benefits, and it wasn't about maintaining the status quo of the Church body, but rather about spreading the Good News; about bringing the sacraments to everybody, and about serving everyone and community.

I'm intersex. I was born neither male nor female. If XX is female and XY is male chromosomes. I'm XXY, and in fact, the church that ordained me said that I should not exist, and that I'm an anomaly and a mutant rather than seeing me, a beautiful part of God's extremely diverse creation. So, the opportunity I felt in the Independent Movement was to embrace the diversity of creation and, as a priest in this Movement to embrace everyone else. Rather quickly, this developed into a thing called Metanoia Ministries here in the Atlanta-Metro area. Opening the door of the Church to everyone.

Suddenly, we specialized in the lesbian, gay, bisexual, transgender, intersex, and queer community. Then the unchurched and folks that thought, "If I walk into a church, I will spontaneously combust." You would be surprised by how many people there are, but especially in the LGBTQ community. They have been told all their lives, by every denomination that they have ever believed in or ever been in involved, that their choices (and choice is a bad word, but we'll run with it) guaranteed them a ticket to hell, and that they were choosing a lifestyle of sin. The thing is, the Bible, Old and New Testaments, does not say much about that, but when it does, it is often taken out of context. Then the Bible is proof texted in a way to develop a dialogue that says, "We're in control and you're not going to produce more offspring and that's what we need for the church. So, you're just wrong." It boils down to power and control and has nothing to do with this new covenant that we have through God, through Christ's sacrifice. Metanoia Ministries started as a Bible study, and it became a chapel, and it became a movement. Then it got to a point where we had to merge with another ministry, not because we got too big, but because we needed to grow in a specific way. That is how Agape

Fellowship was birthed. Metanoia Ministries combined with some folks that were Pentecostal and charismatic and wanted a traditional sacramental experience in their worship while maintaining their ability to be charismatic in their style.

Why the Convergent Christian Communion? This is a two-part response. The first part is, I had been working with a bishop, a mentor and confessor out of England who was wonderful and fantastic and very supportive of me and my ministry but was in England. You know, you have time differences, and you have small cultural differences. It was never a convenient situation for me, and so the idea of having an apostolically correct bishop who could see our faith similarly to how I see it, and then to have that relationship be "give and take" that you can only have with a priest and a bishop was very attractive.

I started looking at several groups within Independent Catholicism. My buddy Don Pratt is with the United American Catholic Church, and so I spoke with Bishop Tony Hash. Gregory Godsey is a Bishop in the Independent world and lives about two hours from me, and we have had several conversations. Just as The Anthem Network was becoming the Convergent Christian Communion, I met Bishop Kenny von Folmar through various Facebook groups. He was talking about creating a prayer and liturgy book for the Convergent Christian Communion. Since we started Metanoia Ministries, and before that, I have been writing liturgies for our use, and for friends, and for specific types of weddings that didn't have a liturgy in place. I said to Bishop Kenny, "I have a bunch of files and you're welcome to them and use them as you see fit." I sent him everything that I had written over the years, since 2006. We started talking regularly and it was spiritually profound to not have to translate.

Sometimes, when I talk in liturgy, in faith, in theological concepts, I have to explain myself several times because. I guess I talk on an academic level, but Bishop Kenny instantly understood what I was saying. There was never any need for translation and that was attractive and appealing to me. As those conversations happened, we got to a place where we both felt like I needed the Convergent Christian Communion, and the Convergent Christian Communion wanted me involved, too. It was such a natural fit.

KLING: It is frustrating having to always translate what you are trying to say. I'm in a Doctor of Ministry program and the people who are my peers are United Methodists, a Lutheran, a United Church of Christ, and a couple of Presbyterians. I'm constantly having to translate, and I even have to translate when I talk to faculty because most of them have never encountered someone like me before in their classroom. It is frustrating having to constantly translate and then trying to provide some insights as to who I am theologically and ecclesiastically.

I need to translate because they will speak to me and I will respond, "That's not really the context I'm in. I can't just call the bishop and ask him, because I am the Bishop and I have no money or resources to throw at a problem."

D'ARRIGO: Exactly. I can call my bishop and I can ask for money, and he can laugh hysterically at me and say, "No." It will change nothing.

My bishop is very giving, and an example I can give you is we had our General Council Meeting in February, and that meant flying from Atlanta to Phoenix and staying in Phoenix for four days, five days. In my home, my wife is the primary breadwinner because I don't know if you know it or not, but Independent Catholics don't really make a big salary or really any salaries. Our son is autistic, and it is a crazy God who provides, and it is amazing and wonderful and I'm appreciative, but you know, flying out to Phoenix is not usually in the budget. My communion came together, and the bishops came together, and they raised the money necessary for me to fly out to Phoenix. Luckily my best friend of 35 years lives in Phoenix with his wife. So, I stayed with them for free. That was my first time with everybody, with most everyone from the Communion, and I taught classes during the Council.

I taught a course on liturgics and a course on the history of the Sacramental Movement down to everything from how it came to pass to how this is how you say the mass, such as these are the things you do with your hands and an instructive Eucharist. It was about the coolest experience I have ever had being with other clergy. It was empowering. It is also when I realized that this was the right choice because the Convergent Christian Communion is truly a family of brothers and sisters in Christ, both in the clergy and the laity.

We all get along like siblings, and functional siblings! I have never had this experience and I feel like, "Was this what it was like to be hanging out in Jerusalem three weeks after Pentecost?" It is the only way I can describe it. God planted us all here together for a reason.

KLING: We are all dispersed, and most jurisdictions don't have a lot of people in the same location. I could just imagine it is the first century and you're in Jerusalem. Someone else is in Antioch and you have the means to text one another. That would have been interesting!

D'ARRIGO: Think about how fast the early church grew without all of that. I think that is one beauty of the Independent Sacramental Movement. We are growing similarly, especially here in the states, like how the first century church grew, and we have the added blessings of Zoom and Facebook and texting and cell phones and video calls. The list goes and goes and goes, but we are authentically a growing Body of Christ. Every time I seem to turn around, there is a conversation on one of the various social media platforms about planting another church or planting a mission, or we have grown too big for this building, and we're going to plant another church. That seems to be different about Independent Catholicism from Anglican or Roman Catholicism is this notion of there being too many people in the parish. Let's plant a whole new church versus we have over 250 people. You know what I mean?

KLING: Can you elaborate on that?

D'ARRIGO: In my experience, especially as an Anglican, let's say you have a worship space that can accommodate 200 people, and you grow to 250 people. Now it is standing room only, and you have some overflow that watches on a TV monitor in the hall. The Anglican answer, traditionally speaking, is let's build a bigger church on this property to make up for the new membership. Whereas it has been my experience in the Independent Sacramental Movement where the thought process goes from a priest's point of view, is that there are too many people in the building, and I can't have a personal relationship with everybody. If there are over 250 people, then let's plant a sister church with another priest. Then we can bring in more people into that parish and then they can plant a second sister church. Suddenly, you have church plants in and around the area that make up this one independent body, and that is how that independent body grows. As far as I can tell, that's a first century model. That is exactly how we went from a church in Jerusalem and a church in Antioch to a church in Damascus to a church in wherever.

KLING: That makes sense. You were talking about the phenomenon of the Independent Sacramental Movement, and the Movement has been around a while, over a hundred years in the United States. I think we are in a unique time now because we're realizing that being insular is not doing us any good. In the past, jurisdictions have stayed to themselves. They haven't networked with other jurisdictions. Bishops have often been paranoid about their priests, having too much contact with other jurisdictions, for fear that other bishops would steal their priests. It's crazy. We are in a different age now. Jurisdictions are starting to cooperate and work together. There is a lot of cross-fertilization of ideas across micro-denominational and jurisdictional lines. People are starting to work together and network in ways that they have not in the past, and it is about time.

D'ARRIGO: That is why the Convergent Christian Communion is in intercommunion relationships with a growing number of independent denominations, jurisdictions, whatever we want to call them. It is part of what I find so empowering. Earlier this summer, I took part in the Old/Independent Catholic Virtual Summer School, 2020. You even taught a class. It was a two week Zoom-based Christian Education program organized Father Jayme Mathias, through his parish in Texas.

It was so phenomenal for me on so many levels. I spent the better part of last year here, in Madison, Georgia, which is about 50 miles east of Atlanta, about 25 miles south of Athens. I live in farm country. It is not suburbia. This is rural. It is all cow pastures, and the town next to us is Rutledge. At the Rutledge Community Depot, I taught some classes there and one of them was an Introduction to the History of the Christian Church. We started in the Book of Acts and moved throughout the year to our current century. It was a cool to attend a class at the Old/Independent Catholic Virtual Summer School that took the basic tenants that I was teaching for this local community center. My class was not for clergy. It was for laypeople. People who may have spent a lifetime in the church, but perhaps didn't know that Jesus was Jewish. Let that sink in for a second. So, it was cool to take this class and to realize not only the stuff that I was teaching was spot on, because it's always good to know that you're not teaching the wrong stuff, but to get such insight on how all the places where humanity made a right turn when God was hoping they'd make a left. That equates to the creation of the Old Catholic Church and, therefore, Independent Catholics. It was fascinating, but the coolest thing about the Virtual Summer School was, we would get together once a week for a social hour on Zoom after the classes on Fridays. I could put not only faces to voices who were asking questions, but have conversations with clergy from across the country and globally because of Zoom. I have made permanent, incredibly rich, and powerful friendships through that class. I don't just have a bishop in my community who I can approach, but I have priests and sisters and brothers in Christ globally where I can say, "You know, you and I talked about Döllinger and I'm stuck on this point, do you have any input for me?" That is empowering, and that is new to our relatively old movement. It is a sign to me that there is more to come, and I think that this is necessary. I think for us to have the impact that we can require networking.

It doesn't require us to become one big denomination. That's not what I'm saying, but it requires communication and networking. For instance, if I have parishioners here in Madison and Atlanta that are going to go on vacation to Ohio, and they are going to be in your jurisdiction then you and I can talk about it and we can send them to a parish that they are going to feel comfortable. That way, they don't have to go worship at an Episcopal Church or at a Roman Catholic parish. How awesome would that be?

KLING: It is awesome, and I think that networking is so important, and the reason I created *Sacramental Whine: An Independent Sacramental Movement Podcast* for that very purpose. If it wasn't for Sacramental Whine, I wouldn't be talking to you, and I wouldn't have talked to scores of other people either.

All the people that I've talked to, I have a relationship with, and some of them, I have built upon that relationship and most them, I am in constant contact and in constant discussion and I think we need more opportunities for this type of networking. This would never have happened 20 years ago, 10 years ago, but it's happening now, and I think it is outstanding.

D'ARRIGO: I'm going to throw this out there and I'm not sure if this is a popular opinion, but I believe that for all the horrible that COVID-19 has caused across our globe, and it is exceedingly hard, as a priest, as a pastor, it has kicked my ministry into overdrive. Agape Fellowship has grown more from March 2020 to now, September 2020, than we did the entire year of 2019. A lot of that has to do with the notion that people are stuck at home and people feel a foreboding and a depression and a sense of hopelessness and confusion, and emptiness. That is an opportunity for the Church to walk in and to offer hope and to offer the three Rs: reconciliation, restoration, and redemption in no particular order. Because of social media and instant messaging and Facebook Live and YouTube and Zoom, we can be in people's living rooms.

Before, they had to come to church, but now they don't have to get out of bed. They can sit up with their laptop or on their TV screen and experience worship., We work between Agape Fellowship and a sister ministry, which is called Glory Tribe, and Glory Tribe is run by a good friend, Pastor Debra Lynn Rodriguez. Glory Tribe is her experiment into ministry, and Deb comes from Appalachia, and she was raised Pentecostal. She's a Christian singer and songwriter. She is married to her lovely wife, Robbie, and helps raise Robbie's kids. Deb's thing has always been music ministry, and she created Glory Tribe and they were getting together once a week on Wednesdays for worship out loud in the middle of the week via social media. She would come on and she would sing some worship songs and people would put in prayer requests. That grew into contemplations, and we started doing advent contemplations, and Lent contemplations, and when COVID hit, I started on a Monday mid-day meditation with Glory Tribe, and now Glory Tribe and Agape Fellowship shares all of our media links and everything that streams in one ministry also streams in the other ministry. Now, we offer programming three and four days out of the week on a slow week and on a busy week we are offering five and six days of moments of reflection and prayer and community building. During this time of COVID, when we are so deeply in isolation and yet our ministries, our folks, talk to each other almost every day.

It is cross-pollination because Deb's group is extremely Protestant and ours is Convergent Catholic. You have this wonderful platform to exchange ideas and different ways of looking at prayer and COVID has been wonderful for pastors to reconnect with our folks and with our local communities, because who else is offering regular programming?

I think there has been such a working of the Holy Spirit through COVID to bring Christianity into people's lives and to unite our Independent Movements, because we are all stuck in front of the computer screen. It is extremely empowering. Have you had that experience too?

KLING: Yeah. Let me give you an example. I work with ten other chaplains, and we all come from different theological backgrounds. I know them from work, but I know little about them outside of work. And one of my colleagues is a Pentecostal associate pastor at a Pentecostal church. When he was talking about how they do a lot of stuff through Facebook live now, I asked him, "What's the name of your church? I'll check it out." The availability of worship services on-line has given me an opportunity to listen to his preaching and to watch their services and to get a glimpse inside of a Pentecostal church that honestly, I never in my life would have ever visited. It has given me an opportunity to connect in a way that I never would have otherwise.

That is one example of many ways that I've been able to connect with other, with other folks through worship, through Zoom that, under normal circumstances, I never would have. I think you raised some good points. I always like to take a negative and turn it into a positive, and COVID-19 is certainly a negative; however, we can learn from it and put a positive spin on the experience and grow from that experience.

The disease itself is not a positive. It's terrible, but the circumstances that we find ourselves in can make be used as a source for transformation. I think that is a good takeaway.

Switching gears a little, can you share what has been your greatest challenge within ministry?

D'ARRIGO: I can give you an early answer and a now answer because they're very different. I, like many people of every generation, have a salty relationship with my parents. I misspent my youth making poor choices that made them very unhappy with me, and I don't think they have ever recovered from it.

Like most people, I know, no matter how old they are, there is this little piece of their personality that is always looking for parental approval for life choices. It is important for me to say that while I understood from a fairly early age that there was probably a calling to some greater purpose, I spent many years running from that or trying to use very secular ways of fulfilling that purpose. Being a substance abuse counselor being on the top of that list. Help people and help people that needed stuff and I got there from my own personal experience. I had a drug overdose in 1993. I was dead for 10 minutes and I have never again taken any illegal substances since. I went through recovery.

Early on as a priest, I think what was so difficult was people taking me seriously as a priest because they knew my background in rock music; I played studio guitar and session guitar and recorded on a lot of records and toured with bands and toured with my own band. You don't associate that with the priesthood, and I did all the things that the rock music lifestyle promotes. And again, you don't associate that with the priesthood. I remember when I first got ordained, many people, especially people I went to high school with, would say, "Really, you're a priest. Why did they let you become a priest? Why?" Early on, I think it was about legitimizing my priesthood.

Legitimizing the notion that I am really called to do this and that I love this, and this is my life; but I'm still going to wear blue jeans with my clergy shirt. I'm still going to have a chain wallet, and I'm still going to wear Doc Martins because that's me, and too bad.

That also reflects on the immaturity of who I was when I was ordained a priest. Perhaps I wasn't ready for the commitment of priesthood. Then life happened, as it always does, and as I left the traditional body, I spent a hot minute in Nondenominational Christianity working as a worship leader, which is a whole different story. That'll be great for a book someday.

I've come to a series of theological and spiritual conclusions based on what I believe scripture says and looking at the ancient Greek and the ancient Hebrew. As you mature as a priest, I think you start to speak more and more authoritatively about doctrine and about theology because your understanding broadens. You start to meet more than people that agree with that understanding, and suddenly you become authoritative on it. I'm at a place now where I not only see who I am as a pastor and how I teach what the Bible says, but also how it is taught by others. Wrong or indifferent. I have gotten to this place for my son. I'm starting to share this theology with the world that maybe there are bits and pieces of scripture that we have really misinterpreted over the years. As an example, isn't it strange that Judaism to this day has no hell, but traditional Christianity does?

Where does the picture of hell come from it. What does scripture say about a reality of hell? I used to be very timid about teaching revelation because it is confusing and you no one really knows and blah, blah, blah. I had all these excuses to not teach it rather than to just teach.

This is what it says, and this is the context of it. Now I feel empowered to say, "This is what it says, and this is the context of it." What that means, I guess what that means challenge wise, is that it is very easy to convince people they need to go to church when they believe they are investing in their salvation. As in what happens when they die, which I would say that mainline Christianity seems to be all about. If you do these things, you will not go to hell, therefore, come to my church and don't go to hell.

What we at Agape fellowship teach is, imagine if you could experience bits and pieces of heaven right now on this side of the veil. If you followed the things that Jesus taught you to do, imagine that the kingdom of heaven is not only at hand, but within reach on this side. The challenge becomes, people have been generationally taught that things like tithing is a way to buy salvation. Tithing is a way to earn, as they say in the south, "Earn jewels for your crown, your heavenly crown."

I'm not screaming that from the pulpit or from the soap box. I'm saying heaven is right here, right now. Now, let's look at what Jesus offers us right now. Change the lens by which we see the world. Then we can see the world through Jesus's lens, and we can treat each other as Jesus did, and whatever happens later is just that, it's later. We need to be here now.

The challenge is breaking. It's breaking that worldview that it is all about the later and not about the now, even though Jesus preached all about the now. My challenge is literally about breaking down people's understanding and view of what they have been taught to let them see what the Bible actually says.

KLING: My final question is what has been your greatest blessing within ministry?

D'ARRIGO: Oh, there is a new one every day. Greatest blessing? I would say it's a combination of the ability to serve and the ability to grow and evolve in service, which is a funny thing, especially in service to Christ. Jesus says, "My yoke is easy. It's light." It's still a yoke. Freedom is Christ, is not American freedom. Freedom in Christ is, "I no longer need to concentrate on all these worldly things that I used to think were important. I am now free of those burdens." Instead, now live in service to my savior and in following what the Holy Spirit instructs me to do. The blessing in that is that has forced me to evolve. When we think repent for the kingdom of heaven is at hand or repent from this behavior or that behavior, that notion of repenting was like groveling before the altar, before an untouchable God who was high and holy. When I studied the ancient Greek, suddenly repent had a new meaning. The Greek word is *metanoia,* and the simplest direct translation would be to rethink, but it is to completely reshuffle your deck to change your paradigm, to see what you have always done and to realize that it is not quite it. Maybe you need to look at it from a different angle. Then suddenly repent and grovel, because the kingdom of heaven is at hand, becomes rethink and shift your focus. Think about this in a different way, heaven is available here. My greatest blessing is in the understanding of what repentance, *metanoia*, means, because it changes everything about me every day.

It changes who I am as a pastor and who I am as a person. It changes who I am as a husband and who I am as a dad to an autistic spectrum child, because you know how you get your autistic kids to do what needs to get done? By continually rethinking the paradigm that you think you are in and try to see things from their perspective.

Rethink ministry, rethink mission, rethink faith, rethink prayer, rethink sacraments, rethink liturgy. The list just goes on and on. If I had to boil it down to one notion, one concept, it is that *metanoia* has struck every fiber of my being. None of that would have happened had I not gone down this path to be a pastor. I don't think I ever would have come to that scriptural understanding without that Greek background. How many people do you know that have a Greek background that aren't employed by a church? My greatest blessing has been service, in the sense of it has forced a great deal of *metanoia* in my life.

KLING: Thank you for taking the time to talk to me today. I love your story. Do you have any closing comments you would like to share?

D'ARRIGO: Thank you for this opportunity. I appreciate this opportunity, and my final comments are that I hope you take away something inspirational from this conversation and I hope it has caused a *metanoia* like reaction within you.

I encourage you to have these *metanoia* reactions to all the parts of your life, but especially in your middle because if we can rethink this and shift the paradigm, the Independent Sacramental Movement could really be a force of true Jesus. True Jesus Freaks. True Holy Spirit driven reform of the whole Universal Church because I'm thinking that the whole Universal Church might need another Reformation, another Reform Movement.

I think it is the voices in the wilderness, the crazy prophets, the renegades, the freaks, the misfit toys. I think it is us who are going to be the voices of this reformation. I encourage you to listen and to get involved and to speak your mind and to connect with others.

And again, thank you for this blessing and this opportunity.

"When a man really gives up trying to make something out of himself—a saint, or a converted sinner, or a churchman (a so-called clerical somebody), a righteous or unrighteous man,... when in the fullness of tasks, questions, success or ill-hap, experiences and perplexities, a man throws himself into the arms of God... then he wakes with Christ in Gethsemane. That is faith, that is metanoia and it is thus that he becomes a man and Christian."
- Dietrich Bonhoeffer

Concluding Thoughts

I have devoted much of my efforts to promoting the Independent Sacramental Movement, but my history is not exclusive to this movement. My history is eclectic and filled with a diversity of thought. My personal spiritual journey is colored with a full palette of spiritual and religious expressions, and for that I am grateful. Being able to see God through different theological and spiritual lenses has been helpful in my work as a chaplain but also as a religious leader.

Several years ago, I served the Yellow Springs Unitarian Universalist Fellowship as their director of religious education. During my tenure there, I had the pleasure of working with the youth. Now, they are all grown up, but we had a robust youth program. One summer, I introduced them to Hinduism, and we spent several weeks learning about Hinduism. We talked about Hindu and Indian culture and explored the various gods and philosophies inherent within Hinduism. It was a lovely spiritual experience that culminated in our visiting a local Hindu temple.

The Sunday after our temple excursion we spent our time together processing the experience. One youth said to me, "I liked your teaching on Hinduism better than the woman at the temple. She kept apologizing." What this student was talking about was how the woman at the temple, who was our guide, had behaved. She would talk about their temple and their spirituality, but in a deferential sort of way and, as the youth had said, it seemed like she was apologizing for their differences. It was as if she was ashamed of who they were and wanted to make light of their existence. That is what the youth perceived, and I felt it too. I'm sure years of British colonialism and feeling marginalized fed our guide's demeanor, it excited the children to learn about Hinduism and as Unitarian Universalists, they had no preconceived notions that Hinduism was inferior.

The world is a diverse expression of spiritual views, and we can learn from each other. The Independent Sacramental Movement is diverse too, and there is much diversity within this movement. Some people close themselves off to difference, and some difference needs to be admonished, such as on-line and Internet ordinations; however, there are other differences that should be explored and honored. I have hoped help shed light on the myriad of spiritual expressions within the Independent Sacramental Movement and to honor those expressions.

For Reflection, Contemplation and Prayer:

- Have you ever found yourself in a position, talking about the Independent Sacramental Movement to a Christian of another theological background, where you have to translate the ISM culture and theology into a context that they can understand? What was that like?

- Father D'Arrigo talked about the three Rs: reconciliation, restoration, and redemption. What are your thoughts on these three words and what they mean? Are they important? Why?

- Do you think the Universal Church is in need of another Reformation? And do you think it will have its genesis in the Independent Sacramental Movement?

CHAPTER THREE

— • —

"MATURE STEP FORWARD"

FATHER JERRY MAYNARD

"And when you stand praying, if you hold anything against anyone, forgive them, so that your Father in heaven may forgive you your sins."
- Mark 11:25

Father Jerry Maynard is an Independent Catholic priest formerly with the Order of Mary Magdalene and now under the episcopal protection of Bishop David Strong. Known as "the People's Priest," he leads a ministry of protest, praise and community organizing in Houston, Texas. Father Jerry works on foreign and domestic issues, teaches the spirituality of non-violence, and serves as founding pastor of The People's Church.

KLING: Thank you for returning. So glad to have you back. I know that one of the things that you want to talk about is your work with justice and advocacy. A little bit of background on my involvement in such issues goes back to 2010 when I was in seminary. We had to do a cross cultural trip, in my case, it was down to the Texas/Mexico border to study immigration and to study border culture. We went over into Mexico and studied labor laws and got to look at where all the factories moved from the Midwest down to Mexico. I learned about immigration, and I was ignorant on the subject prior to the experience. I'll be honest, I was not only ignorant, but some of my opinions were vile. I thought if we are having problems with the border, we could put a landmine field there. That was stupid of me to think that and to make those kinds of offhanded remarks to my peers. I went to Texas and Mexico, and I learned about immigration. I talked to families, I talked to labor leaders in Mexico and in Texas.

I got to see how people lived. I went into the Mexico side and saw the colonies of people living in shacks, working in factories, making next to nothing. I found out that Mexico has stricter labor laws than we do in the United States, but at the border, all those laws are forgotten. All companies have to do is bribe government officials and corporations can do whatever they want. The conditions that people live in on the Texas side wasn't that much better. I mean, it was better, in some areas, they had running water in some areas they didn't. Even on the Texas side. I learned a lot about border culture and about Hispanic culture. I learned a lot about immigration.

In late 2010 I was able to go to a conference in Washington, DC. It was a conference put on by Sojourners, which is more on the conservative side, but the conference was designed to bring conservatives and liberals together. Faith leaders who were progressive and faith leaders who were traditional and conservative coming together on issues that they could agree upon. So, they're not going to agree upon, for example, reproductive choice, that's going to be an issue that they're going to be at odds with, but they may have some agreement on immigration. That's what the emphasis of the conference was about. I was able to participate in that and after the conference, I was involved in a handful of demonstrations in Ohio, on immigration. For example, Senator John McCain was at Ohio Wesleyan University doing the commencement address and we protested his views on immigration.

That's the short version of my "sojourn" into activism and justice work. To give you some context of where I've been and the work that I've done. Most of my involvement has been in immigration. Now, I'm going to throw the ball back in your court.

MAYNARD: I'm glad you shared that because I think you bringing up something that is vital for us in the ISM to remember, but also for the entire Body of Christ to remember that our faith is a faith of encounter, a faith of witness. We experience Christ, we experience divinity in the world that we live in the here and the now and through our senses through the tangible realities that we call creation. Because we worship a God who was incarnate, who could put on flesh and who sanctified our experience. I think that openness to encounter is something that for those of us who come out of a sacramental tradition must remember that is essential to discipleship, to being a person who practices our Christian faith in this context, in this world. Also, remembering that we are not isolated entities or isolated beings. Our faith, our way of being sacred people in the world, is connected to history. What has happened in the past, what is happening now, and what will be happening in the future, and what we are doing here in the now gives birth to the future. Leonardo Boff has talked about this idea where he says that if spirituality can be defined as a "meeting with God and history," then if a new historical epoch is opening, then a new meeting with God is also upon us. A God, that is less war like and less patriarchal, and more concerned with compassion, justice, celebration, beauty, and creativity. That really is really what I try to do in my ministry, and my work is that I try to pay attention to the God of the now, how God has manifested in the now. Not just because I think that it's important to do so. Not just because I think this is one type of theology you can have, but because I think it's crucial to living an authentic life. You know, Thomas Aquinas, one of the Doctors of the Church, and one of the main contributors to Catholic theology, defined salvation as being the act of preserving all things in the good. Aquinas taught that all of us are born into what he called original goodness, that denotes to me a very biblical concept that God created us and created the cosmos, and we were named as very good. For us to practice an authentic faith in the here and now requires that we preserve all things, including creation in the original goodness. Part of doing that in our tradition is understanding the theology of being a part of a sacramental universe that is profoundly transcendent, mysterious, but also deeply capable of being intimate, being close to us, as close to us as our breath.

I think that level of intimacy is what we experience through the sacraments, the sacraments that we have learned and been passed on throughout the centuries from Baptism to Confirmation, to Holy Orders, Eucharist and the Anointing of the Sick. I think all of this is important because we are living in a time where there is a lot of upheaval. There is social uprising, there are challenges that are taking place. These challenges must have an influence on our understanding of incarnation.

KLING: Your description of God as being transcendent and mysterious, but also being in dwelling with us in an intimate way is the classical definition of panentheism. So, my follow-up question for you is do you use subscribe to a Process view of God, like in the Process Theological view that God is capable of change and that God isn't static in the classical sense of God being unchanging.

MAYNARD: Absolutely, I totally hold on to a Process Theology view of God, the Godhead, mainly because if we're going in Sacramental theology, we are taught that the sacraments are the way that we worship because they are by-products of the ultimate act of God, which is incarnation, which we believe is represented by Jesus Christ, the Anointed One, the Messiah. Part of that incarnation, part of that reality of the sacraments is understanding that these are derivatives of incarnation, which includes creation of the world around us. When we look at the way that colonies of ants, the way families of birds, schools of fishes, the way that trees grow, our plants grow, there is nothing but process all around. There are steps that take place when you plant a seed and you nourish it and it grows, and it turns into a plant or a tree or a harvest. It is all around us, and it's quite silly to me, for us to say that the author of all creation is stagnant. It's not static. It's bountiful, it's vibrant, it's robust. So, really having a sacramental understanding of the universe is ultimately a challenge to this idea that God is stagnant. That God stays the same.

KLING: I think as we're talking, and I'm reflecting, I look at God instead of being one or the other as being both and let me explain. If we work with the assumption that God is both transcendent and imminent, then I think you can make the argument that the transcendent aspect of God tends to lean more towards the classical understanding of God, of unchanging. Whereas the imminent aspect of God is what is more malleable and changes and is reflected in nature. So, for example, you have an animal scurrying around doing animal things, and then it dies. It decomposes, fertilizes the ground, new life Springs from the carcass of the dead animal. Then the animal's progeny continues to proliferate, that can reflect the changing aspect of God, as well as the history of humanity. Hopefully we're evolving in such a way that we're learning from our mistakes; although, common practice shows that that doesn't always happen. I'm rambling a bit, but I'm just trying to process this idea of God and how it fits into what you mentioned is the now.

MAYNARD: That's the part that really is the part that clarifies a lot of this. If we're living right now in a time of global pandemic where our global health systems are really at the edge of what they can and cannot do, our expertise has really been challenged and our understanding of how to best manifest healing protocols for people who are dealing with the Corona virus and other viruses that are manifesting all over the place. We're also in a social pandemic of racism, and white supremacy. Whether we like it or not, either we're made in the image and likeness of God, and that includes black, brown, and indigenous people, or we're not. I'm trying to help people understand and struggle with the theology around that because ultimately the whole point of all of this is that what we need to do for the church, for the movement, is to progress more closer to what Martin Luther King Jr called the Beloved Community, or what scripture calls the Reign of God, Jesus Christ called the Kingdom of Heaven. We must shatter the stained glass that separates us from what is happening in our church and what is happening in our streets, because as long as there are black and brown people being choked to death, we can never authentically say with any sort of authority, or spiritual power, that God is for us, and that God is all powerful or that the incarnation actually exists, that we take it seriously. When I look at the altar, my job as a priest is to confess the bread and the wine in the Eucharist, and one of the parts that always shocks me and makes me want to take a step back is, "Take this all of you and eat it. This is my body broken for you."

If Jesus was a great American, like most Christians think, he would have said, "Go and break their bodies for me, to show your allegiance to me, those shed their blood for me to show that you're worthy to participate in this," but Jesus doesn't do that, Jesus does the complete opposite. He does kenosis, this emptying of himself by breaking himself open. We must be able to go to the altar and see that and understand that that is the ultimate form of discipleship for our current time is to allow ourselves to be broken open so that we may be freed from this idea or this desire to be comfortable. This attachment to this idolatry of privilege, this idolatry of power and understand that the sacraments are ways of us getting closer to being able to be like Christ and embody that self-giving sacrificial love that we call agape.

It goes further than that, it requires that we take that understanding from the altar, from the sanctuary, and practice every day in the shadows, as well as in the light, but also in the streets, because I don't want to come off as being that this is just because of political stuff. We must remember that what happens in the church must happen in the street because we are living in a world where there are policies that are actively undermining this beautiful theology of solidarity, of sacrificing ourselves and our wants for the vision of God. So, this must be facilitated. We must confront laws, and great prophets of old, like Martin Luther King Jr and Gandhi, Dorothy Day, Peter Maurin, Henri Nouwen, and many other folks, Frederick Douglass, Harriet Tubman did that by actively putting their bodies into the narrative, putting their souls into the drama. They organized themselves, they took people from the South and they put them through the underground railroad to get to the North. Dorothy Day saw around her the immense poverty because of the global economic depression. She organized the mass food sharing and educated people by creating a newspaper, which still exists to this day. Martin Luther King Jr organized demonstrations. Why? Because we are trying to physically manifest what God's dream is for us, which again, Martin Luther King Jr called the Beloved Community or the Kingdom of Heaven. It's not just about theologizing, it's about getting our body into the story, getting our worship from the sanctuary to the streets.

KLING: I'm going to play Devil's Advocate for just a moment. I do not disagree with anything that you said, however, I think since we're coming from a sacramental perspective, going back to the Patristic period. A side note, you mentioned politics, my politics tends to be progressive. However, lately I've grown weary of the battles and the fights and the constant going back and forth. I grow weary of that, but what I don't grow weary of is the Patristic tradition that placed an emphasis on justice and standing with the marginalized. I don't grow tired of that, but I do grow weary of the constant political rhetoric. I can ground myself in Patristics and still feel connected to working for justice. Whereas, if I look exclusively to the modern political arena, I get burnt out real fast. I don't know if that makes sense, but that's what I have been feeling.

There is a need for active people like Martin Luther king Jr. Clearly, he was needed to do what he did, but there were other people who were a support network to Dr. Martin Luther King, for example, Howard Thurman. I don't know if you're familiar with Howard Thurman, but you don't see a lot of pictures of him. You don't see a lot of pictures of him at demonstrations, but he was the guy that Martin Luther king Jr called when he needed to recharge. So, people like Howard Thurman functioned in a similar way as the monastics of ages past who were in cloisters praying for the church militant who were out doing active work. I think that's important, and I think you also need that difference between the "introverts and the extroverts" in a sense.

MAYNARD: I think that's a great point. Howard Thurman really was the heart of the Civil Rights Movement because he did help by not only being a source of support; he was a source of support and an outlet of meaningfulness for those who showed up regularly in the public forum. He was also the one who helped to develop the consciousness of the Civil Rights Movement. His writings explore the theological, spiritual, and psychological understandings of what the Movement was all about, and the drama that was taking place. I do want to point out though, because while he's not often pictured, Howard Thurman often did go to demonstrations. He was not always present up front, mainly because he was an older guy. He always wanted to be in the back. I don't want to give off the idea that he never went to anything because that's just not true.

I appreciate as a movement organizer, and a movement builder, I do oftentimes point out, in my training, that not everyone has to be at the front of the march, and not everyone has to be at the march at all. We need to have people who are dedicated to challenging narratives that are being promulgated while we are out marching, or getting arrested, or whatever we're doing. I think that's important, and you must do your homework, you have to know why we are stomping on the streets, and really do that internalized work and Howard Thurman really helped to do that, but at the same time, I do encourage people to realize that the prophet, the mantle of the prophet, is not an option for just a select few. It is the mandate of the Gospel and anybody who claims to be a follower or a practitioner of the values of the gospel must take upon the mantle of the prophet. Now, how they do that? One of the gifts of the Spirit is discernment, and how they do that, how they activate their throat chakra to use a Hindu concept, which is the chakra of the prophet, how they activate that is dependent upon their context. Dorothy Day in her final years was not physically capable of going to demonstrations, which she loved to do. She often said that she loved practicing the liturgy of the streets, but when she got older, she used her prophetic way of being in the world by doing as Howard Turman would often do by educating the populous, deprogramming us from an idolatry of the God of power, to an authentic worship of the God who lays themselves down for the lowly as the Virgin Mary said in her magnificent, "You cast the mighty down from their thrones and you lift up the lowly."

I want to give an example of what I'm talking about when we think of the Kingdom of Heaven, or when we think of the Beloved Community. We oftentimes think that it's a thing or an experience that will happen eventually. It's an off in the distance concept. I don't think that is the proper way of viewing it because I think that a sacramental theology, our understanding of the sacraments as avenues of grace, as historic ways of understanding God denotes to us, that the Kingdom of God, the Kingdom of Heaven, the Beloved Community is facilitated, it is co-created, and it is tangible and practical. An example is in Mathew Fox's a book on Thomas Aquinas, The Tao of Thomas Aquinas: Fierce Wisdom for Hard Times. I had the pleasure of writing the Afterward for that book, and in the Afterward, I share a true story that happened to me. It was a very transcendent, deeply personal, and almost mystical experience that took place, where I had a very tangible realization of what it means to build the Kingdom of God. Another instance, where I encountered an authentic expression of joy was when I was down in Houston with my fellow anti-homelessness activists passing out free food. We are part of an international decentralized movement called Food Not Bombs. While setting up on a cold night, a young boy, maybe eight years of age asked me what we were giving out that night. I said it was soup. It was not clear to me if this child had not eaten in days or whether he was just the biggest fan of soup in all of humanity, but when I said the word soup, his entire face just lit up like a light bulb. Later that same night while finishing up my time, visiting with people, I began to gather myself before heading home. I was one of the last volunteers to leave that night. I looked up after answering a text message and was amazed to see a group of unhoused friends laughing, running around and enjoying the fact that they had a full belly. In that moment, I realized that this is what Jesus meant when he said, "Your Kingdom come, on earth, as it is in heaven." The words of the Jesuit priest, theologian and scientists, Pierre Teilhard de Chardin popped into my head, "Joy is the infallible sign of the presence of God." Watching this merriment was like being granted a glimpse into the possibility of what communion really means.

For that night, our soup and our presence were the life force that liberated weary bodies. When we invest in one another, when we choose to affirm each other by being in solidarity with the most vulnerable of our world we are exposed to the deep mystery of communion and we may discover what St. Irenaeus meant when he said, "The glory of God is a human being fully alive!" I think that story deeply moving, and I remember experiencing, and having this unique feeling of, "I'm on this planet anymore." This was all facilitated, this was all a conscious act and is just as conscious as the priest is when he gathers the bread and wine, places it on the altar and says the words of consecration, breaks the bread and passes it on to the people. It is just as conscious as that is, and I'm trying to showcase that this is a bridging that needs to take place in order for us to really understand more fully what our mission is in this current time, as Christians, as people who practice sacramental theology. Does that make sense?

KLING: I think so, I'm trying to process what you mean by mission. For me that goes back to the role of the Church. I think we are talking about ecclesiology. The mission of the Church. What is the Church supposed to do? Obviously, we're supposed to administer the sacraments, because being a sacramental church, the sacraments are important. What does that mean for the greater mission? Do we have a responsibility to do more than just perform the Eucharist and to offer the sacraments? Is there more to it than that? I think there is obviously more to it, but we need to constantly ask these questions.

MAYNARD: Yeah. We need to ask, what is right in front of us? We can't allow our lenses to be covered over by a filter. When we enter a church and all we see is extravagant pageantry in our sanctuaries, of smells and bells and all those things. I'm not opposed to any of that within reason, but if we only stop there, then all we are doing is just playing theatre. You know? One of my favorite lines in the missal of the Roman Church is a general instruction that says that the Eucharist is not theatrical, but it is always dramatic. Ultimately, that's what it is. This is a story. This is an entry into the cosmic story of the universe within this particular moment in this particular church, in his particular instance. So, asking those questions are essential, and I think when we talked about education and formation, this must be a part of formation; otherwise, we become a museum of ancient ideas and practices that are very sweet and pretty. We should become a hospital for the wounded, a place of healing. I oftentimes think priests should be less like doctors and more like street medics, because we have to be willing to get up and go to be disciples, to be artisans of the horizon who take time to envision what it means to be disciples here and now.

I want to hear a more from you. I'm going to stop preaching for the moment. Tell me when you went to the border. You had that experience, did that affect your understanding of being a priest and, or being a follower of Jesus? Jesus, who himself was a brown man with African descent. Did that experience have an influence on your understanding of theology.

KLING: It had a major impact because it humanized the topic for me and put it into perspective. For example, I live in Ohio, in a town called Massillon, not far from Akron or Canton. If I get sick, I can go to a doctor or I to the hospital and while I have terrible insurance, I still have insurance and they will treat me. Even if I didn't have insurance, they will treat me; however, down at the Texas/Mexico border, they didn't have hospitals. They had urgent care facilities the size of hospitals. Because an urgent care doesn't have to treat you. They don't have an emergency room. They have an urgent care, which is like an emergency room. But if you don't have insurance, they don't have to treat you.

That was one thing I noticed. Another thing I noticed is that there were birthing clinics where pregnant women could go and deliver their children because Medicaid will cover a pregnant woman even if she's undocumented. They were there to cash in on that Medicaid check, and once the child was born, they are done because the mother and child are no longer covered. I learned that our society functions differently at the border based upon privilege and other factors. But my point is that I have a sense of privilege living here in the Midwest and knowing that if I must go to the emergency room, they will still treat me even if I don't have the money. They may not do surgery If my insurance won't pay for it, but I'll still get some treatment. Down at the border, you may not get any treatment, if you don't have insurance.

So, it's a different climate to navigate. There are probably a lot of people who are undocumented, and if people can't make money, they are not going to provide services. That bothers me. I looked back at a time when churches, namely the large, big box churches, like the Roman Catholic Church. When they had hospitals and their mission was to treat people regardless of insurance or ability to pay for services. Even now you have large hospitals that are technically non-profits, but they are there to make money and they are going to make money. My views have changed. I look at things much more compassionately than I have before my trip to the border.

One of the things that I learned in conjunction with immigration was human trafficking. Human trafficking is a horrible problem, and it exists everywhere. It exists all over the United States, and when we think of human trafficking, we usually think of people who are trafficked as sex workers against their will. That certainly exists, and that's certainly a problem, but a lot of our agriculture is also done through human trafficking. People will bring other people from Central and South America over into the USA with promises of a better job and a better life. They will take them to a farm, and they will become indentured servants. They're told that if they leave that ICE would be called on them. They are fearful to leave and become prisoners at the farming compound. All documentation or identification is held, keeping them held hostage. They work for very little wages in order to pay rent that it's exorbitant, and it is a system designed to keep a person enslaved. This happens a lot, a lot more than people realize.

So, it's not just a young teenage girl who's being trafficked. It could be a 50-year-old man who's expected to work in the field. I learned all about human trafficking and it breaks my heart. I think we need to fight injustice and the church needs to be a part of the fight.

MAYNARD: There is an assumption in a lot of our theology. In many of the established mainline churches there is an end point to the truth of the theology that there is the theological principle of the incarnation only applies to some people. Excluding some groups, whether it's women, black people, poor indigenous folks, immigrants, people with differing abilities, or the LGBT community. I think that we, whether we know it or not, have adopted that understanding of theology and it's completely an affront to God. The God that I've already said several times is a god of solidarity, a God who shows up for us. One of my favorite saints is Saint Bartolomé de las Casas from Latin America, who said, "God is the one who always remembers those who history has forgotten."

Part of this whole endeavor is having a theology of liberation. Having a theology that is all-inclusive, non-retaliatory, and expansive in love. Agape, is to actively remember, a Greek word, which means to bring back to mind and to remember those people that history has forgotten. Those beloved children of God who have, whether we like it or not, the imprint of God upon them, which relates back to our understanding of the Eucharist. There's a reason why in the Catholic and Orthodox tradition, we have always been taught that the source and the summit of our faith is the Eucharist, because the Eucharist tells us in the words of the ritual that you are to "do this in remembrance of me," you are to allow your body to be broken for me, your blood, to be shed for me.

I don't necessarily mean physically, doing that in most cases, that won't happen, but there are places in the world where the Body of Christ, including our streets like in Minneapolis or in Selma or on the border in Texas. Where the beloved Children of God, their bodies are being broken and their blood is being shed. The life force, the pneuma, the breath of God, the ruach is being taken away from them. Their intimate connection to the Divine is being forcibly taken away. In my Pentecost message this year, I said that we are living in a time where unholy spirits are actively manifesting and taking away that Breath of God from the Body of Christ. It's our job to enact the gifts of the Holy Spirit to help protect others, and to remember those people who history erases, who history forgets, who our society forgets. Ultimately, our spiritual and ethical ways of living need to be worthy of the beauty that is to come, because at the end of all this, our story will always end in glory. That's what the resurrection teaches us, that this will all end in glory. This will all end with a good old fashioned camp meeting in the stars as Pentecostals like to say. That's the end, that we know how the story is going to end, but we can't get there without first going through the cross. That includes confronting the people that we elect being conscious about the people whose policies they are applying or voting for, or what we are teaching in our churches. There was a time when Catholic parishes did not allow black people into the sanctuary. There's a reason why we have the Knights of Columbus and the Knights of St. Peter Claver.

I want people to take a mature step forward, and be willing to be available to this experience that we are having right now, which is an experience of God invading and interfering with this idolatry of hatred and this idolatry of abuse that we live in.

KLING: Before we adjourn, I want to share something about my jurisdiction, the Community of Saint George. We are a part of the Young Rite, which is within the Liberal Catholic Church tradition. The founding of the Community of Saint George was inspired by a prayer, and the theology behind it. The prayer is a troparion sung within the Romanian Byzantine Rite and goes,

As a saviour of the enslaved, benefactor of the poor, doctor of the sick, guardian of kings and bearer victory. Oh, Great Martyr George, pray to Christ our God to save our souls, now and always, and forever and ever. Amen.

For the Community of Saint George, I interpret the characteristics of this prayer as a commitment to justice, to those who are marginalized, a commitment to service towards the poor, and those who are suffering, a commitment to healing those who suffer from what I refer to as spiritual pain, and a commitment to Christian Unity, a commitment to our view that Jesus Christ is victorious over death, and a commitment to humility. We believe that understanding our intentions is important and to strive to live by the ideal of "In all things, may God be glorified." If we can truly do this, then we can start to erode away the hate and injustice we encounter.

"The things that we love tell us what we are."
- St. Thomas Aquinas

Concluding Thoughts

I mentioned in my discussion with Father Jerry that while in seminary I took a cross cultural experience down to the Texas/Mexico border and studied such things as immigration and border culture. It was a fascinating experience but one of the major "take aways" dealt with friendships. During the trip I spent time with a half dozen other people and got to know them and learn about their hopes, fears, and ambitions. I remember spending time with a friend named Kathy Hammitt. She was wise beyond her years, and she was a few years older. The trip took place in January of 2010 and sadly, Kathy died on June 5th of that same year from a tornado. She had gotten out of her car and was trying to get to safety and got caught in the winds of the tornado. Her death was a sad time and years later I still think about that trip and the friendships I made and how friendship is an important glue within the Independent Sacramental Movement.

During the trip I kept a journal. Instead of writing in a narrative style I wrote this journal exclusively in haiku. The first haiku about friendship is here, titled *"Good time with Kathy,"*:

Good time with Kathy
Conversation can be fun
When had with a friend

The second haiku about the importance of friendship is titled, "*Important friendships,*":

Important friendships
Vignettes of time here and there
Those who care thank you

I think about Kathy and the friendships I made on the two weeks of that cross cultural trip. I think about the friends that I have made over the years and how I have been influenced and enriched by those friendships. I mentioned that friendship is an important glue within the Independent Sacramental Movement. What I mean by that statement points to how small this movement is and how important friendships have become in creating a stable environment across jurisdictional lines. In the past, it has seemed the bishops wanted to insulate their clergy from other jurisdictions out of fear that someone would "steal" their clergy. Some of this, I think, still exists today but it is my hope that this fear will be replaced with friendships and the various jurisdictions will learn to work together and stop trying to reinvent the wheel.

With the advent of the podcast, *Sacramental Whine*, I have had the pleasure of talking to a lot of people. Many I probably would not have to talked to if it wasn't for the podcast. It has been a true blessing to me to be able to make so many connections and establish friendships where I would not have been able to in the past; however, you do not need a podcast to reach out to someone across jurisdictional lines and say, "Hey, I would like to get to know you. Can we talk?" Take the time to make connections and build friendships that will hopefully last a lifetime.

For Reflection, Contemplation and Prayer:

• Have you made friends within the Independent Sacramental Movement? Have you crossed jurisdictional lines?

• Are you willing to take a mature step forward and fight hatred and injustice? What does this look like?

• What is your vision of being a disciple in the "here and now?"

CHAPTER FOUR

— • —

"FOOL FOR GOD"

CHAPLAIN MIR PLEMMONS

"As each has received a gift, use it to serve one another, as good stewards of God's varied grace..."
- 1 Peter 4:10

Chaplain Mir Plemmons is a Deacon in the Ecumenical Catholic Communion and a novice in the Order of Ecumenical Franciscans. He has been a Franciscan for over 28 years and has served as a chaplain for over 34 years. Mir and his wife live *almost* far enough from Seattle to enjoy the natural terrain Washington has to offer, and he teaches high school special education. He does disaster mental health as a Field Traumatologist. He has extensively taught socio-emotional skills. He is a writer and an editor and serves and advocates for Intersex, QUILTBAG+, and Science Fiction & Fantasy Fandom. He volunteers extensively in multiple organizations including, but not limited to, the Society for Creative Anachronism, Civil Air Patrol, and Okanogan Fire Protection District 12.

He tries hard to pay attention to his wife's reminders to get enough self-care and rest to at least not be a bad example... [Note: in August of 2021 Mir was ordained to the priesthood.]

KLING: What is your elevator speech? How would you describe the Independent Sacramental Movement to somebody who has no idea what it is?

PLEMMONS: I talk about how we are Catholic, but not Roman, which is the first thing I get out of the way. I tend to point us back toward the early church and Old Catholicism and the unity of the early church councils. If someone gives me one of those eyebrows, that sounds like they are going to stand for Rome, well it is not productive to get into an argument about Rome. I try not to say anything inflammatory, such as, "I think we are the authentic Church.

KLING: My second question deals specifically with your jurisdiction. Can you talk about the Ecumenical Catholic Communion and also talk about Franciscan spirituality?

PLEMMONS: Well, there are many Franciscan houses and families. There is one within the Ecumenical Catholic Communion, but so many beyond. It is its own thing. I'll separate those out. The Ecumenical Catholic Communion is a collection of regional congregations following the old traditions of a bishop knows their region or a region knows their bishop, and both know their needs better than a huge outside organization. The structure really comes in at that regional level, and from there those regions come together into a family and we are coming up on our synod next week in which we will all gather. We have a presiding bishop, and he is part of an episcopal council. He makes decisions in consultation with his sibling bishops. This is something that is very important to us.

We have congregations in Poland, in the Netherlands and larger pieces of the "new world" as well as in the United States, which is our largest group. We have something on the order of, I think, it is 60 different congregations.

KLING: Wow. That's impressive. You mentioned the Franciscans. I'm curious about Franciscan spirituality. Can you elaborate?

PLEMMONS: Franciscans, there are many Franciscan Orders and families. Saint Francis is fascinating the most popular saint. A popular myth of Francis sees him out with a couple of birds and a deer, and if I'm lucky, a wolf, because I'm fond of that wolf and Franciscan theology. There is more to it than a statue of St. Francis in the garden with birdseed in his hands, although that is a pretty suitable metaphor. So, we have an academic Franciscan tradition and dear God go play in Duns Scotus. So many wonderful things that we have done in our scholarship as well, but there is a piece of us that really is the friar wandering the back roads or the conventual friar working in the factory and teaching the students of the poor. You can probably guess that I'm more like the second. I teach students about Franciscan spirituality, which is about the beauty of creation. The beauty of God's work, the joy of God, and the willingness to be a fool for God, and to honor and acknowledge God's foolish, which is an extravagant love for us. That is a large piece of being a Franciscan.

KLING: That's fascinating. Now, in your bio, you mentioned that you have been a Franciscan for 28 years. I'm assuming that's not been 28 years with the Order of Ecumenical Franciscans, but with a different order?

PLEMMONS: I am a novice within the Order of Ecumenical Franciscans. I was previously a part of one of the many other Franciscan Orders.

There is an old joke that the three things that no one knows is how much money does the Pope have; how many heresies do the Jesuits have; and how many different Orders of Franciscans exist? No one knows how many Franciscans there are! So, I have followed Saint Francis and had Franciscan vows in an Order that didn't manage to make the bridge of a generation, which is hard. When that Order collapsed in on itself, I needed a new Franciscan home. I went looking, and the Order of Ecumenical Franciscans is a delightful group of people who can go deep or go goofy in the change of a moment and have so much love in God, and in each other that it is a beautiful, and fully Franciscan thing. I am very glad to have found this home.

KLING: It sounds like Franciscan spirituality is a major part of your identity? It is amazing that you have carried on for 28 years. You also mentioned that you have served as a chaplain for 34 years. This leads me to my next question. I'm particularly interested in your volunteer chaplaincy work, especially within different forms of science fiction and fantasy fandom. Can you talk about that?

PLEMMONS: The science fiction and fantasy community, known as fandom, is a group of people that gather around a desire to immerse themselves in stories and metaphors of a future that is possible, or maybe something that isn't possible at all. One of the fascinating things is that fantasy stories, when you free yourself of lining up with a specific geography and history of a place, what you are left with is the human story. Human hopes and fears and worries and struggles. They are purely human stories, and that's part of what I love.

You end up with this group of people, who are usually quite happy to call themselves geeks and who are immersed in that subculture get together at conventions four to six times a year, depending on what region they are located. This means that they have a kind of episodic friendship, because you see these people every few months. You share all the news, you do all the connections, and then you won't see them for another few months. As you might guess, these interactions can be intensely good and intensely moving, and sometimes heartbreaking. You hear about losses and deaths, and you occasionally see breakups and things like that. A chaplain in that community is someone who knows their fellow geeks. I know them because I am one of them. I'm going to find the person crying under the stairs and plunk down next to them and offer them a tissue. I'm going to step in when a conversation has gone a little too far and suggest that maybe we stop and change directions. I am the person who might bring somebody who has just had something bad happen to them into a hotel room and calm them down and be with them until the police come.

All these things are traditional chaplaincy things that need a fandom flavor and vocabulary, and that is what I can do. It also means that I can help people integrate their geek identity with their full identity and tell them that God loves their creativity and their imagination too. This is some of the most amazing things I've done. Being able to serve mass to somebody in a Klingon costume and watch them integrate themselves as a whole being and watch that settle. Maybe I'm the first person who has ever acknowledged someone who is exploring being transgender, and to give them the Cup under the name they have chosen for the weekend. There are so many stories like this.

KLING: Can you share some stories and tell us what type of fandom that you were working with? I'm interested in specific stories that you can share.

PLEMMONS: I've given mass to a Klingon and to somebody who used the name Noel for the first time and watched that change. I rapidly came up with a blessing for fun. It was a good time when SCAers (note: Society for Creative Anachronism) were having a demo at a convention and wanted a battle blessing. I was like, "Let me change that up just a little bit for you. Okay, not going to go all church militant. Thanks." But it was fun to do. I got to bless someone in armor. It was pretty rocking. I've had opportunities where I've talked about social and emotional wellbeing, as decisions were made about leadership in various fan clubs in science fiction.

I'm the person who is the advocate and unofficial ombudsman within the Royal Manticoran Navy, and there are a fair number of us that are Independent Sacramental clergy who are members.

I have been a member of the Society of Creative Anachronism for a very long time, which means that I have done critical incident stress debriefings for event's steward teams. This would be at events that had a crisis and then I will check in with them for the next few months to make sure they are processing well around what had happened. Also, I am still the theoretical head of the first aid team, the Chirurgeon's guild.

I have been able to bless someone who is a devout Christian and to attend his laureling ceremony, help with preparation and be his chaplain along the journey, which was amazing. There are so many of these moments, when you are in a community that is beautiful.

KLING: I have a Star Trek story to share. When I was in the US Navy, back in the late 1980s and early 1990s. I had just transferred from Washington, DC, to the USS Dwight D Eisenhower. At this point in my life, I decided I wanted to be Roman Catholic, and I had been reading a lot of Thomas Merton and other things. I approached the chaplain on the Ike. He was a full captain and I believe he was the head chaplain for all the chaplains on the ship. I told him I wanted him to be Catholic. He asked me, "Are you getting married?" I said, "no." He said, "Well, why do you want to be Catholic?" I responded, "Because I want to be Catholic." He thought there was a reason, such as I was getting married or there was a girl or something. And I kept telling him, "No," but I don't think he believed me. He never made time for me. I wasn't impressed. I really wasn't impressed.

At the time I was a member of a club called Starfleet International. I had been active, as best I could from a distance well before the Internet. I started in a chapter in Columbus, Ohio, to a chapter in the DC Metro area, and then when I transferred to Virginia, I found a chapter in Norfolk, Virginia.

When I was talking to folks at the Norfolk, Virginia chapter about my struggles and my frustrations with the ship's chaplain and wanting to be Catholic, someone said, "We know a priest up in Richmond, Virginia, who is a member of the chapter there." It was 30 or more years ago. I was put in touch with Father Joseph Terry Marks. Father Marks was part of the Traditionalist Movement, a subculture within the Independent Sacramental Movement.

Traditionalists reject Vatican II and celebrate mass according to the Tridentine Rite in Latin. Father Marks had been with the Roman Catholic Church in the diocese of Louisville, Kentucky, but left because of liturgical abuses he observed and could not live with. He affiliated with the Society St. Pius X. He helped with some mission work in Norfolk, and served as pastor of a parish in Richmond, Virginia, "Our Lady of Fatima Traditionalist Roman Catholic Parish. The people who put me in touch with Father Marks did not know the difference between the traditionalist Catholics and "the canonical church."

So, they put me in touch with Father Marks and I discovered he was serving a SSPX mission in Norfolk twice a month. I was baptized by Father Joseph Terry Marks and confirmed by Bishop Richard Williamson of the SSPX. After I left the US Navy I joined a traditionalist Benedictine Monastery, Christ the King Monastery, that Father Marks recommended.

My involvement in the Traditionalist Movement and becoming Roman Catholic in 1991 was ultimately because of my involvement in Star Trek fandom.

PLEMMONS: I have had a lot of conversations at conventions where I would recommend the exploration of "this or that particular path" to someone. A path that seemed well suited to what they were seeking.

KLING: It is interesting how people find meaning and purpose. When I was in seminary, I took a course called *Theology in Film*. The reason this class was important is that many people have stopped going to church, but they still find meaning and purpose somewhere. Often it is in pop culture. In my hospice work, I had a patient who watched the film Dune every day. If you were to ask him if he believed in God, he would tell you he was an atheist. There was something about the movie Dune that spoke to him spiritually, especially while he was dying. There is a lot of need in these little niches that you've mentioned.

PLEMMONS: I totally agree. I have done a Tolkien memorial service, which was easy, and I did a Game of Thrones memorial service for my partner/teacher. That was a little more challenging. I had to go to Game of Thrones fans to find readings that were going to say what I needed to say in a memorial service. That was what she held on to as she fought cancer. I needed to honor what she had found truth in.

KLING: My next question deals with your greatest challenge. What has been your greatest challenge within ministry?

PLEMMONS: My greatest challenge is that I have the heart and reflexes and skills of a chaplain. I can see the need for a congregation here in my area of Independent Catholics, of those who have been burned by Rome and need a home. I haven't got the first idea of how to successfully put out the word and gather people. I'm great at showing up at a street corner, making it a holy place and giving some comfort. I do not know how to recruit. Advertising? That isn't quite the right word for that kind of outreach. I don't know.

KLING: Well, advertising and marketing, that's all a part of new church planting. We may not like those terms, but I'm sure if you had an MBA (Master's in Business Management) that would probably help you out a lot better than if you had an M.Div (Master of Divinity).

PLEMMONS: I think that's very true. I've tried "this," and I've tried "that" and it's still obvious that I'm fumbling. I'm not entirely sure how to bring people together.

KLING: I'm no expert in new church planting, but one thing that I would recommend is consistency. If you are trying to facilitate a new church plant and you say that you are going to celebrate mass at nine o'clock on Sunday or six o'clock on Saturday evening and you do it a couple of times and nobody shows up, don't get discouraged. Keep doing it. Consistency is very important and just keep doing it. Eventually, if it is blessed by the Holy Spirit, you will get people, but consistency is important.

It is when people get discouraged, and they hold a service once or twice, and then they stop. Keep doing it even when you think no one is going to show. You are doing it for the greater glory of God, not for your own ego. Just say, "No matter who shows up, we're going to do the best we can. We're going to give glory to God."

PLEMMONS: When the plague ends, my intent is to start a street and homeless and outdoors and park ministry and see if I can get somebody to come along with me and work in the vineyard. See whether it may be what I can build as a ministry team.

KLING: When I formed the Community of St. George, which is part jurisdiction, part religious order, we had one person and that was me. Now we are doing fine. Be consistent and do good work and it will pay off. Be patient, and sometimes that is hard because we don't live in a patient world. My last question, what has been your greatest blessing within ministry? [Note: The Community of Saint George was dissolved and has become the Ancient Apostolic Church of Alexandria.]

PLEMMONS: So many blessed moments. So many times, when God has used me to touch, or heal, to speak that one word, to reflect back what that person has said to you and watch them straighten up a little, find a little light. Take a breath and go back to their battles. Those times when I can be a Theotokos, and bear Christ to this person and see them touched and helped.

KLING: That's a great blessing to have and to carry around. It sounds like you have had plenty of opportunities to see the Spirit working within you and your ministry. Do you have any closing comments or thoughts?

PLEMMONS: We are all struggling with hard times right now, our resilience is normally meant for short runs, and we are in one heck of a marathon right now. Give yourselves grace, give yourselves patience, go do the self-care thing and then do your buddy checks. This is a long run we are in, but remember that we can walk in love and we can bear light and together we can walk out the far side.

Most High, be with your scattered people who seek to hear your call. Be with our people in a wilderness time, in a hard time, remind them of your precious love, of your deep compassion and your abiding strength, that wraps around each one of us. As your family, give to each one of us, your breath, your Spirit, that we may breathe your Spirit to the world. We ask these things in Christ's name. Amen.
[Prayer by Chaplain Mir Plemmons]

Concluding Thoughts

Popular culture is a powerful agent within our society and living during the age of streaming services, we see so many great programs being produced. I grew up in an "unchurched" family, so popular culture became the source of my personal spirituality. Much of what was popular in my youth, in the 1980s, is becoming popular again and exciting. In my work as a chaplain, I have many patients that are also "unchurched," and I find I can navigate through their quirks easily because of my upbringing.

Now that I find myself in my fifties with a four-year-old daughter, it has become my intention to raise her in the best of both worlds.

Embracing the best that popular culture offers, the power of myth and what it means to be a hero, along with a spirituality that embraces openness and acceptance. Vivianne loves Disney princesses but is also being introduced to Star Wars and Star Trek and has taken a particular interest in my Austin Powers' bobble head.

As I get older, I find I'm more and more like the guy who would shout, "Get off my lawn," and there is a lot from my youth that I remember fondly and wish my daughter could enjoy. Such things as going outside and playing and just being a kid; however, there are things about today's society that I cherish, such as great wi-fi. It is a good paradox. People will make meaning out of life regardless of church attendance. I'm trying to embrace the change.

For Reflection, Contemplation and Prayer:

• Finding meaning and purpose is important. What are ways you find meaning and purpose?

• Are there types of fandoms that appeal to you? What aspects of popular culture feeds you spiritually?

• Have you approached someone for spiritual support and guidance only to have them question your motivations and ultimately dismiss you? How did you reconcile this experience?

CHAPTER FIVE

— • —

"TAKE YOUR TIME"

DEACON KAREN GORDON

"Now Deborah, a prophetess, the wife of Lappidoth, was judging Israel at that time. She used to sit under the palm of Deborah between Ramah and Bethel in the hill country of Ephraim, and the people of Israel came up to her for judgment. She sent and summoned Barak the son of Abinoam from Kedesh-naphtali and said to him, "Has not the Lord, the God of Israel, commanded you, 'Go, gather your men at Mount Tabor, taking 10,000 from the people of Naphtali and the people of Zebulun. And I will draw out Sisera, the general of Jabin's army, to meet you by the river Kishon with his chariots and his troops, and I will give him into your hand'?"
- Judges 4:4 -7

Deacon Karen Gordon is a student for the priesthood in the United American Catholic Church. She is a veteran of the US Navy having served from 1984 until 1989. She has worked for the University of Tennessee at Memphis in the office of the Dean of Students, she has worked in public affairs at the United States Naval Academy in Annapolis. She has done an impressive amount of volunteer work and she holds an associate of arts from Anne Arundel Community College and a Bachelor of Arts from the University of Maryland in Interactive Electronic Publications. She is currently a Master of Divinity student with Nations University. [Note: Karen was ordained to the priesthood in October of 2020].

KLING: My first question is, what is your elevator speech? How would you describe the Independent Sacramental Movement to someone who has no idea what it is?

GORDON: For me, the Independent Catholic Movement would be described as something that upholds Roman Catholic Church traditions that I was raised with but without all the limitations on women and allowing LGBTQ and others into the worship service. That is the closest I can get.

KLING: What you're saying is a more inclusive Roman Catholicism?

GORDON: Yes. Taking away the limitations because I don't believe anyone should have communion withheld from them. If they are a faithful Catholic or Christian, I don't believe that's the priest job, to withhold communion.

KLING: Thank you for sharing. My second question has to do with the life you have lived. How has that life revealed to you your vocation to ministry and to holy orders? You have been in the military, done volunteer work, and several things to make a living. How has all of that revealed to you your vocation to ministry and holy orders? Can you talk about your vocation?

GORDON: Sure. My vocation is different from most priests. I was raised in a lower middle class income family and was looking for a way out of that situation where you live paycheck to paycheck. I wanted to go to college, which no one in my family had done before. I decided the best way to do this was to lead with faith and join the military. It was the same feeling I have when I worship, and I had going into the military. It was that deep love of doing something that was helping other people. I was doing some things for the good of my country. Now, I do things for the good of the church. It's a very similar situation. My military service was typical, you go in and do your job. I was discharged with an injury that resulted in my inability to work for over twenty-five years. I spent time in a wheelchair. That was the biggest lesson for me. Going into a wheelchair and learning limitations. I couldn't get up and dress myself. I couldn't go out walking with my dog, not being able to go to college and participate in classes without thinking about, "Can I get up? Do they have a wheelchair ramp, or am I able to keep up with the classes mentally?"

Because of all the medical conditions that were ongoing, that difficulty taught me how to deal with other veterans and other individuals who say, "You don't understand." I do understand. I've been in that position, and I do believe that God walked into my life in a deeper sense, allowing me to be healed so that I can help other veterans. This is my mission. My mission is to go out and to work with veterans. I want to help them find the inner peace that I found. To reconcile moral injury, dealing with military sexual trauma, and with other incidents that occur in the military. I have that ability, only because I suffered through it for twenty-five years.

KLING: It sounds like your vocation to the priesthood is tied to the work that you've done in the past. Tied to your military service.

GORDON: Much of it is tied to the work I have done. I have always worked with the homeless. I have gone out and fed the hungry and given clothing. Clothing drives or baked goods to sell to raise funds for a Christmas tree project. These things have always been integral to me and it's a continuation of going out and helping veterans too. My mission, the way I see it, is to go out and help people regardless of who they are. With my personal affiliation with the military, I feel a deep affinity for people in the military who have suffered moral injury or trauma, and who don't know how to deal with it. So, yeah, I guess it is.

KLING: Thank you for sharing, it sounds like you're committed to not only an inclusive ministry, but a ministry of service to those who have suffered in some way.

GORDON: Yes. That would sum it up clearly.

KLING: My next question continues to look at your story. Even though most jurisdictions within the Independent Sacramental Movement allow for the ordination of women most are still heavily populated by men. As a woman, how has it been for you navigating through the ordination process as a woman? Has it been different?

GORDON: I believe it has been different. One of the incidences that became a problem was being assigned to write three or four papers on women as clergy. I shouldn't have to write four papers on women in ministry. On Martha, Priscilla, and on Mary of Magdalene, just because I'm a woman. If you're going to require these papers, then require them of everyone and maybe more so for men. Require the men to write about women so they understand that women were integral in the history of the Church. It has been a sore spot with me, because they are more concerned with men. Clergy and seminary students learning about the practicum of what they are doing, and with the women, it seemed like they were more worried about the touchy feely of, "What do you need to do today? What are we going to teach you?" I was not receiving the necessary training.

KLING: You felt like you were singled out and given an alternative track?

GORDON: I know I was! The other female in the program were too; because I went through the previous training that was held and it had none of these "required" papers. The previous woman who had gone through the tracks, also I believe, had to write one or two papers that were different from the papers the men were being offered.

KLING: I went to an accredited seminary, not part of the Independent Sacramental Movement. The seminary was affiliated with the United Methodist Church. Most of the professors I had were women. I did have a couple of men. I had some African American men. I had two Korean men as professors but at least three women professors. There was a diverse faculty. When I was in college, I took a course called The Women of the Old Testament. Everyone in the class had to write about a woman in the Old Testament. Something I thought was interesting, and I'm thinking about now as you were talking about your story, was the women in the course. The women of the Old Testament they picked to write their papers about. It seemed like the men picked women who were strong within the Hebrew Bible, or Old Testament. Women who had a story to tell, that put them in a positive light. Most of the women in the class, at least the ones in my little discussion group, picked women who they could look down upon. It was strange, except for one person in our group who was a women's studies major. I think she wrote about Deborah, but the rest of them were, very different. I thought that was interesting.

GORDON: Well, that kind of fits though, because unfortunately humans tend to look down on people to try and build themselves up. That may have been a way that they were doing that to show that they were stronger. It's hard to say, but it makes sense to me somewhere in the back of my mind to say, "Yeah, you could choose that."

KLING: I thought that was interesting, and they picked women that they could pick apart and show all the things that they did wrong. There was one exception, one woman who was a women's studies major. She picked the most powerful woman in the Hebrew Bible, Deborah. She was a strong figure. I wrote about the necromancer or witch of Endor who summoned up the spirit of the Prophet Samuel, for Saul. The group dynamics were interesting and which women the women in the group picked tow write about versus the men.

GORDON: I'm not like most women, or I don't believe I am, but many of the women I know are what we call catty, and that is typical process. You want to be better than someone else. You're going to pick someone who's less than you. So, when you want to go to the bar you pick someone a little less pretty to go with you because you want the guys to look at you. This is the same type of situation where you're going to pick someone that you're better than them, and you're going to show how they messed up and you're not going to make that same mistake.

KLING: I've noticed that same cultural dynamic between men and women. It is just interesting. I find that what's interesting about your story is that when you studied in different jurisdictions and as you made progress towards the priesthood that you were assigned writing assignments based upon your gender and not upon what you needed to know to be a good priest. I find that troubling.

GORDON: It was a sticking point for me, and my reason for leaving the second place.

KLING: Let's transition to the next question. What has been your greatest challenge within the Independent Sacramental Movement?

GORDON: My greatest challenge has been finding somewhere that is legitimate seminary formation program. The first place that I was accepted into seminary, I declined their invitation. The reason I declined is I was interviewed at the location. I interviewed at the chapel where the archbishop lived with his wife. I visited with my husband, and the archbishop was one of the most pompous self-aggrandizing individuals I've ever met, and I've met a president and a pope and they were not that self-aggrandizing. That is why I declined the invitation to start seminary with them.

KLING: Well, you've probably narrowed it down to about three fourths of the Independent Movement, just kidding.

GORDON: Well, he came out with his pom-pom hat, and full regalia as if it was a High Sunday mass. It could have been Christmas Eve services, the most formal high church you have attended. I was told to ensure that I called him "your grace," and to ensure that I showed him the appropriate reverence. I was there for an interview. I wasn't a seminary student. I was applying and when I was accepted, I noted to him that I had heard him make statements at the interview about firing or suspending four or five priests and I wanted to know why, because he only had 12 priests and he suspended four or five. That gives me pause. He said it was not my place to question a bishop.

He knew what he was doing. He was the only bishop, and I would not be involved with that, which gave me pause. The next step was signing up for seminary courses at his non-accredited college and pay $10,000 per semester to attend. I could go to a real seminary and get a degree for $10,000? That was not a legitimate church, if you asked me at that point.

KLING: Wow $10,000, I'm doing it all wrong.

GORDON: He offered me a 15% discount if I was a seminary student with them. So, it would only be $8,500. My guess is that the students attending this non-accredited college were paying for his priory.

KLING: Sure, vestments aren't cheap.

GORDON: That's the only thing I can figure. Being a bishop was his only job. So, he had to be making money somewhere.

KLING: I'm sorry you went through that, and you said that was the first? What about after that? How did it go?

GORDON: The second church was better. It took a substantial length of time to get my application looked at, since there was a problem going on with one of their bishops. I believe they had six or seven bishops out of 20 clergy. So, they're a little heavy on the bishop side. They finally got to the application and were in the process of approving it, and said, "We'll start your study and finalize everything at that point." I figured, "Yes! I've been accepted." So, I decided to do it, and everything was fine at the beginning, until I started realizing there was no practicum. I had to request to work at the altar in order to shadow a deacon prior to my diaconate ordination. I was never formally trained on the altar. It was all "OJT" which I had to request. I asked, "Hey, when can I start doing a homily? I want to start practicing," and was told, "Okay, you've got this date." No one asked to look at it. No one questioned it. No one asked what I was talking about. I just gave the homily.

KLING: So, no training in homiletics before they wanted you to preach?

GORDON: No. I never read a book about it, but I had a good idea of what I wanted to say. Thank goodness it was well received. It was received well enough, and by my third homily a woman had seen my name on the list and drove over an hour to hear me speak. My third one, I totally thought I blew it because there was not a sound to be heard, and I couldn't figure out what was I saying that had been so horrifying. I discovered that they enjoyed it so much, that they were listening intensely. I was so thankful for that.

KLING: It sounds like you're happier where you're at now. Third time seems to be the charm.

GORDON: Third time's the charm. The bishop and the church I'm working with is smaller than the second one. The training included a list of books. There are assignments each week. So much better, I'm learning in depth knowledge. I've done practicum for the mass service. I will be giving my first deacon service in two weeks. Very different.

KLING: There's been a lot of talk on the topic of formation lately. What are some of the things that you think are essential for formation to the priesthood? You don't have to come up with an exhaustive list, just some of the things off the top of your head that you think priests should know before they're ordained

GORDON: Well, the sacrament 100%. People need to know the sacraments. What they are, how they are provided to people. When do you use them? The different prayers you use before services, such as the rite of marriage. I know priests who have ordained in the Independent Movement that go out and will marry anyone, no matter what they ask. Some say, "I want to have candles," or "I want to do Pagan ribbon wrapping around the hand in the middle of the service. I don't want the word God." These priests just go out and do these things. I don't think that's what the Independent Movement is supposed to be. I thought we were supposed to be providing a Church, not just filling a gap for people who don't go to church but still want a church wedding by a priest.

That is one of the problems I see that we are not necessarily being trained in the discipleship and mission work. I think this needs to be forefront. Most Independent Churches don't have churches. How can you fill a gap for people that want to be Christians or Independent Catholic if you're not using the church? You must have knowledge of missional theology, evangelism, going out and finding the not-yet Christian or not-yet Catholic and bringing Christ to them. Discipleship is a hundred percent necessary!

KLING: I speak of formation often. It's nice to have different view on the topic of formation. My final question is what has been your greatest blessing being a part of the Independent Sacramental Movement?

GORDON: The greatest blessing for me is being able to serve at the altar equally with men and other women. The fact that I can put on an alb and a stole and reverence the altar as a full-fledged member, brings me to tears. It's something I've wanted my whole life and never thought it would be possible. I can share my love of Christ with people that I normally wouldn't have. My position is now one of authority; whereas before, if I shared my love of Jesus, it was just one person to another. Now, as a priest, it means a little bit more. It has more authority to it. I'm taking the steps to go through seminary. To do the training, to learn my role, and be able to share this with others.

KLING: Thank you for sharing some of your story with me today. Do you have any closing thoughts that you'd like to share?

GORDON: Well, for the women out there, if you truly desire a part in Christian mission work and being part of the priesthood, take your time. Find the right place. Ask a lot of questions and avoid the pitfalls of paper churches, and hollow bishops. For the men out there, to accept women with the full authority that you accept men. Don't look at them differently. We want to learn things and we want to work in the same way y'all do.

"Nothing great was ever achieved without enduring much."
- St. Catherine of Siena

Concluding Thoughts

Homiletics is the study of preaching. Initially, I resisted having to take a course in homiletics. I thought, "I've preached before, why do I have to take a course in something I already know how to do?" I had an unhealthy amount of arrogance back then. When I looked at the book list I rolled my eyes, "Why do I have to read 'Black Preaching: The Recovery of a Powerful Art,' by Henry Mitchell? I'm not black!"

Little did I know, but that homiletics class would change my life. The course challenged me from the first day of class when the professor walked in the door. He carried a basket and had each of us take a piece of paper from the basket. On that paper was a single line of scripture and he told us, "You have five minutes to prepare a one-minute sermon." Not as easy as you would think, especially when done in front of your peers.

I realized I was okay as a public speaker, but I lacked the passionate zeal of a true preacher. I came to desire being filled with the Holy Spirit in my preaching. As time went on, I felt the need to talk to my professor where I said, "I feel guilty. I was critical of having to read Henry Mitchell; however, I loved the book. When he wrote about class struggle it resonated with me. I love the book, what else do you recommend?" He recommended I read Howard Thurman.

Howard Thurman was a Baptist minister who was a friend of Martin Luther King, Sr, and his son. He was a civil rights giant, working behind the scenes. I started reading Howard Thurman and ultimately specialized my M.Div in Black Church and African Diaspora Studies. My specialization project was a comparison of the theology of Martin Luther King, Jr. and Howard Thurman.

I resisted having to take that homiletics course because I knew better. I resisted the reading selection for the course because my whiteness was threatened. When I opened myself up to different perspectives, and recognized my own privilege, I could not only learn and grow, but could be transformed.

For Reflection, Contemplation and Prayer:

- Finding the right community can be challenging. Community is important and finding the right one can truly make a difference in your life. What has been your journey in finding the right community?

- Women have struggled to find acceptance and equality. What are some ways you can support women and promote better acceptance and equality for women?

- What is a time when you resisted something, only to find that your resistance was your own pride holding you back?

Chapter Six

— • —

"A Pastor's Heart"

Bishop James St. George

"For we do not have a high priest who is unable to sympathize with our weaknesses, but one who in every respect has been tempted as we are, yet without sin."
- Hebrews 4:15

Bishop James Michael St. George, also known as Father or Friar Jim, serves as a Bishop within the Old Catholic Churches International and is the Bishop of the Diocese of Saint Bernard of Clairvaux (which includes Pennsylvania, New Jersey, and part of New York) and serves as Pastor of Saint Miriam Pro-Cathedral Parish, and is a professed Franciscan.

He was born and raised in Erie, Pennsylvania and graduated from college and became a licensed Funeral Director and returned to help run the family funeral home before going back to college to attend formal seminary in Washington, DC. In addition to his prior funeral and business professional experience, his career has allowed him to serve as a youth pastor, nursing home and hospice chaplain, and as a Certified Trauma Chaplain focusing primarily on trauma and triage emergency services. Friar Jim served as a Trauma/Triage Chaplain at Lehigh Valley Hospital, a nationally recognized trauma and medical center in Allentown for over six years.

In addition to his serving as Pastor at Saint Miriam Parish, Friar Jim is an Adjunct Professor and Instructor at two Philadelphia area universities teaching in the areas of Ethics, World Religions, Philosophy, Introduction to the Bible, Religion, and Culture, Catholic Theology and Urban Studies and Justice. Friar Jim serves now, or has previously served, on the Adjunct Staff for Community College of Philadelphia, Chestnut Hill

College in Philadelphia, University of Phoenix, and has lectured at The University of Pennsylvania and various churches and inter-faith groups in the Philadelphia region.

Friar Jim is an alum of Gannon University, Pittsburgh Institute of Mortuary Science, Howard University, Howard University School of Divinity, and completed additional course study and received certifications at Virginia Theological Seminary, Catholic University, St. Louis University, Canterbury Cathedral International Studies Centre, the Benedictine Abbaye Notre-Dame du Bec in Normandy France, Sibley Hospital in Washington, DC, Lehigh Valley Hospital, Allentown, PA, and Albert Einstein Medical Center, Philadelphia, PA, with a Residency in Clinical Pastoral Education.

KLING: My first question is, what is your elevator speech? How would you describe the Independent Sacramental Movement to somebody who does not know what it is?

ST. GEORGE: Oh boy, this is probably going to get me in trouble. I really don't have an elevator speech, and what I mean by that is I remember when I was interviewed by Father Rick Romero one time. He asked me that and he asked me about the Independent Sacramental Movement and then the Old Catholic Movement. I said something that I think set him back. I said, "I really don't care about it," and he was like, "What do you mean you don't really care about it?" I said, "I have so much to do with my parish. I'm trying to build this parish from nothing, and I've been rather successful at it."

My whole point was, and is that in this area, when somebody comes up to me and says," Oh Father, where are you at? I say I'm at St. Miriam. I don't have to go any further anymore." I've laid all the groundwork. What I find helpful is I tell them where I'm at. They ask if I'm part of the archdiocese, I tell them no, that I'm independent of Rome. I tell them about our Franciscan heritage and what St. Miriam is all about. That's as far as it goes or else they will take me to where they need answers to questions. I often find that what we are and what we represent is what a lot of Catholics of all stripes are thirsting for. I hate to disappoint everybody, but I don't have a magic elevator speech.

KLING: You segued well into my next question, and that is you seem to be a very successful pastor. Can you talk about your work at St. Miriam's parish?

ST. GEORGE: I'll let you get away with a successful pastor thing, Oliver, for a minute. I think that St. Miriam is probably one of the most successful parishes in the Movement. We've been around a little over 13 years. This coming March, God-willing, we'll enter our 14th year. We started off as a thought and an idea built first on paper, while I was a chaplain at Albert Einstein Medical Center, my first calling after seminary was chaplaincy. Even though I reluctantly went into it only because I couldn't find a job anywhere else, and so I became a chaplain in a CPE program. Then I ended up finding my way, and God wanted me there. I ended up becoming a Board-Certified Chaplain. Then I ended up becoming a trauma chaplain, and then I trained trauma chaplains at some of the nation's largest trauma centers.

I enjoy that work, and I thought that's what I was going to do. I often told people that my ministry was done in 12 to 24 hours or less. St. Miriam is different. When I got burned out from trauma chaplaincy and seeing all that horror that most chaplains don't like to talk about. I prayed about it. I wanted to do something different, and I remember speaking to the bishop back then, and I said I'd like to build a parish. They gave me all the reasons I should go to an opening that they had in Virginia, or I should go somewhere else. I shouldn't try to start something on my own, but what I wanted to do at St. Mariam was create something and to have intentionality with the entire process. The only way that I could do that was to build it in my mind's eye. Translate that over to paper, and then I did something that was crazy. I had no money. I was struggling to make ends meet on a chaplain's salary. I paid for a website, and I built a website that wasn't released to the public to feel what St. Miriam would be, and what I realized in doing that, which took well over a year, was that it gave me some touchstones that I wanted to always have in a good parish. I wanted polished liturgy, but I wanted liturgy that was accessible. I wanted to do form and manner that made sense to anyone coming off the street that knew anything about Catholicism, but I didn't want it to be restrictive and I didn't want it to be harmful.

I also wanted something that honored the Blessed Mother. I started right off the bat by having a Thursday rosary after a Thursday mass; we chose Thursday; I wanted Wednesday, but we were in a synagogue and the Jews had Wednesday locked up and so they pushed me over to Thursday. That Thursday liturgy is still, to this day, with adoration and rosary and mass. Then we did Sunday and for the first six years of my life, as a pastor of St. Miriam, I never took a vacation. I was never absent. I was always there every Thursday; every Sunday I lived and breathed building up this parish. Then we went from rented space in a synagogue to leased space in Blue Bell, PA. After renovating it, we had about 6,000 square feet, and I thought to myself, "Dear God, what have I done? How are we going to fill this? And how are we going to afford it?" Within three years, we were out of space.

Then God brought us to Flourtown, PA, to an opportunity that we weren't looking for. We were going to purchase the corner lot property from a Lutheran church that, unbeknownst to us, we made the offer on the property that they were selling was really in dire decline. After meeting with them and negotiate a meeting with them to purchase this wooded lot property of about three acres to build a little church; they offer to sell everything to us. I remember that day sitting in the church's fellowship space. The president of the board said, "Father, have you ever seen Willy Wonka and the Chocolate Factory?" I said, "I have. It's one of my favorites." She responded, "Well, you're our Charlie." I said, "What are you talking about?" And she said, "We have an offer to buy this property three times, but we're going to sell it to you. We want it to remain in the hands of someone who will keep it a religious institution, a house of prayer for everyone, and we know you and we know your history, and we want it to be you."

That started a negotiation process, and we ended up purchasing 12 acres, a cemetery, a closed school, and an almost closed parish. Over the last six years, we have invested well over $2 million in the property. We have a vibrant school and a wonderful parish. We just renovated the last untouched part of the parish by going to our heart and literally renovating the entire sanctuary to give it a Franciscan liturgical feel that fits and matches with what we want as a parish community. We have a cemetery; we have a pet cemetery; we have a friary. Recently, we also acquired a retreat center. We have a retreat center up in Starlight, PA. We literally, in almost 14 years, went from a budget of $500 a month, and we didn't even really have $500 a month, to a budget that's right now approaching about $1.3 million a year.

People sometimes look at that and say, "Oh, you're very successful." I don't know if I'm very successful or was stupid enough not to stop. I think somewhere along the line you get to a point where what you've built is so big, no matter what the size is compared to others, a pastor has to decide, and what I had to decide was, do I take it from this little family church, do I take it to the next level? And then I did. Then, after I got it to the next level, and I started a community church, do I take it to the next level? Now, I'm at a corporate, structured church size, and every step along the way somebody would ask me, "Why didn't you stop if you thought you might?" And I said, "Because people were at stake, people that loved it, people that brought their children to our school, people that found and made a home, LGBTQ people who were rejected or harmed at other parishes and found a home with us."

It was always about the other, and what I realized was that was one of my touchstones. My touchstones have always remained the same. Strong, identifiable polished liturgy honoring the history of the church. I don't mess with the core elements of it. I'm not that bright, and many people have worked a lot harder on that than me. So as somebody who's studied liturgy, I know it and I love it for what it is. I want the history of the church to be there, but also to be welcoming. I often say, "We fling wide our doors, open for anyone. Anyone can come." The only caveat is you don't even have to believe, like we believe, except that you have to love like we love. That doesn't mean that you're going to like everybody, but you well better to love everybody. Even the person you may not agree with is welcomed in our parish. We welcome everyone. The only caveat is that you cannot harm another individual.

By way of a quick segue, I had someone that came to mass, and he almost always was drunk. I'll call him John. One day I said to him, "John. You're always welcomed at St. Miriam, but you're never welcomed here drunk." And he said, "You said everyone is welcome." And I said, "And everyone is welcome, but you're not welcome here if you're going to harm someone. And sometimes when you're intoxicated, your words harm others." He left angry, and I walked away from him sad, but I realized it was a hallmark of being a good pastor, knowing that somebody could be harmful to other people in the building.

The other touchstone is good outreach. I always thought that I would build a parish in the inner city and serve in areas like Kensington or in the forgotten areas where nobody wants to go. But God brought me to one of the richest counties in Pennsylvania, and yet what we do is we still have done outreach. Outreach is a hallmark of who we are, our Blessing Bag Program and our Hot Food Program to the streets of Kensington and Center City, Philadelphia, even during the pandemic, are strong. Then we also have an outreach to children. We educate children and we provide the regions only S.T.E.A.M.M. (Science, Technology, Engineering, Arts, Music, and Math) school for our age group. If families cannot afford to come to this private religious school, we subsidize them.

We have children in our building that are there for a hundred dollars a month, and we have those that can afford it and pay the full amount of $1600 a month. The wonderful thing about St. Miriam School is that nobody knows who they are, everyone is treated the same. Even our educators don't know which children pay full rate and which children are there on a scholarship or a subsidy. Only the administration knows, and I want it that way because I want every child to be treated the same.

I wanted a place of respite, and that's what we have through our devotions. The devotions of the church, having people come and reflect using a day of prayer, rhythms of prayer. That's why the retreat center has been such a blessing to us because now we have the opportunity to outreach to a whole new group of people that allows us to move the mission of the parish forward.

Now, in all of that, people might say that I'm successful. There are also people who say that I'm too hard on people, or I'm exact. This is one thing that I often hear. I have to do that in order to protect the lives and the well-being of those who come. It's a very hard thing to do when you have so many moving parts in a parish, the size of mine. Right now, parish size people say, "Oh, we have 1,000 families, or 100 families, or 60 families." We use what we call units, and the reason that I call them units is that I didn't want to say, "Oh, families, if I use the word families, then that means that, people in their head, they automatically, gravitate towards a mom and a dad and a child or children." I have gay and lesbian people who are families. I have gay and lesbian people with children who are families. I have a transgender family. I have multiple families in different forms that make up the complexion of St. Miriam. The other problem that I have is that sometimes people call them giving units. Well, giving units is a way of segregating those who give and those who don't. I also recognize that if you're a so-called giving unit, one thing that happens is if you are married, you're really not 2 giving units, you're a combined giving unit. So, we just call them units. We have 215 units, and those units, if you extrapolate them out, because some are families of six or eight, and some of them are single individuals, and some of them are husband and wife or married gay couples, and so on. We have probably a little over 600 persons that call St. Miriam home, plus 75 kids in the school and so forth. So, is that successful? I think it's successful and

I'm proud of it, but it also is replete with the complexities of running a parish. I often say, "I don't know if I have, knowing what I know now, would I have gone? I miss the days of 20 people. I missed the days of standing around an altar and celebrating mass in the midst of people. I miss those days." But I also know that I wasn't the designer. One thing I often say when asked, "how did you build it?" I say, "I didn't. I just learned to listen well, and I pray I listened to God."

When we first started in the synagogue, I had a couple of older women who came, and they brought this barrel into the synagogue. And I said, what is that? And they said, "oh," that we're going to collect cans. I said, for what they said, the homeless and what I realized, and what I said to them was, "I don't know what God wants us to do for outreach. But if we just donated a dollar to the soup pantry, they can do a lot more with that dollar. Then you soothing your consciousness by emptying your pantry of year-old expired food." They kind of took umbrage at that. And then they looked at the cans and they were all expired. And one thing that I said is when God is ready, God will tell us what to do. You can't walk before you crawl. Let's worry about keeping the doors open, and God will bring outreach and ministry as God sees fit. And that's what God has done.

God brought us to the homeless outreach. God has brought us to the children's education. God has brought us to welcome the immigrant and the refugee. I've literally done weddings in my sanctuary as INS was in my parking lot. Ministry and sanctuary come in many forms. And I try to remember that as I built St. Miriam, is St. Miriam perfect? No. Does St. Miriam have a lot of issues that every parish does? Certainly, But what I will say is that there's a feeling about St. Miriam, and there's a tenor of the people that truly do welcome everyone else. And if you don't, then you find your way to the door because it's just not a good fit.

KLING: Thank you for that story. For me, it's very inspiring. I work as a chaplain, I've been doing it for seven years, and I'm getting that itch that I really would like to do congregational ministry. I'm listening to your story and comparing it to my own and thinking if I could do half of what you have done. If I did a quarter of what you've accomplished, I would feel successful. So, kudos to you! Very inspirational.

I want to switch gears a bit. You wrote an essay recently in Convergent Streams: The Premier ISM Magazine, and you titled the essay, *"Empty hats, the Silent and Ever Pervasive Scourge of the Old*

Catholic ISM Movement." Can you give a synopsis of the essay and maybe reflect on some of the key points? Let's stir the pot a little.

ST. GEORGE: I was very clear in my essay that one thing that saddens me after all that we've built here. And I want to make sure that that's, stated clearly, I may have been the bus driver, but there were many people in that bus to create St. Miriam people that are with us still. I think my core team is almost all still intact. So, after 13 years, my core team on the board is still present with me and still believes in the vision. There's many people that not only were in the bus, there were those who had to carry the bus often when we ran out of money and we ran out of steam and we ran out of faith, which comes to any ministry team and especially pastors.

So, with that said, the thing that I've often been accused of is being too hard. Use the colloquialism with you, that some people think that I'm a hardass or some people think that I'm a little too exact. But the thing that I won't do, even as an ordained priest and a consecrated Bishop, is ordain those who aren't ready. And there are many people in the Independent Sacramental Movement and Old Catholic Movement that will ordain whoever comes along, and they almost say as much on their websites. What happens when you do that is you create a church that people can find a lot of faults with. I have to remind people you can kill people with a collar on your neck. You may not kill them as quickly as if you stabbed them or shot them, but they will be just as dead either inside, or literally if you harm them because you are not trained in what you are doing.

There are many people who wear a collar or ordained rapidly in succession after literally sometimes days or months with little or no qualification to all the various positions within the church. And then what that does is it allows the bigger dogs on the course, like the Roman church, and so forth to look at us with disdain and they have actual fodder to point at and say, look, look at these people. My biggest issue with the Independent Sacramental Movement is everybody wants to have a hat. I have a hat. I rarely wear the hat. I'm only acting in my episcopacy when I need to, and then the parish becomes vibrant, as a pro-cathedral, I won't even let it be a full cathedral because it's a working parish.

I chose the nomenclature of pro-cathedral and when I'm in my chair with all of my regalia on, for an ordination or confirmation or whatever that requires the diocesan Bishop I'm there, but the moment it is over, I remove all of that regalia and put my hat away for another, hopefully year. We go back to being the parish of St. Miriam and I become a working pastor. I like that, and I love what I do.

I don't enjoy seeing people who somehow figured out a way to get a hat, to make more people and more hats as quickly as they can. For whatever reason, it doesn't impress anyone. You can't even ask the average Catholic what Catholic means, let alone what it means to have valid apostolic succession and so forth. The thing that I have recognized is that we need worker priests and priests that will sacrifice everything in order to build the church in little ways and in big ways. Whatever God wants them to do, they have to listen. I would almost always bet that God doesn't need more hats. What God wants his people to do is save souls in big and small ways every single day.

As a pastor, I can be both a pastor and a seated bishop ordinary at the same time and not be arrogant about it, admitting my own sinfulness, admitting where I fall short, and still build a parish that allows people to come. I learned to grow through the Roman church for ordination when I was younger, as I was always afraid of the bishop. Bishops and magisterium and hierarchical arrangements. All of that is fearful to most Catholics. I didn't want people to be afraid of me. I want people to come to me in *persona Christi*. I want them to bring their shame and show that I also have it and forget the fancy attire and stop this social media ministry of celebrating in a bedroom. Instead of getting out onto the streets, or building what you are supposed to build, and I've listened to your podcast and I enjoy it.

One thing I often hear is people who want to be critical of the movement, or they want to be critical of what is happening, and they temper it or they try to soft-pedal it by saying things like, "Oh, I'm not trying to be hard, but blah, blah, blah, blah." I am being hard. I built something that many people haven't built. I think that gives me a place at the table and with my place at the table, I just want people to stop making hats and start doing pastoral ministry. That's what I'd like to say!

KLING: Amen. I think you're right. The idea of toxic masculinity is something I have talked about. I think that is true in the sense that if you think about toxic masculinity, just amongst men, and one aspect of that could be "the more children I have, the more viral I am, the more manly I am." I think a lot of bishops think the more people I ordain or especially consecrate, I'm more of a bishop." With you, you're busy serving a parish, you don't have time for that. In my work, as a chaplain, 40 hours a week plus on call, and I also adjunct teach. I don't have time for that either. With a lot of bishops, that is the only thing that they have time for.

ST. GEORGE: Exactly. And I hate to burst anyone's bubble. But if you think for one moment that people don't know it, that somehow you are fooling someone, everyone knows it. I have refused to buy into that, and that is hearkening back to my interview with Father Rick Romero. My point of not caring about the Independent Sacramental Movement wasn't that I don't care about it. It's that if I do my job well, and I build something, and I didn't know how big we would get, but certainly, we were probably a third of the size of what we are now, but if I can continue to build what I'm building if even when the archdiocese in Philadelphia tried to put us out, when people wouldn't come and you name it, we battled it. If I could keep my head in the game and not lose sight of what we are and not become prideful, if I could do that, then I am much more valuable to the Movement than if I do all the things that many people do and set up Facebook live in my bedroom and fancy myself as a metropolitan or put on a pallium. People don't want that and if there's one thing we've learned in this pandemic, Oliver, is people are learning two things. They are learning the value of the relationships they had with the church or they are learning to do without it. The second part, the latter one it scares me to death because look at what the Roman Church said, we're giving you a dispensation from mass, through the pandemic. Then they revoked it and they put it back out there again.

The average Catholic is going to sit out there when this is over. They are going to say, wait a minute. I was okay not to go. My soul wasn't in jeopardy during the pandemic, but now suddenly that's revoked and I have to go, or I'm fried. Well, that's what we've created. The church has created that fear and that power struggle. What I want to do is to ask all of my fellow bishops and all of my fellow clergy to remember that, to be a good priest or to be a good bishop, you've got to remember what it was like to be a good deacon. If you can't remember what it's like to be a good deacon, you have no business putting a hat on your head and you sure as hell shouldn't be making more hats. That is my whole disgruntlement with that entire system. You literally hear it all the time, "Oh, you can join so-and-so's church and they'll ordain you." The problem with that is if you're not well formed and you have no experience, you can literally kill people. I have a good problem with that.

KLING: That's a good point. One of my professors in seminary, Linda Mercadante, used to say, "Bad theology kills," and that's so true.

ST. GEORGE: Yeah. That's exactly true. When I was in chaplaincy, I looked around at my other trauma chaplains and I went from Sibley Medical Center, National Children's Hospital to Lehigh Valley Hospital, the largest hospitals known with 140 some thousand traumas a year. I worked 12 and 18 and 24-hour shifts, mostly 18 and 24-hour shifts. Then I was recruited by Einstein. I worked at Einstein until I was diagnosed with a brain tumor and God told me to pause again, but as I was exiting trauma chaplaincy, I looked at other trauma chaplains for the first time and I saw they were stoic and no longer felt empathy or sympathy. They were just so stoic about everything, or they were falling into a bottle. I didn't want either of those choices.

God led me after a good ministry in chaplaincy to pastoral ministry. Now my relationships last for years. During the pandemic, Einstein asked me to come back. They needed chaplains they could pull from when they needed them, especially because of the pandemic. They had to make sure that people knew what they were doing. I'm back in chaplaincy now just as needed *per diem* by phone call, either virtual or also I'll go to one of the Einstein Medical Centers. What I realized is that the lessons I learned in my formation as a chaplain were far more valuable than anything I learned sitting at Howard or Catholic University or St. Louis. All of them, it was invaluable. What God did during that time was enable me to understand in reality the difference between empathy and sympathy. I became more empathetic toward people, especially in those traumatic situations.

That's made me a better pastor. Had I just gone from being ordained a deacon to right away being ordained a priest without that hiatus of almost 15 years and then waiting almost another eight years before I was asked to be a bishop. Now where I am today, had I not had those what I call a kind of pause moments, I would have probably hurt somebody. I would not have been prepared. I would not have been ready. I sure as hell would have never built St. Miriam that I'm almost positive.

KLING: Thank you for the reflection on your essay. I agree with everything that you had to say, especially your work as a chaplain, making your parish ministry better. When I was in seminary, I did the opposite. I served a Unitarian Universalist Fellowship and then I completed a chaplain residency. When I reflected on my work in the parish, I think I dropped the ball with some pastoral care opportunities that I learned while in the residency. I dropped the ball when I was serving the parish because I didn't know what to say, didn't know what to do. Now, I know what to say and do. I deal with death and dying all the time in the seven years that I've been a hospice chaplain. I've noticed that, as a chaplain, parish clergy are often not equipped or prepared to deal with death. They don't know how to deal with grief, and they struggle with how to be helpful. Chaplaincy has "upped my game" so much that I can't speak highly enough about the value of Clinical Pastoral Education.

This brings me to my next question: What has been your greatest challenge in ministry?

ST. GEORGE: I often say that the thing that I most admire about the people that have stuck by me and then St. Miriam is their ability to stay in the water. What I mean by that is we live in such a throwaway, instant gratification society. People gravitate towards the commercialization of religion. People don't know how, because they haven't been taught or because they have missed it along the way. The value of long-term staying in the water relationships, the people that have been around me and are strong people, they are the people that tell me I'm being stupid. They're the people that tell me, no, that's a dumb idea. They're the people that tell me to keep my head up and things are going to be okay, and there are people that say, "Don't give up."

Those people stay in the water even when the water is almost over their nose. I value those people. When people leave the parish... I'll give you an example. We recently renovated the sanctuary and just gutted it but left all the wonderful things that were there and uncovered some things we didn't know. Like we had two hidden Tiffany Glass windows that somebody decided would look better literally with tar over it, and wallboard, we resurrected, no pun intended, all the beauty of the parish, but we also stripped down to what is fitting for our Franciscan ethos at St. Miriam. One of those things that we did almost prophetically as we went from pews to chairs and during the pandemic, it's a lot easier for me to distance you with chairs and try to figure out the right combination of distancing people in pews as a lot of parishes are finding right now.

So, we renovated that, and I had two parishioners that left my parish. One was a couple, one was a single guy, and they left in a huff, and they said, "We want pews, and that's what we grew up with. And if you won't bring the pews back, then we're leaving the parish." On their leaving, I felt sad. I felt sad for them. I felt sad for them because they put themselves before the parish, which is against everything that we are. But more to the point is I felt sad for them because they left the parish angrily and they put the hardwood of a pew before the hardwood of the cross. That made me feel like a failure. My most admired thing about parish minister, those that stay in the water, even when it doesn't look so clear.

The hardest part of ministry is letting people go when you know you need to see them go. I once had a woman who sat in my library, and we were becoming bigger. I don't know what year it was. We were at our current location. It was at least within the last six years, but I'll make a long story short. She said to me, "I don't like that you're so welcoming to gays and lesbians. I understand that you have to let them in the pews. I give a lot of money. If you're trying to be so welcoming to the gays, I will not give you the $10,000 that I give twice a year."

It stunned me for a moment, and then it was almost as if peace came over me. I'm not overly pious. I'm not going to tell you it was the Holy Spirit, but I felt peace. And I stood up, and said, "Mary the wonderful thing about the invention of a door is it lets people in to a church, and it also lets people out." Then I said, "You're welcome to use it to leave." I walked away. In that moment, I realized I was a pastor. I was protecting the most vulnerable. I was protecting those that could be most hurt, and that have been the most hurt and the most maligned. I rejected this white privileged moment of power. Now look Oliver, I wanted that money. I'm not stupid. I wanted that money. I wrote a letter, and I talked to her at a later date. She never came back, and the parish continued to go forward.

So, what's my hardest thing about parish life? Having to say goodbye. Sometimes you have to say goodbye. I have a funeral mass for a long-term parishioner tomorrow morning. I have to say goodbye to a parishioner because they've died. Sometimes, I have to say goodbye to parishioners because they move or they retire or they move on or they move to another state. Sometimes, I say goodbye to parishioners directly or indirectly because they're angry or they're disappointed, or I won't give in to them. We have a rule at St. Miriam, and you can give money to anything, but you don't own it. If we're raising money for an altar and you give money towards the altar, we appreciate that. No names are on it, and if I want to move it from point A to point B, I can move it. When I'm gone, the new pastor can move it to wherever they want. We are not going to play, "Oh, I gave money for that, and I own that baptismal."

I've learned that in parish ministry, you're always saying goodbye. That's hard for someone like me that literally cries every time somebody leaves. I've grown in ministry and I've learned that sometimes people have to go. It's just not a good fit. It's not a good fit for you. It's not a good fit for them. I've learned to say to myself, "It's not your fault, and it's okay." Sometimes you have to let them go, and you pray for them. It's my fault sometimes. Sometimes I make a mistake and I have to make amends for that. I will do that, but more often than not, what I've learned is the sadness of parish ministry is always having to say goodbye.

KLING: Saying goodbye is rough. I'm sure you saw it as a trauma chaplain. In my work as a hospice chaplain, dealing with 10 to 30 deaths a month. Some of these people I've gotten to know well, and it's a challenge. Let's try to end on a positive note. What has been your greatest blessing in ministry?

ST. GEORGE: I think the greatest blessing is being able to look at what we've created and know that we've had a positive impact on countless lives that we may never even know that we did. It's amazing to me how many times I hear what St. Miriam means to a family or to someone that I'd never even met because of an impact that we had on somebody else. It's kind of like we're only six degrees removed from everyone else. I have to remind myself of that when we're in the trenches, like this pandemic has taken a lot, one of the wonderful things about having a home church, or like a small church that you either have no rent or very minimal rent is you're very limber. You can literally close for a year and survive.

We've got $44,000 a month in debt service. If I closed down, this pandemic has taken a lot out of us because the schools had to close for four months, and then we could open again. Then the parish was closed and then opened again. Now we're closed again to in-person worship. Not everybody gives electronically. We're right in it, but what gets me through that is my greatest joy. It's that when somebody comes up to me in those few times that I often hear it, or I receive an email and they say, this is what you meant to me, or this is what St. Miriam means to me, or meant to me, that is a powerful feeling. It only could have happened if I listened to God and move forward, even when I was afraid and my feet were stuck in the mud.

When somebody asked me once, "Father, when you die are you going to be cremated?" I responded, "I want to be cremated, but I want to be laid out here in the cemetery somewhere." And they said, "Well, I'm sure you're going to have like a big stone. You're going to be up near that new St. Francis bronze statue." And I said, "No." I said, "I'll be in some grave that nobody else wants." Then I said, "My most thoughtful wish would be that my name is on the stone and underneath, it will say, 'he was a good pastor.'" If I could be known as a good pastor, then I know that I have done my job. one reason I don't beat people up about not giving money in the way that a lot of churches do, we talk about money because we have to, but we don't beat people up about it.

Why we circle the wagons to keep this place going is when I was in seminary, Monsignor Kreider was at Catholic University. He was teaching a liturgy class. One day we had lunch together, and he said, "You know what makes a pastor a good pastor?" And I said, "What?" He goes, "That he's a good shepherd." I said, "Oh yeah, yeah, shepherd. Yeah, I like shepherds." He said, "No, no, no, no, no, no." He called me James. He said, "No, no, James. You're not listening to me. When a shepherd is leading the flock of sheep and they come across a body of water or a river, do you know what a shepherd does? He builds up a dam on both sides of a space of that river to stop it from flowing so hard, to make it smooth so that the sheep aren't afraid to drink from the water. That's the job of a pastor, no matter what's going on in the world, no matter how bad things get, you have to hold that. That's the yolk that you promise when you put this stole on." He went on to say, "When you are ordained a priest, and I know you're going to make a good priest, one day when you put that yolk on your job is to make the way smooth, no matter what's going on in the world and in the lives of others."

That's my job, and I try to do that every single day. I don't always succeed in my brokenness. I've succeeded far more than I failed. My goal is to find someone like me, not as caustic as I am, not as hard as I am, but someone a little softer for the next generation to pastor at St. Miriam. I pray now that God brings in the next five or 10 years, someone that can come and sit with me and be groomed in a good way in order to become the next pastor of Saint Miriam, because they have that same heart and that same ability.

Deacon Pat, who's been with me for a long time, she's one deacon in the church. She sat in my office one day when I was ready to quit.

I was so down. I don't even remember what was going on. She got up, and she came over and she put her hand on my arm and she said, "Monsignor, do you know what makes you so good at what you do?" And I said, "What?" And she said, "You've got the heart of a pastor," and I've never forgotten that. That is the joy of being in pastoral ministry. It's this long-term joy filled relationships you don't even know your impact until somebody reminds you of what you've done for them in their lives.

KLING: Thank you for taking the time to be with me today. Do you have any closing thoughts or words before we adjourn?

ST. GEORGE: I think that your primary audience is probably going to be people like us, people that are interested in the Movement, people that are looking at the writing on the wall and realizing that, God's not done speaking and that things are happening. The church isn't stagnant. It's not meant to be; the church is dynamic and vibrant, and we're part of that church. One thing that goes all the way back to the beginning of your question with your elevators is that I take umbrage with when I see new websites is, we're not affiliated with this, so we're not affiliated with this. We're not affiliated with the Roman church. So, we're not this. Instead of telling people what you are not, celebrate what you are. People don't care what you're not. They don't, despite what the Roman church says, they don't really care about you either.

What we do by saying, we're not this, and we're not, and here's all the doctrine of the church and why we're valid. We take away our authority and we give it to somebody that calls us valid and sufficient, but illicit and who decided that the Roman Church was the only arbiter of power and the word Catholic and church. My parting words, and hopefully not a shock, but more of advice, is don't tell people what you are not, tell people what you are. When people ask me about St. Miriam, I don't tell them we're not this and not that, but I talk about what we are and what a wonderful community it is. What we do as far as outreach and children's ministries and families. My primary makeup of my parish right now is what we would consider being mainstream families, mom, dad, and children.

We welcome everyone into that mix, and they welcome everyone into that mix. They came to us because of what we are, not what we are not. I would hope that we could grow together. I guess if I could have one more stab at it, I'd like us to be more collegial. Put away your miters, put away your croziers. None of us care about them and let's just be colleagues and help one another. If you're going to open up a church, why don't you call someone that's done it and ask to pick their brain? The one thing I love to do is tell you what I did wrong. So I can save you some of those missteps. I did a lot of things wrong in building St. Miriam, but obviously, being one of the larger parishes, I did something right.

Despite what you might have heard, one thing is that we are people who build. We love to have other people build, too. I would hope that we would find a better way to be more collegial. These little microcosms that we've created, little mini-diocese and archdiocese throughout the land, fine. Good for polity, bad for communication and openness to others and all we're doing is we're creating a little mini-Rome. When we do those things, we don't need to be powerful. We need to be pastoral, and we need to be pastoral to our flock, and we need to be pastoral to one another. Oliver, I can't tell you the last time I heard from another priest in any jurisdiction that asked me what I did, how I did it, or how I am. I think that probably tells you a lot about where our focus is and where we need to repair.

KLING: Absolutely. Well, thanks again so much for being with me today. I've appreciated our time.

ST. GEORGE: Thank you Oliver, I appreciate you.

"Life's most persistent and urgent question is what are you doing for others?"
- Martin Luther King, Jr

Concluding Thoughts

Bishop James St. George talked about the difficulty of saying goodbye and seeing people go. I know he was talking about parishioners and with the necessity of letting some people go, but his words have caused me to reflect upon lost friendships and relationships I have experienced within the Independent Sacramental Movement. As a presiding bishop, I have experienced several people join or affiliate with my jurisdiction to see them leave. Often a departure is done violently, with the burning of bridges and pointing fingers. The saying of goodbye is rough. Often there isn't an opportunity to even say goodbye, as it is common for clergy friends and colleagues to just depart from the Independent Sacramental Movement without a trace.

I recently preached at a nursing home that I frequent in my work as a hospice chaplain. During my sermon, I shared that if you had to reduce every teaching in the Bible down to one word, to one teaching, you would get relationships. The Bible is about maintaining a proper relationship with God, and with maintaining proper relationships with one another. Therefore, I usually preach the same sermon repeatedly. We need to work on our relationships with each other and focus on our relationship with God, according to the sermon I usually preach. The reason this message can constantly be preached is that we always, as a society and as a Movement, continue to fail to sufficiently follow the command of Jesus from the Gospel of Mark [Mark 12:30 - 31], *"And you shall love the Lord your God with all your heart, and with all your soul, and with all your mind, and with all your strength. The second is this, you shall love your neighbor as yourself. There is no other commandment greater than these."* Do we always keep this "great commandment?"

I know I often fall short in keeping this commandment and I suspect most of us do, too. In the fluid and unstable waters of the Independent Sacramental Movement, I have seen many estranged relationships. What do you do? You just keep trying to do the best you can. You keep trying to be the best Christian you can by continuing to love God without reservation and love your neighbor as yourself. This is not a simple task. When I was a Benedictine monk, we had a maxim that we lived by, "In honor preventing one another," which is a way of honoring the great commandment of love your neighbor as yourself. Monks can be vindictive and proud, like people of the "world." Therefore, it is important to constantly be reminded to love one's neighbor. Even when you don't want to.

For Reflection, Contemplation and Prayer:

• Does the Independent Sacramental Movement have too many bishops? Is there a solution to this phenomenon? What are your thoughts?

• Saying goodbye, even when necessary. What are some experiences you have had with saying goodbye to people you have cultivated a relationship with? How do you manage the feelings you have after saying goodbye?

• Not everyone can afford expensive seminary educations or clinical pastoral education. What are some ways a would be priest can prepare for ministry? What preparation and formation is necessary to prepare for ministry?

CHAPTER SEVEN

— ❖ —

"BE A PRIEST"

BRIAN ASHMANKAS

"Do not be conformed to this world, but be transformed by the renewal of your mind, that by testing you may discern what is the will of God, what is good and acceptable and perfect."
- Romans 12:2

Brian Ashmankas is a native of central Massachusetts. He is a former politician and former Roman Catholic seminarian for the Diocese of Worcester. He has two master's degrees, one in political science and the other in theology. He was dismissed from sponsorship by the Roman Catholic Diocese of Worcester in December 2019 after sharing with his bishop that he has a well-discerned call to be a married Catholic priest in Worcester. He is currently an aspirant for ordination with the Good Shepherd Companions, an Ecumenical Catholic Ordinariate formed from the joining of the Ecumenical Catholic Diocese of America and the St. Barnabas Mission with roots in the Married Priests Now movement started by Emmanuel Milingo. He is recently the founder and facilitator of the "Community of the Hyphenated." This group meets weekly on Zoom to share and listen to each others' spiritual insights and stories and aims at self-reflection, self-betterment, learning from others' experiences, camaraderie, and ultimately social and ecclesiological transformation – building a new world and church in the shell of the old. [Note: in June of 2021 Brian was ordained to the priesthood.]

KLING: My first question is, what is your elevator speech? How would you describe the Independent Sacramental Movement to somebody who has no idea what it is?

ASHMANKAS: I think I would describe it in terms of Peter Maurin's quote, that is hanging in the Catholic Worker House I'm currently living in. It talks about the point of the Catholic Worker which is to rebuild a new society in the shell of the old, based on a philosophy that seems new because it is so old. I think that is the same thing as the Church. I see the Independent Sacramental Movement as a way to build a New Church in the shell of the old. There's so much within Catholicism that I love, and I can never not be Catholic. I love the tradition; I love Catholic Social teaching and the sacramental worldview; and yet, it's so mixed with Roman Imperialism left over from Constantine and the patriarchy. There is so much stuff that is contrary to the Gospel and yet mixed in with it. When I discovered the Independent Sacramental Movement, it seemed to be how Church was meant to be lived.

KLING: I like to describe the Independent Sacramental Movement as the best kept secret within the Christian tradition, and I think that's true. That doesn't mean it doesn't have lots of problems, but I think it's a best-kept secret.

ASHMANKAS: Yeah, I think that's true, and I think that's more of what the early church was, right? It was such a wonderful, vibrant community that was almost dismissed by the authorities, but then it just grew.

KLING: Here's a follow-up question for you, and it's a question that I've never asked before, but it goes back to the first question I just asked. How would you describe the Independent Sacramental Movement to your former Roman Catholic Bishop in an elevator? Imagine that he asks you, "So, what are you up to now?"

ASHMANKAS: Wow. A little context. I shared with my former bishop that I was called to be both married and a priest. He said, "Yeah, that's nice. But if you're called to one, you're not called to the other and you're no longer a seminarian." I think I would say, "You know, Bishop, how I told you I was called to be married and a priest? God made a way, and God made a way through wonderful people who have set the groundwork. It's a way that I can be the married and a Catholic priest that I was always called to be, and you never let me be."

KLING: Can you describe that conversation? That you had with your Bishop when you shared with him how you felt called to be married and a priest? What was going on emotionally? How did you feel?

ASHMANKAS: I felt strangely ready; although, because I had been preparing for it for so long. Especially in my last year of Roman Catholic seminary, there was this real pull and push and pull for marriage and priesthood and everything that was going on, and it felt unstable. Maybe I'll be one of the married deacons? Or maybe I'll be an episcopal priest? It's so many things and all of them are somewhat appealing but not quite right. Throughout all that instability, the one thing that just seemed so clear in my prayer was once the Amazon synod is over, I have to talk to the bishop. I have to tell him what this is, and it was so clear that I said, "God, if you want me to do this. I guess you're going to work a miracle, right?"

So, I went into it with a real sense of peace. I had been preparing for it. Thinking about it. I felt that this was God's will. I went there, and he said, "The floor is yours." I think he had some idea of what I wanted to talk about, but I was able to detail exactly why I felt called to be a priest, exactly why I felt called to be married, and why I felt called to be in Worcester and why I still felt Catholic. I don't think he listened because his response was, "Oh, if you're still thinking about marriage then you're not called to be a priest," was the short of it.

He said something about how celibacy was mandatory. Celibacy permeates every aspect of Catholicism. I think what I said was that I agreed, but it's not a good thing. I think that was one of the other things that gave me a lot of courage to speak to him was that it wasn't just my own call to marriage. It's a recognition that, while some people may be called to celibacy as a legitimate call from God, to mandate celibacy for all who want to be priests or called to be priests is the foundation of so much of the clericalism and so much of the exclusion of women. It is part of the repression, and the other problems that exist in the church. It was interesting that he said it permeates everything because I think it does, but in a really bad way.

KLING: Thank you for sharing! Let me share with you my experience. I spent some time at a Traditionalist Benedictine Monastery, and when I say Traditionalist, I mean a part of the Traditionalist Movement. They rejected Vatican II. The abbot of the monastery had been a monk at St. Bernard's Abbey in Cullman, Alabama, and he had been there since the 1940s. So, he was trained as a Benedictine prior to Vatican II, but was a part of the Vatican II Church. In the 1980s he left. When he retired as the pastor of Sacred Heart Church in Cullman, the abbot of the monastery allowed him to live as a hermit at a house the parish bought him. Eventually, some folks asked him to say the Tridentine Mass and form a monastery and ultimately, he did, and he got connected with the traditionalist movement. He founded Christ the King Monastery, which was the monastic community that I had joined. When I left, someone connected me with the regular Roman Catholic Church through the Byzantine Rite. I could not stomach the Novus Ordo liturgy, so the Byzantine Rite was my best option.

I ended up living with a priest in the Byzantine Rite. He is now the Bishop of the Romanian Byzantine Rite Greek Catholics, John Michael Botean. I used to live with him. I served at the Divine Liturgy every day for two years. I remember there was a clergy retreat, and I was there taking notes and helping. Every single priest at the retreat was married except for the one priest who I was living with. Rome had appointed Botean as Apostolic Administrator and Archimandrite because, I suspect, he was the only priest who was celibate. John Michael Botean ended up becoming the bishop for the diocese or eparchy. When I said to him, "Can I get married and be a priest here?" He responded, "Well, the Roman Catholics don't like it, but if you go to Romania and you live there for a while. You can find a wife in Romania. Get married, and then get ordained in Romania. Then come back to the United States, you can do it that way."

That was incredibly confusing to an ex-Traditionalist Benedictine monk, now a Romanian Greek Catholic. I was being told, "You can be married and a priest, but you have to do it under the radar of the Roman Church." It was really confusing. A sad story was there was a priest who I was familiar with, and his name was Father Emmanuel. I don't remember his last name. He was married and had five children. He had been ordained by the Melkite Catholic Patriarch of Antioch and came back to the United States. The Melkites didn't give him faculties because he was originally Roman Catholic. He couldn't get faculties from any of the Roman Catholic bishops. He was serving as a chaplain for a while, but once John Michael Botean became a Bishop, he gave Father Emmanuel faculties, and he became pastor of the Cathedral parish for a while.

Talk about confusing! So, when you're talking about your former bishop saying, "Clerical celibacy permeates the entire church," I'm going to call shenanigans on that because there are plenty of married Byzantine Rite priests out there that are in full communion with Rome. The Roman Catholic hierarchy, the bishops, all over the country don't want people to know about the Byzantine Rite. They do not want people to know there are options. It's frustrating and a paradox.

ASHMANKAS: It strikes me how many hoops that one must jump through. So, it's either totally closed off, the opportunity to get married, or you must jump through all these confusing hoops. It's hard to understand what their purpose is other than to make it difficult. It reminds me of the married, permanent deacons in the Latin Rite. In the sense that they're allowed to be married, but they must be married before they're ordained. If, God forbid, their wife passes, they can't get remarried. That always struck me as a strange and unnecessary rule. Why you must be married first but you can't get remarried?

Are they married deacons or not? Why this extra rule? And then I imagine it's one reason you have so few young, permanent deacons within the Latin Rite. Obviously, no one wishes their wife to die, but things happen. To think that you just be alone for the rest my whole life. Because even though I have this solid marriage, maybe I don't take that risk? It's such a strange, complicated and convoluted thing. Like you said, in one way, it is total shenanigans, and yet it permeates the Church in the sense that it affects even the Byzantine Rite, even though they have had married priests. Rome doesn't like married priests; how do we walk through that hoop and walk a tightrope? It's strange.

KLING: I hope no one gets offended by this, but within the Byzantine Rite there seems to have developed a type of "ghetto church" mindset. For example, I was in the Romanian Byzantine Rite, and what I mean by "ghetto church" is that there is an unstated obligation for them to keep their Romanian ethnic identity. Because it's easier to disappear and not be taken too seriously by the Romans If they still see you as an "Other." As an Eastern European Other, as Ukrainian, or Romanian, but not quite Roman Catholic; instead, on the periphery within the Eastern Rite. It gets complicated when people are born and raised in the US. People who don't have an accent and who don't identify with an Eastern European ethnic identity but identify as American.

Because then people question the need to live this ethnic identity. Why do I have to learn Romanian? Why do I have to learn Slavic or

Ukrainian? That becomes a big disconnect. If they keep the Eastern Rite in the periphery, it's okay. If the Eastern Rite becomes more mainstream than I think the Roman Catholic elites will be afraid. This idea of married priests will become like a virus and infect the Roman Church, with too many people who will point and say, "What about them? They're Catholic and their priests are married." The elites in the Roman Church do not want that, they do not want that at all.

ASHMANKAS: Yeah. We shouldn't underestimate how much they don't want it. Also, I want to reemphasize that some people are truly called to celibacy. I don't think it's a lot of people, but some are called to be celibate. But the system creates a kind of insider club. It's the celibate male priests that are the elites, as you said. They have the power. You can be in the Church If you're a married white person. You can be the Church If you're Byzantine Rite, but you don't have any power. It's that sense of control which isolates. One way it is bad for the people; authoritarianism is bad for the authoritarians and the oppressed in the sense that they're stuck and isolated within their own group. Yet, all they have is their power, and it creates this thing where they're isolated from people and isolated from women and they have their own insular club. It's sad because there are many holy and good priests within it, but having that kind of power and that kind of isolation ultimately corrupts.

KLING: Agreed and I think being called to clerical celibacy is linked to a call to a religious life. What the Roman Church does is it forces men, since it doesn't ordain women, to embrace a religious life, even if they're not called to the religious life. They're forcing people into a pseudo-monasticism. When these men may not be called to be monks. You can be a priest without being a monk. I think it is a disservice to the Church, forcing a religious vocation when someone may have a priestly vocation, but not a vocation to religious life, monastic or otherwise. That is problematic for me.

ASHMANKAS: When I was in seminary, they were always praying for vocations. I always felt, God is sending plenty vocations! They keep saying no to the ones that don't want to be monks, or who are women who don't agree with the Catholic Church's stance on women's ordination. You say, "God send vocations," and then turn them away. Of course, you are going to have a crisis, but it's not a vocation crisis. It's an acute exclusion crisis.

KLING: Right, and in some respects, I think a lot of the discipline within the Roman Church is bizarre to me. I'll give you an example.

We are talking about ordination and priests, but even when it comes to laypeople, the whole annulment situation it baffles me. I knew a couple. Both have master's degrees in theology. One of them taught at a Catholic high school teaching religion, Catholicism. The other one was a chaplain certified by the national chaplain endorsing body that endorses Roman Catholic chaplains, the National Association of Catholic Chaplains. They got a divorce. Now they are getting an annulment.

You have two Roman Catholic theologians, even though one's on a high school level and one's a chaplain. If that's not a valid Catholic marriage, I don't know what it is. Yet, it will get annulled, and they will move on. If they don't get it annulled and they moved on, they would technically cut themselves off from the sacraments (excommunicated) by the fact of getting remarried without having an annulment. To me, that's absurd. Just let people get divorced and get remarried and, like the Orthodox, do and say, "The human condition is flawed, and these things happen."

ASHMANKAS: Yeah, it's a sad thing. I don't think anyone's arguing that divorce is a good thing or that we are happy when divorce happens, but I think that when Christ said, "You know what God has joined together let no human separate," that it is more of an "ought statement" rather than an "is statement." I think the Roman Church interprets that as a statement where you can't be separated. When I think it is really saying that you shouldn't separate it. Also, this is the same Christ that is forgiving and understands that we are weak, and we are flawed and that things happen.

It's sad that divorce causes so much harm, but is also sometimes necessary. Sometimes, it is painful. Again, it is like you said; it is another way to keep the system as it is. Dealing with annulments, it is this entire process that every one of these people has to go through that keeps them "under our thumb."

KLING: I wonder if the issues such as marriage and annulments, and clerical celibacy for the priesthood, results from scholasticism within the Church. Are you familiar with Saint Gregory Palamas within the Orthodox Church?

ASHMANKAS: A little. I know we've talked about him here and there, but...

KLING: There was a conflict between St. Gregory Palamas, and another monk named Barlaam. Barlaam was advocating for scholasticism and Gregory Palamas was advocating for mysticism.

In the Orthodox Church, the mystics won the battle. In the Roman Church, the scholastics won. In the Roman Church you have the primacy of St. Thomas Aquinas. There is a reason the Dominicans were some of the main inquisitors for many years, and then later replaced by the Jesuits as a sort of "shock troopers" of the Church. I think part of it was because of the emphasis on scholasticism, or a rationalizing of the teachings of the Church. The intellectual exercises of scholasticism helped to shape theology and codifying canon law.

I wonder if that is the reason why we see some of the legalisms we do. Even after the Second Vatican Council, the legalisms are still very much a part of the Church. The legalisms are just as bad within the liberal wings of the Roman Catholic Church, as well as the conservative wings.

ASHMANKAS: That's true. All the different ways of putting God in a box. St. Thomas Aquinas has said things that are inspirational and helpful, and yet there are other things that I find frustrating. I don't doubt that St. Thomas Aquinas has led some people toward mysticism, but ultimately, the goal is to get God out of the box.

KLING: Another Question for you. Can you tell me about your experience at Catholic University in Washington, DC? In what ways did you challenge the establishment?

ASHMANKAS: That's a good question. Ultimately, I have to say my experience in Washington, DC, was good, not perfect, but good. I had good friends. I felt mostly free there, which contrasts with the experience I had a few years before at Catholic University. I spent pre-theology at St. John's in Boston. That was a very challenging place. You mentioned the inquisition. I won't quote all the details, but as we say, "The inquisition was alive and well at that seminary." I could give my former Roman Catholic Bishop credit. He allowed me to switch to Catholic University in Washington, DC, and I was happy there. They allowed me to be who I was. There were challenges. We didn't all agree, but it wasn't a sense of inquisition. I made some good friends.

I was in politics before seminary, and it was a great opportunity to get involved with social justice. I would get emails about a protest in favor of social justice and rallies in DC. I could get on the Metro and head there. I always wore my clericals as a witness. It was a good experience. I tried to bring social justice issues to the forefront.

The challenge when I was there was probably the last thing I did while there. The inquisition briefly found its way into the seminary.

I hadn't had an issue with it the whole time, but there was a point when some seminarians, and I purposely never sought to find out who they were. I never wanted to know. They took it upon themselves to write a letter to the faculty, stating all the ways in which they thought I didn't fit in. They said I was heretical, based on what they overheard in conversation and, some of it they hit on the head and some of it was a misinterpretation of my words and some of it was totally off.

I know one of them wrote that I didn't believe in the Eucharist. Where did they get that? That's not true. I totally believe in the Eucharist and in the true presence. It was a list of things within this letter and all their concerns. To the faculty's credit, the seminary at Catholic University, they didn't believe that the letter was appropriate. They didn't think it was okay for seminarians to take it on themselves, to police each other's orthodoxy. They didn't take it seriously. but it was. My response was, "I've been through this before. I'm on my way out. I'm not going to worry about it." I was talking to a good friend of mine there about it, and he said to me, "When you leave, am I the next target? You have to say something about this." It inspired me. I wrote a goodbye email to the house, it was good. I said, "That's why I'm leaving, because of celibacy. No other reason." I wanted to head off the idea that they had pushed me out. Their letter had nothing to do with me leaving, and I wrote how grateful for the openness of the theological college and everything. Then I wrote, "This one thing came to my attention. I want to leave with a note of warning, of caution, that I came from a place where this was common practice, and it really destroyed the community. It really harmed us. We lived in a culture of fear. Don't let this happen to theological college, which is so wonderful." Then I attached the letter they wrote against me to the entire house. I felt like it was kind of like, "what they do in the darkness, put in the light."

I think it made a difference. I am committed to non-violence. I'm involved with PAX Christi, and non-violence spirituality is the core of who I am. I felt like my letter was a kind of non-violent civil disobedience. From what I heard; people were impacted by my letter. They reflected on it, and they thought, "Wow, I can't believe this kind of stuff would happen at Catholic University." Like I mentioned, I never knew who wrote the letter against me. Someone I know, who knew who wrote it, told me that the person felt a certain repentance. I think my letter helped.

I remember it was this amazing thing. One of the faculty members came up to me at the Christmas party. I think it was the day or the day after I sent the email out. He said, "Brian, I've been in formation for six years and I've been a formator for six years and that's the most impressive thing I've ever seen." I think there's a million reasons I was still in seminary. I got a degree out of it, and I learned a bunch. I had spiritual direction. There were so many reasons I wasn't meant to be there that many years to get to where I am now in the Independent Sacramental Movement. Yet that alone made it all worth it. To have made that kind of impact, and to walk out the door and say, "Don't let this happen here." To make people conscious of how harmful that can be.

KLING: Well, thank you for sharing that. I'm sure that was a painful experience.

ASHMANKAS: It is strange how it was more painful all the other times it happened earlier. At that point, I was desensitized. It really was my friend who encouraged me to say something. By the time I got there, I was, "Yeah. Okay." Also, I think it is a kind of pain. To think that you can get desensitized to something that awful. Is it okay? We should be keen to that kind of injustice.

KLING: Well, now that you're involved in the Independent Sacramental Movement, can you share what has been your greatest challenge thus far? Within the Independent Sacramental Movement.

ASHMANKAS: It has been such a short time, and it has been almost all good. There is a movie that came out, a documentary called *A Perfect Candidate*. It was about Oliver North's campaign for Senate. The documentary followed the campaign. There was a scene in the film that gives the movie its name. It is where this black pastor endorses the Democrat, even the establishment Democrat, really wasn't his cup of tea. The pastor wanted to endorse him against Oliver North. In his sermon, he talks about a person looking for the perfect candidate is like the person looking for the perfect church. He tells the story of this person looking for the perfect church. He goes from church to church saying, "I would love to join this church, but it's not perfect." As he is about to give up, he stumbles upon a small little church and walks in to discover it has one member, Jesus Christ. He says, "I found the perfect church." Jesus says to him, "Come on in, but it won't be perfect anymore."

I just think of that scene in the film, and I feel so thoroughly called to this Movement. It is a literally a godsend that this Movement exists.

It gives me an opportunity to follow my calling. I feel open. I feel like I can be myself within the Independent Sacramental Movement. I have found support there, but it is not perfect. My group is not perfect. There are people in it and we're all part of Jesus Christ, but we're not all Jesus Christ. Even wonderful people have their rivalries and differences. Sometimes there's infighting and power plays, and occasionally, some sexism. All of that comes with it because we're all people. That means we work at it, we address it, and I think they are working, working on that. It is not perfect, but it's where I'm meant to be.

KLING: I agree. One thing that keeps me grounded in the Independent Sacramental Movement is that it is a place where I can be authentic. I went to a United Methodist Seminary, and I have a Master of Divinity degree from Methodist Theological School in Ohio. While I was there, I struggled with how am I going to pay the bills when I finish? I thought, "I can go United Church of Christ? I could go United Methodist or, since I was serving a Unitarian Universalist parish, I could stick with that." However, a lot of what I discovered with the Unitarian Universalists was that many of them were Secular Humanists or Atheists. I'm a theist and I have been attached to the Independent Sacramental Movement loosely since 1991 and ordained since in the early 2000s.

So, here I was trying to figure out how am I going to make a living? Then I discovered chaplaincy, and that allowed me to reaffirm my involvement in the Independent Sacramental Movement strongly while also making a full-time living in ministry. Being in the Independent Sacramental Movement allows me to be 100% myself, not to put on some sort of disguise to survive as a pastor. I have had many United Methodist friends since I went to a Methodist seminary who put on a pastor disguise to make it, to just survive. They're not able to be authentic. They're not able to be who they are or who they want to be because they fear that they'll get stigmatized, and they won't be able to make a living. I don't have that fear and I love it.

I told someone recently, "God has always given me what I've asked for, just not always the way I want it." Almost thirty years ago, when I was in the Benedictine monastery, I thought I would be an old, seasoned monk and priest by now, saying mass every day. That didn't happen. When I was living at the Byzantine Rite Cathedral with the Romanians, I thought, someday I'll be married and serving a parish within the Byzantine Rite as a priest, and that didn't happen. I always had a vocation. God honored that vocation just differently. When I was in seminary thinking, how am I going to make it? God found a way. I work as a chaplain and I adjunct teach at a college. Everything worked out, just in different ways than I had expected. It goes back to what you were saying when you were talking about your elevator speech to your bishop.

ASHMANKAS: I can be myself. I can be my authentic self in a way that has always felt a call to be a priest, and I have felt a call to marriage, and to be Catholic. There has been a tension; as I approached the meeting with my former bishop, I remember having a realization that I could go forward, and I could give up everything to be a priest in the Roman Catholic Church. Everything as in a life with children, a wife and family and everything that goes with that. If that's my call, that's my call. I realized they didn't have to reciprocate. The second I say something about how there should be women priests or something similar, they could cast me out. I have to give up everything, but they don't have to make the same commitment. Now, I still have to give things up, since the work of a priest is difficult; but I can be who I am and authentically do the ministry I'm called to do and accept whatever challenges come to me.

KLING: Speaking of ministry, what has been your greatest blessing within ministry?

ASHMANKAS: As you asked, I had to separate and distinct things came to mind. The first is I remember the ministry that led me to the seminary. Where I had a mystical experience. I try to be clear to people. I don't hear voices, but I heard the voice of God say, "Be a priest." That was in prison ministry. I had done prison ministry for a few years, once a month. The inmates built their own chapel, Our Lady of Guadalupe Chapel out of an old weight room. We came in to start a PAX Christi group, a Catholic non-violence presence, within the prison, and as far as I know the first time that has ever happened. I remember every time we walked in there, the presence of the Holy Spirit, which is so overwhelming and so present with so much caring and listening. That experience plus that of the mystical aspect of it really led made there. I first think of that, but I also have to think of my current ministry, which is very new. It is tough to say exactly how it is going to develop, but part of the thought process as I approach the diaconate and eventually priesthood within the Good Shepard Companions, which is the diocese for lack of a better word, that I'm a part of within the Independent Sacramental Movement is that ordination comes out of the Holy Spirit at the hands of a bishop, but also out of a community. You are called to ordination to serve a community. So, the thought was, "Okay, I guess I start a community and start a ministry."

Of course, there is COVID-19! So, I started a Zoom ministry. I emailed 53 people, and that list has grown since I started. We meet on Sunday afternoons and Thursday evenings, two different groups depending on schedules. We are building a new church out of the old. There is an opportunity. There are many people who are on the periphery of the Church, who, for good reasons, have been repelled by the Church or directly excluded by the Church or have felt unaffirmed by the Church. They come and we talk, and I facilitate, and we converse with each other, and we listen to each other.

I try to emphasize that listening is such an important thing. You mentioned being a chaplain. I briefly served as a hospital chaplain while in seminary, and I realized how much people are not listened to in this world. How unused to being listened to people are, and how valuable it is to offer the opportunity to actively listen to someone. We share stories; we share our reflections, and our reactions and responses, and let the Holy Spirit move. It's wonderful, and we will see where it goes from here.

KLING: Thank you for sharing part of your story with me today. Do you have any final closing thoughts before we end our time together?

ASHMANKAS: I'm so grateful to have found a place among this Movement, a group within a Movement. That is so wonderful, and I look forward to seeing what God does in my life and my ministry and in the whole Movement going forward. I think it's still evolving and still growing, and I'm really excited for the future.

"Be at peace with your own soul, then heaven and earth will be at peace with you."
- Saint Jerome

Concluding Thoughts

Clerical celibacy was not a problem for me when I lived as a Benedictine monk. The monastic system lends itself to celibacy since the word monk itself comes from Latin and Greek, with the Latin word being *monachus*, which means single or alone. Saint Benedict also refers to a wandering monk as a *gyrovague* and refers to this type of monk as the most wretched. The monk with no abbot, who instead of taking the vow of stability, wanders without an abbot. In the Independent Sacramental Movement, I have seen a fair number of men who are not necessarily celibate and who not only have no monastery but no abbot as well. Like Saint Benedict, I too find this practice wretched.

Within monasticism, especially Benedictine monasticism, there are two virtues that are prominent. Holy obedience is the first. The monk does not do whatever a monk wants to do, but falls under the mantle of holy obedience. The monk's will is subject to the will of his abbot, and ideally, the abbot is prayerful and obedient himself to the will of God. Humility is the byproduct of obedience and the monk learns to curb and control pride through the practice of holy obedience because a calling to a monastic vocation differs from a calling to the priesthood. Saint Benedict was never ordained; he was a monk first and did not see the priesthood as a necessary component of his monastic vocation. The monk's vocation is to solitude, even in community, and is one of prayer. The prayer that the monk is devoted to is the prayer of the Church, the Divine Office, and the monk prays the liturgical office daily. The monk's vocation is not posting memes on Facebook to illustrate how holy they are, but silent contemplation and prayer. In our world, the spiritual practice of *Lectio Divina* has become popular, but for the monk, this meditative way of reading religious texts is normative practice.

Second to Holy Obedience is the virtue of stability. Unlike Franciscans or Dominicans, who are mendicant friars, the Benedictine monk takes vows of stability. Obedience and stability are the remedy against the *gyrovague!* The *gyrovague* is always searching for the next shiny spiritual thing and will wander and roam perpetually looking for something that does not exist. The virtue of stability forces the monk to plant roots to better grow in his monasticism. Stability is essential to the monk and without it the monk is no longer a monk. The wandering monk is a friar, and the mendicant spirituality of a Franciscan differs from the spiritual foundation of a Benedictine monk.

In the Independent Sacramental Movement, I do not have an issue with the many Franciscans I see because the spirituality of Saint Francis differs from the spirituality of Saint Benedict. The friar, by nature, wanders and preaches by their example. You may see a single friar, like in the pages of Robin Hood, or you might see friars grouped together. Franciscan spirituality has developed over the years and you have the major orders of the Order of Friars Minor, the Capuchin Order, but you also have diocesan third orders for men and women and various Franciscan orders for women. Within Benedictine monasticism, you have the Benedictine Order and its offshoots, such as the Cistercians and Trappists; however, the monastic orders that have branched off of the Benedictine Order only attempt to get back to "original" Benedictine monasticism, not a lessoning of restrictions. In the Independent Sacramental Movement, I have noticed many men who use "O.S.B." behind their names. Some of these men have asked me questions and I respond, "Ask your abbot." Every time, the response is, "I don't have an abbot." Then I want to shout at them, "Stop using O.S.B. behind your name because you are not a Benedictine!"

I can have an affinity for something, but to claim membership in an order without having received tonsure within said order is the definition of disingenuous. There is an initiation within monasticism. The would-be monk goes through stages of initiation, starting out as an observer to the monastic community. The observer petitions the abbot to join the community and, upon acceptance, the monastic guest puts on a cassock and becomes a postulant. After participating in the life of the community, the postulant for six months to a year the postulant petitions the community to enter the novitiate. The abbot then calls the monks to chapter, and they discuss the viability of the postulant becoming a novice. Depending on how the discussion goes, the postulant is tonsured a novice and takes upon a new name. After a year, or more in some cases, the novice, under the direction of a Master of Novices, takes on simple vows which last for three years. After this three-year probationary period, the monk in simple vows takes solemn perpetual vows which last a lifetime. It should take five years, or more, for a man to go from being a guest at the monastery to being a monk in solemn perpetual vows. This five-year period is a time of strict formation and education. All the "monks"

I have known in the Independent Sacramental Movement have not undergone the monastic process of becoming a monk. Stability is unknown to them as many migrate from one jurisdiction to another at will, and most would never subject their will to that of another, let alone an abbot. Those who choose to use the term "O.S.B." behind their name within the Independent Sacramental Movement would do better to use "O.W.G" instead, "The Order of Wretched Gyrovagues."

——————

For Reflection, Contemplation and Prayer:

• Have you ever been in a situation where you felt like you needed to challenge the establishment? What was that experience like? What was the end result?

• Authenticity is important. Have you ever had to make a tough decision in order to maintain your own sense of authenticity?

• Our spiritual journey's are often accompanied by painful experiences that often lead to growth. What are some painful experiences you have had to negotiate on your spiritual journey and how did you work through them?

Chapter Eight

"Ah ha Moments"

Laura Hayes Marsh

"You shall treat the stranger who sojourns with you as the native among you, and you shall love him as yourself, for you were strangers in the land of Egypt: I am the Lord your God."
- Leviticus 19:34

Laura Hayes Marsh is a Seminarian at Ascension Theological College. She has worn many hats in life, such as mother, divorcée, and widow. Her previous educational pursuits include an associate degree in Chemistry and a Bachelor of Science degree in Biology with a minor in Psychology. She currently works as a paraprofessional in a self-contained elementary classroom for students with Autism (ABLE) and works on weekends and holidays as a Pharmacy Technician.

Her spiritual formation began in the United Methodist church; however, the Episcopal Church offered a part-time job in the late 1990s, after which the liturgy spoke to Laura's soul, and she became a member of an Episcopal parish. After Confirmation, God nudged her to do more than just singing in the Chancel Choir and in 2015, she served as a Lector, a Eucharistic Minister, and as a Lay Eucharistic Visitor in the Episcopal Church. Serving in various church ministries led her to community service as an on-call Justice Court Chaplain and participation in the Behavioral Health and Suicide Prevention Taskforce. In 2017, a pilgrimage to the Holy Land opened her heart and mind, and she acknowledged a call to the Priesthood. She began discerning a vocation in the Episcopal church and working with a Spiritual Director. During the process of discernment, an unfulfilled need was discovered. Finding a Spiritual Director who was a better fit led her to pursue a Master of Divinity with Ascension Alliance. Her ministry goal is in Healthcare Chaplaincy.

KLING: My first question is what is your elevator speech? How would you describe the independent sacramental movement to somebody who has no idea what it is?

HAYES-MARSH: Currently I'm still working on that as this is a new venture for me, I would say that it is all-inclusive, It doesn't matter what walk of life you come from, where you've been, as long as you are willing and able to come to the table reverently and willing and looking to accept God and to be a part of Jesus and his sacrament and his body and the blood.

KLING: Well, you mentioned that this is new. This leads into my next question, and I usually interview bishops and priests. I've interviewed some deacons and subdeacons in the past, but I'm hoping to talk to more deacons and seminarians like yourself who are training for the priesthood. Can you talk about your call to ministry and why you got involved with Ascension Alliance? Why not just remain in the Episcopal Church? You'll make more money that way.

HAYES-MARSH: Money doesn't always buy happiness.

KLING: Good answer.

HAYES-MARSH: I got a call around 2017 and I saw the workings within myself. Around 2015 when I had gotten confirmed into the Episcopal Church and I was nudged to do more, more service in the church, more service in the community. I went on a pilgrimage to the Holy land and that changed me. I will tell you honestly that I am the biggest skeptic. I didn't think it would change me. I came back and scared my kids with my sense of peace and calm.

KLING: What was it there at the Holy land that changed you?

HAYES-MARSH: I couldn't tell you. More grace, more God? Something within my soul had changed and I can't put my finger on it. I'm still looking for the answer.

KLING: What was that experience like at the Holy land?

HAYES-MARSH: Magical.

KLING: Where were some places that you went to that spoke to you the most?

HAYES-MARSH: Bethlehem spoke to me, Jerusalem spoke to me. We had also visited Qumran and Masada; the peak was very high and that one scared me.

KLING: How so?

HAYES-MARSH: It was a trolley ride to the top, and I'm not one for heights.

KLING: So, you're now involved with Ascension Alliance after experience with the Episcopal Church. I'm going to ask this question again. Why not remain Episcopalian why Accession Alliance. What was it about Ascension Alliance and the Independent Sacramental Movement that drew you?

HAYES-MARSH: There was a portion that was missing. There was something, a something in my soul that had an empty space that needed to be filled, that longed and yearned to be filled. A sense of spirituality in a different sense is the best way I can describe it. There was something missing that is being filled, and I still can't put a name on that something, but it is being filled by the Independent Sacramental Movement, and don't get me wrong, the Episcopal liturgy speaks to my soul, but there are similarities enough in the Independent Catholic liturgy that I can use that liturgy as well. My understanding is that by the end of my seminary studies, I will have to develop my own mass and therefore I can take the best of all worlds and make it my own to invite a welcoming, a new and personal worship experience.

KLING: Archbishop Alan Kemp, when I interviewed him, he mentioned that the students at Ascension Theological College have to write a Eucharistic liturgy, and I think that's an excellent exercise.

HAYES-MARSH: That is my understanding.

KLING: So, what you're saying is that there was something missing within the Episcopal Church, in your involvement there, that you could find with your involvement with Ascension Alliance.

HAYES-MARSH: Correct?

KLING: Now, how did you discover them? Was it just an internet search? Did you know somebody?

HAYES-MARSH: I knew somebody.

KLING: Who?

HAYES-MARSH: Monsignor Steve Grubbs. He sang with me in the Episcopal Church at Trinity Episcopal in the Woodlands.

KLING: You had a contact within Ascension Alliance. Now, did you know about Ascension Alliance while you were studying with the Episcopalians? Tell me about that story.

HAYES-MARSH: Nope. I met Archbishop Patsy Grubbs through my late husband Palmer Marsh, and it's been a wonderful experience. He introduced me to her and there was something there that was drawing me. I've heard that when you are looking for a teacher that one will be brought to you. At the time in 2017, I was discerning with the Episcopal Church for a vocation in the ordained ministry. I was not happy with my spiritual director and I asked Archbishop Patsy if she would work with me? She agreed, and I have grown spiritually by leaps and bounds almost exponentially in the three years that I have been working with her. I have experienced things that were beyond my comprehension. It's been the most wonderful experience.

KLING: That leads to my next question. Ascension Alliance has one of the best educational institutions within the Independent Sacramental Movement. What has it been like as a seminarian at Ascension theological college?

HAYES-MARSH: Wonderful, it has been academically challenging, but I have support from my formation committee, which comprises a formation director who I'm blessed enough to have as my spiritual director as well, and two other members on the committee to provide support academically, spiritually, and then myself. I've also had support from the professors, as I call we discuss things. Although the coursework that I've had so far has been independent study, when I got stuck, I can contact the professor and they get back to me in a timely fashion.

KLING: Do you feel like your education there is going to prepare you for ministry?

HAYES-MARSH: I do.

KLING: Because I know a lot of priests and bishops too, within the Independent Sacramental Movement have been loose on formation, and I know Ascension Alliance emphasizes formation and education, and they do so through their Theological College. I suspect anyone who has gone through their program will be well-versed in the things that a person needs to know in order to function sufficiently as a priest or a member of the clergy. And for that, I think they're doing a wonderful job in setting an example within the Independent Sacramental Movement when so many jurisdictions fail in doing adequate formation. What are some hallmarks that you've experienced with your work with your spiritual director and in your formation with the Ascension Alliance? I'm curious about that.

HAYES-MARSH: In my formation, I had to pause in the middle of my class. I had read the textbook, and it just wasn't sinking in; I contacted my professor; we discussed things, and he said, "Hold on to this, let it sink in, listen to the additional resource that were listed in the syllabus." That made all the difference. I just took the class, Introduction to Jewish Mysticism, in which they passed a lot of knowledge by telling stories. That's an auditory thing. You can read stories, but if you're not a visual learner, it might not make sense to you. If you listen to CDs, listening to the stories might help it sink in, and then you have a better understanding of the concepts that are being taught. I'm very thankful that Archbishop Alan asked me to stop and let it sink in because it's not just an academic venture. This is also a spiritual journey, and information is important. Some things you just can't get intellectually, some things just have to be felt in their fullness.

KLING: It takes time for things to sink in sometimes.

HAYES-MARSH: Correct.

KLING: Now you're interested in health care chaplaincy. Is that right?

HAYES-MARSH: Correct.

KLING: What is your goal for ministry? Hospital or hospice? Where do you see yourself let's say in 10 years when you're finished with your seminary education and you're ordained to the priesthood, where do you see yourself?

HAYES-MARSH: I will see where the pandemic goes and 10 years that's so far out. I really want to leave that one open to see where God leads me. I've got a basic idea of the path that I'm supposed to go on, which is in chaplaincy. I know military is out, I'm too old, too broken physically, but I have gotten the call to go towards either hospice or hospital care. I've taken the first step in volunteering and community service with Judge Wayne Mack in precinct one of Montgomery County, Texas. I would highly suggest you Google this person he is a righteous Christian human being who invites prayer into his courtroom prior to legal proceedings. And he needs prayer because he is being sued personally for this action.

KLING: So, you led prayer in the courthouse?

HAYES-MARSH: No, I am an on-call chaplain for emergencies after hours.

KLING: Can you talk a bit about your work there? That's interesting. I want to know more.

HAYES-MARSH: Unfortunately, I haven't gotten to go out on any calls. I have had training, but just as I had gotten to go through a couple rotations, I did not receive any calls and then the pandemic hit and that put the program on pause since we did not want to endanger our lives?

KLING: What kind of work would you do? I mean, what calls would you receive?

HAYES-MARSH: Fatalities, suicide.

KLING: That sounds like great work. Hopefully, when the pandemic is over, you'll get used and you'll get some really wonderful experience with that. That will certainly help you if you pursue healthcare chaplaincy down the road.

HAYES-MARSH: Correct. I was one of the few that was a lay person.

KLING: I know you're new to the Independent Sacramental Movement, but since being a part of the Movement, what has been your greatest challenge?

HAYES-MARSH: I have not come across too many challenges to be honest. I have found the Independent Sacramental Movement to be very welcoming.

KLING: That's good news to hear. I mean, you're in a good jurisdiction, Ascension Alliance. I'm sure you're insulated from some of the drama that some of us witness within the Movement. My recommendation is to stay with a good jurisdiction like Ascension Alliance. It sounds like you have a great spiritual director, and you have a great community. I have affiliate status with Ascension Alliance, and I consider myself also a part of that community. I value that connection that I have with the Ascension Alliance. So, stay with them because they know what they're doing and they got it right. But my last question is what has been your greatest blessing?

HAYES-MARSH: My greatest blessing is witnessing "the ah-ha moments" and the exponential growth in my formation. I recently had an experience of having lunch with two of my dearest friends from college, and for a moment I transcended time, transcended place, and for lack of a better word, I spent a moment with God while the other two were carrying on a conversation. I understood the blessing at the end of worship, at the end of the mass where the priest blesses you and says, "...and the peace of God that transcends all human understanding." I get it. I get that peace. I get that joy. If just only for a moment. Unfortunately, I had to snap back into the conversation. That was just the most wonderful thing I had ever experienced in my life. I got it. I don't think that's something that many people get unless you invite God to take you there.

KLING: Yeah, I think you're right. Well, thank you for being my guest today. Do you have any closing thoughts or comments for the listeners?

HAYES-MARSH: Just an attitude of gratitude. I'm thankful for where I'm at. I'm thankful for the opportunities that I've been given and just to trust in God whole-heartedly, because there are places you'll go that you would've never thought that you would be led to.

"Jesus said: If those who lead you say to you: See, the kingdom is in heaven, then the birds of the heaven will go before you; if they say to you: It is in the sea, then the fish will go before you. But the kingdom is within you, and it is outside of you. When you know yourselves, then you will be known, and you will know that you are the sons of the living Father. But if you do not know yourselves, then you are in poverty, and you are poverty."
- Gospel of Thomas

Concluding Thoughts

I meet with a spiritual director every month and have been doing so for almost seven years. She has been a therapist for my soul all these years and walked with me in my spiritual journey. There were several "ah ha moments" during spiritual directions. However, in the past year there have been less and less of those "ah ha moments" and instead we just talk about how God is working in my life.

I have become more settled in my work, in my ministry, and in my life and have moved to a different phase of my spiritual life. I have had some angst filled days as I struggled with my spiritual life. Trying to figure out what God wanted me to do, and where and how to find my way in the world as a spiritual and religious person. I have had many struggles in my spiritual journey and having a spiritual director to walk with me in those struggles has radically helped me navigate the spiritual storms I have endured.

I am grateful. I am grateful for the many blessings that God has given me, and I have often said that God has given me everything I ask for, just not always in the way I thought. Sometimes we are surrounded with blessings but not always see them. I have had to open my eyes wide to see how I have been blessed. Sometimes we don't always notice the subtle "ah ha moments" that are right in front of us. It is hard being fifty one years old with a four year old daughter, but when she runs up to me and in her sweet toddler voice and says, "I love you, daddy," it makes it all worth it.

For Reflection, Contemplation and Prayer:

- What are some "ah-ha moments" in your life? Have you experienced moments of growth in your formation as a Christian that you can look back upon and recognize as an epiphany?

- Have you felt periods of spiritual emptiness, only to have that emptiness filled? What was that experience like and what was it that helped you feel whole?

- What has been your experience with mentors? Who have been the most influencial mentors in your life? How did they help you?

CHAPTER NINE

— • —

"PROPER ACTION"

FATHER WILLIAM EDDY

"Forget the former things; do not dwell on the past. See, I am doing a new thing! Now it springs up; do you not perceive it? I am making a way in the wilderness and streams in the wasteland."
- Book of Isaiah 43:18 – 20

Father William Eddy was ordained a priest in October of 2018 within the Ascension Alliance and he has lived an eclectic spiritual life. At eight he challenged his Sunday school teacher. He had intuitively known that what was being told to him was not the truth. In his early teens, he read J. Krishnamurti, "On Education and the Significance of Life." This was his first intellectual exposure to the concepts of enlightenment and the limitations of individuality. This affected him.

He learned about Transcendental Meditation in 1972 and has greatly benefited from it. He learned the advanced program and moved to Fairfield, Iowa. The home of the Transcendental Meditation movement. He started doing copious amounts of meditation in various modalities; however, his heart was getting restless. He had a lot of experience of spirit and consciousness, but his heart was not fulfilled. He started exploring other avenues of spiritual progress. He explored several things including the local Liberal Catholic Church parish.

In December of 2012, he became aware of a calling to become a priest after growing in the Liberal Catholic Church over the years. While he was supported there, he had an epiphany that lead him to Spiritus Christi a nearby parish within the Ascension Alliance.

Spiritus Christi is a very open and welcoming community. There are many similarities to the Liberal Catholic Church but more inclusive. There are women priests and gay clergy. It is theologically diverse and allows for individual growth. Father William has done several things in his 71 years of life.

KLING: What is your elevator speech? How would you describe the Independent Sacramental Movement to someone who does not know what it is?

EDDY: We welcome people to enjoy the sacraments. If they are attracted to that, they like that, they can enjoy it with us. We don't tell them what's right and wrong. We don't tell them what their theology has to be. We don't deny them the sacraments because of some aspect of nature in the past or in the present, we just welcome them.

KLING: Sounds like you're very inclusive?

EDDY: Jesus Christ was inclusive. I mean, the fulfillment, his process is the whole family of humanity is one. He said, "I'm one with the father. I'm one with you. And you are one with me." That is one of his ultimate purposes.

KLING: There are more things that bring us together?

EDDY: Yeah. When we reached that goal, absolutely.

KLING: That brings me to my next question. Who is Father William? What makes you who you are? What makes you unique?

EDDY: Well, I'm a very independent person. I'm iconoclastic. I'm obsessive with efficiency and still am at 71. I'm still modifying my life to make it more efficient.

I'm a direct communicator. This has been challenging because when I deal with people, they are very indirect. I have trouble understanding them. I don't know if they understand me or not. I've been a seeker my whole life. I want truth, period. Jesus Christ said the truth will set you free.

When I was a kid, I was an introvert. Now, I'm probably an extrovert. I've gone through so many changes in my life.

KLING: Can you talk about one or two changes that have influenced who you are today?

EDDY: This process is going on my whole life. I was the shy, reclusive person and there was another part of me that wanted to spring forward and be who I could be.

When I was 23, I started my own business. I was serving people since I had a service business, and it made me come out of my shell. That was the beginning, and there has been many other things since. I've been a member of Toastmasters for over 20 years. I've been a member of different mutuality groups that have helped me come out of my shell. One reason I came to Fairfield, Iowa in 1986 was to be part of a group. To be a part of a higher quality group and develop a higher level of mutuality than what is experienced in our culture, and I'm still working on that.

KLING: Was that your involvement with Transcendental Meditation?

EDDY: Yes, that was one part of it.

KLING: Can you describe Transcendental Meditation and its impact on your life, and how do you weave that into your work as a priest?

EDDY: Well, it's interesting. *The Science of Being and the Art of Living* by Maharishi Mahesh Yogi talks about spiritual growth. In one area, he specifically mentions that what is needed is you need to transcend (i.e., meditate) and you need to practice your religion, whatever it is, to have spiritual growth. If you don't have both, then both will fail. We've seen the history of Christianity! Failure after failure, of fulfilling the potential of humankind. This is one technique for creating balance.

In the community where I live, there are many people who are into Transcendental Meditation, and there's a lot of progress here. It is not perfect. All the human weaknesses are alive and well, but there is progress here. There is more in life than there is elsewhere. Transcendental Meditation is going back to self. When I talk about self, it's the spirit. The basic nature of who we are. Most people are concerned with themselves as their body, their personality, their beliefs, and so forth. That's just the surface, the real depth, the spirit needs to be known. You need to know that that is who you are, and that is what Jesus Christ taught. That is my understanding and somewhere along the way, I think it was lost.

KLING: Can you go deeper in discussing Transcendental Meditation? If we were to engage in Transcendental Meditation, what would that experience look like?

EDDY: It is a very simple, easy practice. It doesn't depend upon belief or posture. You sit comfortably, you close your eyes and then you introduce a mantra and there is a way of dealing with that through the process.

Most people meditate for 20 minutes, twice a day in a quiet place. It's simple and easy, and there are many other techniques out there for meditating these days.

KLING: Can you explain what you mean by mantra for those who may be unfamiliar with the word?

EDDY: Well, it's a simple word. A word without meaning because we don't want the mind to get caught up in some great dialogue. We want the mind to settle down to a simpler and separate state of being. That's the purpose of the mantra.

KLING: Is it repeating a word over and over in your mind to settle yourself?

EDDY: That's one way of putting it, but you don't force it. It's not an exercise, and seeing how many times you can say the mantra is not the point. You just use it to settle down, and sometimes the mind settles down easily, and sometimes it doesn't. That's part of the process.

KLING: It sounds like it is a practice that synchronizes well with whatever religion a person might follow.

EDDY: Absolutely. Of course, it depends on the person and how open they are to seeing possibilities. Within Christianity, there is a lot of rigid, small thinking.

KLING: In your biography you mentioned having read Jiddu Krishnamurti at a young age. What was it about him that spoke to you, and continues to influence and speak to you? How do you incorporate those teachings into your work as a priest?

EDDY: I read Krishnamurti at my local library in Cortland, New York, when I was 13 or 14 years old. Somehow, I came across him, and his thinking was so clear, and so basic. The book was *The Education and the Significance of Life*.

He went into great depth about the limitations of the individual. We all have limited intelligence. We all have limited experience and therefore we don't really have a comprehensive basis on which to create perfect action. Because of our experience, we're going to do something that may not help our neighbor, or may do damage to somebody some way, somehow rather than only being good in our environment.

Proper action is a very important part of who I am. When I went to the Transcendental Meditation's first lecture, what I heard was a way of learning to act properly. Krishnamurti was a woke person in the Eastern tradition and he talked about "just be." His followers couldn't relate to that. They did not learn to transcend by just trying to be. Krishnamurti was very interesting to me because I read his biography years after I read his work. He was Indian, and when he was young, he did a lot of mantra meditation, a lot of asanas, which is Hatha Yoga, a lot of Pranayama, which is breathing techniques. Then, after he woke up, she says, "I don't need that anymore. It's just another attachment," which is what happens to some people when they wake up, "I don't need that path anymore." That's a slight tragedy because it was the path that got him to where he was and his followers didn't have that anymore; however, he had incredible insight.

How do I use that? It helps my expansion of awareness. Like my theology. The way I like to look at theology is God is infinite. There's always more to know. I don't care if you're a Fundamentalist or Unitarian or Unity Church. Whatever it is, there's always something more to know. It is good to emphasize that because it's so easy to get caught up in our limited ways. We all do that, and the more we get caught up in it, the more diversity we create between ourselves and other people. Look at our conflicts, and politics, and conflicts of religion in the world.

It is a sad road that humanity has gone down and it's unnecessary. This sort of understanding can help ease that. Of course, one has to be able to go down that path, which is a level of spiritual development. They go hand in hand. The more you evolve spiritually, the more open and broader your perspective becomes, and the more tolerant your perspective is. It used to be, if somebody came at me in a Fundamentalist tone, and judge me, it could be very painful. Now, it's much easier to tolerate such thinking because I understand the limitations of it. I may try to share something with a person if there's any receptivity. It certainly affects my homilies (preaching) because this is who I am.

KLING: I'm interested in your journey to the priesthood. Can you talk about your experience within the Liberal Catholic Church and then what compelled you to ultimately pursue studies within the Ascension Alliance?

EDDY: Let's go back to when I read Krishnamurti. My parents were Methodists and when I was eight years old, I told my Sunday school teacher, "You don't know what you're talking about." I was right, to some extent. And I saw the behavior of the people at my parent's church as hypocritical. I shared that with my mother, which she was open to hear. I never adopted that tradition. When I visit, I go to church with them, and usually I get angry afterwards.

I started learning Transcendental Meditation and after about a year, I intuitively knew that "God was." It wasn't about belief. I just knew it. That was a real shift for me. I still didn't like churches. I came to Fairfield, Iowa in 1986 and got involved with a lot of meditation hours to advance my spiritual progress. There was a lot of progress on the level of spirit, on the level of consciousness, but there was some dissatisfaction in my heart.

I started exploring. I went through a transition, becoming much more social. I got involved in ballroom dancing, and in Toastmasters. I got involved in men's work, which is an organized process that helps you understand what it means to be a man. To have greater interaction, and quality interaction between men.

I had felt separate, and wary, but that changed. A friend of mine said, "You want to come to church with me? So, I went to the Liberal Catholic Church, St. Gabriel's and All Angels Church, in Fairfield, Iowa. I started going regularly. The charm just kept building up over the years.

I pray a lot. There is a teacher here in town who is incredibly astute at teaching people how to pray. How to build a deep connection with the Divine. I was in prayer, and it was December 12th, 2012. While praying, Jesus Christ showed up and said, "Have you ever thought about being a priest?"

It is interesting that he put it that way because he obviously understood. I have had some thoughts about the priesthood, but hadn't taken them too seriously. So, after that I leaned into it and after a few days I realized, "Yeah, that's what I'm supposed to do." I talked to the rector and told him, and he was surprised. He didn't expect this from me and he said, "I'm willing to help you on this path. It will probably take about four years." After a couple of years, it became questionable whether I was going to get the support I needed. There was another church nearby, Spiritus Christi, a parish within the Ascension Alliance. I knew the bishop there for years, but not very well.

I just showed up at Spiritus Christi and Bishop Michael Adams says, "Do you want to serve?" So, one thing led to another, and I started the studies and being independent, an efficiency-oriented doer, I like to get things done. There were plenty of challenges, but I survived the process, and I became a priest and I'm happy. It's very dharmic. I assume you know what dharma means?

KLING: I know of dharma. Can you describe it? I'm interested in your definition of dharma.

EDDY: Dharma means action. It's used in many ways, but basically means proper action. Some people are meant to be carpenters, others are meant to be teachers. While some people are meant to be priests and it became obvious what I should do in my mid-sixties.

KLING: Can you describe the process that you went through with Ascension Alliance?

EDDY: It's a very academic organization. Archbishop Alan Kemp is a professor, and several of the priests and bishops are teachers of the courses. They gave me some credit because of the work that I had done previously.

KLING: Can you talk about your greatest challenge within ministry?

EDDY: One of the things I did during the recession was to become a life coach. That was good for me because it helped me listen more deeply. Toastmasters also helped me too. The most important part of communication is listening, and listening has been an enormous challenge for me.

KLING: What has been your greatest blessing within ministry?

EDDY: Being able to say Mass. Christmas has always been uncomfortable for me because of the superficial reality of various things. The first time I was able to say Mass was on Christmas day. This is what Christmas is about, and this is what really needs doing. Now, I say Mass three times a week.

KLING: Thank you for allowing me to interview you. Do you have any closing thoughts you would like to share?

EDDY: The best thing I can say to people is to be true to yourself. That is an ongoing process because it's always different and deeper levels of who you are. Being true to yourself is very important because if you're not true to yourself, you're going to betray yourself and you're going to betray other people, and that's a waste of time.

"Happiness is strange; it comes when you are not seeking it. When you are not making an effort to be happy, then unexpectedly, mysteriously, happiness is there, born of purity, of a loveliness of being."
- J. Krishnamurti

Concluding Thoughts

Dharma, or proper action, seems like the Greek word orthopraxy, which means right action. Orthopraxy is often invoked when officiating sacraments and is the right way of administering a sacrament. The recent case of Arizona Roman Catholic Priest Rev. Andres Arango comes to mind. He had been performing baptisms using a different form than what was authorized. In performing baptisms, he said, "We baptize you in the name of the Father, and of the Son, and of the Holy Spirit," instead of the prescribed, "I baptize you..." The local bishop stated that the baptisms performed by Father Arango are to be considered invalid, he broke from the authorized form of the sacrament. The interpretation of the Roman Catholic authorities states that it is not the congregation, the "we," that are performing the baptism but Jesus Christ through the priest and therefore it is proper to say, "I baptize you," which really states, "I, acting as a proxy for Jesus Christ, baptize you..."

In various circles within the Independent Sacramental Movement, many people are critical of the decision that the Vatican made on the sacrament of baptism. I have heard virtual shouting to the unpastoral decision by Rome against this priest and the effect that the decision must be having upon all the people who were baptized by Father Arango. As a chaplain, I am in the business of compassion and fully understand the seriousness of this situation; however, orthopraxy needs to mean something, and one responsibility of bishops is to safeguard the efficacy of the sacraments. Therefore, I am also sympathetic to the authorities in Rome who had to make the tough decision to invalidate all the baptisms performed by Father Arango. The two perspectives, I hold in tension because both perspectives have validity.

As a bishop, it is sometimes necessary to make decisions that others do not like. Likewise, as a sacramental Christian and a self-proclaimed theologian I will sometimes make statements that others do not like. Statements such as, "I view all on-line or virtual ordinations as non-sacramental." I have had people accuse me of being conservative or traditional because of my views opposing the use of technological advances in the administration of the sacraments. I do not consider absolution done via a Zoom call as valid. I do not consider virtual Eucharistic celebrations as a valid means of fostering transubstantiation (i.e., the priest on one end and the elements on the other). In our age, these views are considered unpopular by some. I am fine with that!

For Reflection, Contemplation, and Prayer:

- Being able to officiate at the Eucharist is an honor and a privilege of the priesthood. What are your views of the Eucharist? How do you feel when you attend the Eucharist?

- Meditation is often seen as an Eastern religious practice; however, it exists within the Christian tradition. Do you meditate, perhaps upon scripture? Eucharistic adoration is a type of meditation. How do you view meditation and do you incorporate it into your spiritual practices?

- Sometimes we receive a calling later in life, like Father William's call to the priesthood later in his life. Do you feel like you are answering a calling from God, in whatever phase of life you find yourself?

CHAPTER TEN

"SACRAMENTAL JUSTICE"

BISHOP CATHY CHALMERS

"Do nothing out of selfish ambition or vain conceit. Rather, in humility value others above yourselves."
- Philippians 2:3

Bishop Cathy is a bishop in the Ascension Alliance/Community of Ascensionists, and a Board-Certified Chaplain (BCC) under the auspices of the Association of Professional Chaplains (APC/BCCI). She works full time as a professional healthcare chaplain (both hospice and hospital chaplaincy), currently with the inpatient Palliative Care consult service at Providence Regional Medical Center in Everett, Washington, and serves as Director of Chaplaincy for the Ascension Alliance. Bishop Cathy also serves as a member of the Interfaith clergy staff at Unity in Lynnwood, Washington, in liturgical and teaching roles. She holds Master of Divinity degrees from Vanderbilt Divinity School (with Honors) and the Ascension Alliance's seminary, Ascension Theological College, where she now serves as faculty. She holds a Bachelor of Science in Biological Sciences from Florida State University and a Diploma in Professional Music from Berklee College of Music in Boston (summa cum laude). Prior to entering the ministry, Cathy had a lengthy career as a professional scientist and has also worked in the music industry professionally as a performing and recording musician. She has spent time over many years as a volunteer political activist for the LGBTQ community.

KLING: What is your elevator speech? How would you describe the Independent Sacramental Movement to someone who has no idea what it is?

CHALMERS: My elevator speech has morphed over the years as I have morphed over the years, but it's pretty basic, and I think predictable. I talk about Catholic, but not of Rome necessarily, and that's a whole other conversation. You don't have to be Roman Catholic to be Catholic. What makes us Catholic the three S's. Saint, Sacraments, and Succession. I explain those things, and if people don't know what they are I talk about them, especially being sacramental in our orientation. I talk about us recognizing seven sacraments, perhaps rather than the Protestant two in case there's some question about what it means to be Catholic if you're not Roman and not calling yourself Protestant, even in a Lutheran sense. Depends on who's asking.

Then I talk about why I remained Catholic rather than becoming an Episcopal priest or a Lutheran minister or something that's closely related and sacramentally available to me in terms of Holy orders. I think most people who ask don't know that much about Catholicism, I'd say about half and maybe the other half or a little less than half are Roman Catholics who are astonished that we exist. Then I talk about Rome being sort of the "silverback," or as a Father Jayme Mathias likes to say, "the supertanker and we're a little dinghy behind the supertanker." I like his imagery.

KLING: I love what you said about the three S's, saints, sacraments, and succession. I love that. I also like how you brought up the why, and I've often wondered, about that. I have thought about asking this question of the people that I interview which is, "why the Independent Sacramental Movement. Why not the Episcopal Church?"

CHALMERS: That's a valid question, because in some ways it would have been much easier to go that route in terms of legitimacy or support. Financial support, material support, administrative support, and all those things that you would want in congregational ministry. I'm a chaplain, I don't need those things. I think, for me, it's a matter of theological integrity. That is why I am not a Mainline Christian. I am solidly Catholic in terms of mysticism and the saints, the Communion of Saints, and their efficacy as spiritual entities, angels included. My line of the ISM certainly has emphasis on the esoteric and the mystical, and that's why I landed where I landed.

KLING: I think for me, it's about authenticity. I don't want to have to hide who I am. I don't want to have to put on a face or an image to appease some Board of Ordained Ministry that's interviewing me for ordination. I want to be who I am 100%. Authentically and not having to hide any of my theology to be accepted, either to a congregation who's paying my salary or a hierarchy who's got me under the microscope.

CHALMERS: Yeah, there it is. That's very well put and that's exactly where it's at for me as well. I can be exactly who I am on every level of my personhood and be acceptable in the eyes of my peers. It's not even accepted, it's cherished and loved and empowered and enabled to follow the call that feels real to me.

KLING: Yeah. I'm with you on that, and that leads into my next question. Tell me about your experience with the Ascension Alliance. Can you talk about it and go anywhere you want with it?

CHALMERS: Well, if you've read "*The Other Catholics: Remaking America's Largest Religion*" by Julie Byrnes the Ascension Alliance is prominently featured. Sadly, the Ascension Alliance, maybe not sadly, for me it's a mixed bag because we, those of us who were of the original flock of Ascensionist had been members of the Catholic Apostolic Church of Antioch. We split which is common knowledge and published in Julie's book and otherwise well-known. I would imagine in the ISM world, that time was excruciating and heartbreaking. A lot of us are still grieving and hurting over everything that went down in that period. I'm thankful that Archbishop Alan Kemp and his co-founders, the plank holders who created the Community of Ascensionist and the Ascension Alliance, when they did and how they did it because our polity is helpful. If it weren't for Alan being attentive to worldly matters of legitimacy, I wouldn't be able to do the work that I do professionally as a chaplain, because I wouldn't have had anywhere to land in terms of an ecclesiastical endorser for my ministry that would be valid in the eyes of the Association of Professional Chaplains.

My gratitude to Alan for that goes beyond my ability to articulate it in words. I would not be doing ministry right now, if it hadn't been for that, it's been a great blessing to me to be with the Ascension Alliance. I want to talk a little bit about Richard Gundrey, who was the presiding Bishop of the Church of Antioch when I came on in 2003, as a seminarian. I was dormant for a couple of years and then got active in 2005 when I attended convocation for the first time. This was well-described in the book, *The Other Catholics*, because that was the convocation that she first came to and where bishop Patsy Grubbs, Kera Hamilton, and Diana Phipps were consecrated together. That was quite an occasion. A lot of attention gets paid to Herman and Mary Spruit, for good reason, as the parents of the ISM. Herman Adrian Spruit was the original ordainer of women as Catholic priests and bishops and their legacy speaks for itself; however, Archbishop Richard Gundrey has been a huge influence on my own ministry because of his origins in the Episcopal Church, but also in Religious Science and Science of Mind. He is a mystic in his own right, and we have a beautiful connection to classical Catholic mysticism but also a way of thinking about energetics and unity and unified fields, and with my background in science I think that way too sometimes. I have a scientific way of looking at some of this stuff. All those things come together and resonate in a way that's powerful.

I don't consider myself just of Ascension because I joined Ascension near the end of my seminary education and had been with the Church of Antioch up until the time that it fell apart for a while. Richard was an influence on me, both Richard Gundrey and Alan Kemp. Our current presiding Bishop, Archbishop Roberto Foss, has been an influence on me too, and I had the fortune of being in seminary with him. I have learned so much from him and have been well supported spiritually by him. Also, by Archbishop Patsy Grubbs as well, she's been a mentor to me as a woman, a lot of mentorship from her and from other women priests, and bishops, but primarily from Archbishop Patsy. I wouldn't be sitting here talking to you without those people and certainly without Ascension Alliance coming to life as it did, and when it did was lifesaving for me.

KLING: You mentioned the work that Archbishop Alan Kemp has done, I'm assuming that you mean getting the Ascension Alliance listed as a viable ecclesiastical endorsing body. When you went for board certification through the Association of Professional Chaplains, you were able to show that you were ordained by an ecclesiastical organization that had done its homework.

CHALMERS: Yes, that's right, and had IRS accountability, and everything that it took to be an ecclesiastical endorser for chaplaincy.

KLING: Can you explain why that's important? There are a lot of jurisdictions that are composed of just one bishop in his house, and they haven't done any work to become "IRS accountable." There's a big difference between those jurisdictions and those like the Ascension

Alliance who have done the work. Why was that important to you and what would have happened if you were with one of the other jurisdictions that didn't do the work?

CHALMERS: The short answer is I would not be able to work as a professional board-certified credentialed healthcare chaplain. I wouldn't be working right now, at least not in my chosen ministry or my chosen way of expressing my call to ministry. Congregational ministry does appeal to me and I enjoy doing it occasionally, but my calling is to be a healthcare chaplain. In the hospital world you have to be a Board-Certified Chaplain (BCC). It's like a social worker that's a licensed clinical social worker. It's just like a nurse being a registered nurse (RN). It's like a doctor passing their boards. It's required for me to be able to work in hospital chaplaincy.

Some health care agencies or ministries don't require their chaplains to be board certified, and usually that's for budgetary reasons. That happens more so in hospice than in hospitals because of Medicare and the pay structure and things like that. Another conversation still, and as you well know, as a chaplain yourself, you know how things work. So, that's the short answer, I wouldn't be working.

KLING: Thank you. I asked the question, but I knew the answer. I want to be able to talk about this because I think it's important. I think more ISM jurisdictions need to do the work.

CHALMERS: Right, I agree with you. I think it's important, not that I crave legitimacy relative to say Rome or even other large mainstream churches. In a way, that's useful out in the world and while I don't personally crave it, I need it professionally. I also think that others and perhaps the movement itself would greatly benefit from being seen in the eyes of other denominations as being more legitimate. I know that's debatable.

KLING: Well, here's my thought on that, and I don't disagree with anything that you've said. I agree with you. For me, it's not about being more legitimate. I know plenty of clergy within the movement who are not part of jurisdictions that have done the work, and many are good clergy, but I think the reason why more jurisdictions need to do the work is because there are a lot of good clerics out there and they need to be in jurisdictions that will give them opportunities. We can be judged on our own merits. I'm counted as a colleague by ten other chaplains. I work in hospice, and I work with ten other full-time chaplains. I have ten colleagues who respect me as one of their own, and they don't care who I'm ordained with or what jurisdiction or church I'm with, but it's important that it doesn't become a problem.

CHALMERS: Indeed, and I think more to the point that you are alluding to, for those of us who are not chaplains, but doing congregational ministry, I think that that kind of work to be done creates opportunity for people to find us.

KLING: That's right.

CHALMERS: And that's so important to me. Even though I'm not doing congregational ministry very much, I am doing it in a different way as an interfaith clergyperson at a New Thought, or Unity Church. I think that the people that I have ministered to have been so grateful to find liturgy without the dogma, because we crave that liturgy and that ritual and that familiarity and those beautiful words of institution and the beautiful Body and Blood. If we, like myself, have not been welcomed in the Roman Church or have been there when our welcome was revoked, if we say come out as queer or some other thing, that's part of why I got into ministry. I think my initial calling was for what, Julie Byrne calls, "Sacramental Justice." I felt a burning desire to bring the Eucharist to people like myself who were not welcomed in the Roman Church unless we were in the closet.

KLING: Yeah. Thinking about the big box denominations out there the closest to us is the Episcopal Church USA. I know there's a lot of people out there that have a strong affinity for Anglicanism, and what I'm about to say is probably not going to sit well with them, but if you look at how the Anglican Church, how the Church of England was formed, it was because King Henry VIII wanted a divorce, and the church wouldn't give it to him. His daughter still became queen. His misogyny would not allow him to just say, "My daughter is going to succeed me, let us be good Catholics." His ego said, "I'm the head of the church. I'm going to have a son," and biology doesn't work that way. He never had a son and his misogyny lost, and his daughter became queen. She became Queen and the Church of England was now the church of the land, and not the Roman Catholic Church. That's my problem with the Anglicans. I know people will say, "Yeah, but that was a long time ago. That was like almost 500 years ago." I get that, but I still can't get over the fact that they raided all the monasteries. They did some terrible things.

CHALMERS: Yeah. History is not pretty.

KLING: It's like my colleagues at work, I mentioned that I worked with ten other chaplains. They know if they want to push my buttons, all they have to do is mention Martin Luther. I know that there are some wonderful, lovely Lutheran clergy out there, but whenever I hear Martin Luther, I go back to Martin Luther's essay, "On the Jews and their Lies."

CHALMERS: Yeah, absolutely. I could never be a Lutheran for that reason.

KLING: That's exactly why, and people will defend Luther claiming that he was a product of his time. Yeah. He should have stayed Catholic if he was a product of his time, but he chose to rebel against certain things just not other things.

CHALMERS: Yeah, and I struggle with all of that myself and I ironically teach church history with Ascension Alliance in our seminary. I'm grinning that you're talking about all this and I'm right there with you. Even when I think about our history, Old Catholic Church of Utrecht, and I love all that, but I'm not even sure they ordain women. Does the Dutch Old Catholic Church ordain women these days?

KLING: I want to say I think so, but I don't know definitively if they do or not.

CHALMERS: I can't say either, but that's the reason I went to the Church of Antioch. I didn't know I could be a priest because I was Roman Catholic, and then I met somebody in my studies along the way that said, "Yeah, you can be a priest." I was astonished and greatly relieved. I think that's a theme in the Independent Sacramental Movement. That woman can follow their calling. It's a big deal.

KLING: Well, you had mentioned Ascension Theological College. The seminary for the Ascension Alliance. Can you talk about that and your role there?

CHALMERS: I serve in an advisory capacity, as one of the vice-rectors and on the committee that oversees the individual formation committees assigned to each student. The important thing about ATC is that it's not limited to people seeking ordination, either with Ascension Alliance or elsewhere. If you want to study with ATC, you can, anyone can apply. The cost is nominal. You can take courses or get a degree or seek ordination or not, seek membership in Ascension Alliance or not. It's open to all comers, and I think that's a cool thing. I teach Church History, Introduction to Pastoral Care, and Theological Reflection, which is like field education.

I enjoy teaching. I don't do it a lot because we don't have a lot of students and thank goodness because I wouldn't be able to keep up, but it's a real pleasure to have that dialogue, with colleagues regardless of status or rank or ordination status or whatever. Anybody that wants to learn more is okay by me, and let's chat. I love doing that, especially in the Introduction to Pastoral Care course. It has to get personal if you're going to care for other people, and especially in caring for their souls. My own passion is to help people see their own stuff so that they don't bring it into a pastoral encounter. It's what you and I both have experienced in Clinical Pastoral Education. I'm very passionate about the priesthood or for anybody who would do ministry, lay or ordained, is that we do no harm.

KLING: Amen! Thank you for talking about the Ascension Alliance. I know for myself, I'm an associate member of the Ascension Alliance and I value that membership. I love you guys. My next question is what has been your greatest challenge in ministry?

CHALMERS: Several things come to mind, so I'm going to name them and then I'll try to pick one. Right now, it's just COVID. I don't think anyone was prepared for what we're dealing with right now congregationally or in chaplaincy. I can just speak from my own experience at the hospital, that there is such a level of moral distress right now, and such a level of exhaustion, emotionally and physically, and spiritually in this pandemic for healthcare workers, myself included. Even though I am not doing the work of a nurse at the bedside, but supporting them, it is difficult because of the work that they're doing and the intensity of the illness itself and the intensity of dealing with the number of deaths that we've seen and the ravaging of people. Even if they recover, and I use the term recovery broadly because some people seem to have a mild case and some people do get ravaged by it and take months, or years to recover from it. We've had a low survival rate among patients in my hospital that have been ventilated in the ICU. It's been a challenge to stay resilient as a caregiver, to patients, family, and staff.

KLING: The pandemic has really hit us here in Ohio, too. We have a color-coded system that the governor uses to distinguish those counties that are doing good and those counties that are doing not so well during the pandemic. We just hit purple, which is the worst. A couple of weeks ago, I blocked off three hours of time at one of the facilities I visit and had the facility staff make appointments to do one-on-one pastoral counseling. I had three people and I met each one of them for an hour. They're struggling. A lot of these people, the staff, they're struggling. It's hard for them because one of the facilities before the pandemic, had a full census. They had 90 plus patients, and then by April or May, they were down to 40 something. It was all COVID related.

CHALMERS: Yeah. I'm wondering too if you've lost staff out of fear because I know that our local hospices have been struggling to keep chaplains who have moved exclusively to tele-ministry and they're making phone calls and doing video calls with their patients and their family members. The nurses, and the hospice aids, they have to show up, because they're doing personal care.

KLING: That's right. I had a chaplain intern. She was in seminary, and she lasted two weeks. She's said, "I can't do this anymore. You go into facilities; you're going into homes. I can't do that." She was too petrified. So, she dropped out. She said, "I'll just either find another internship or I'll take this class some other time." It's really been rough. I'm with you on that challenge.

CHALMERS: It's been challenging. I think though, that I owe you at least an answer that has to do with my ministry in general and not related to COVID. I want to say this because I feel very passionately about it, even though I'm a member of Ascension Alliance and we have lots of women clergy and it's wonderful. My brothers in ministry are wonderful, and I have no issue with my colleagues in the Ascension Alliance. I do want to say that sexism is still a problem, even though we are ordaining women. If you ask a woman priest of any stripe, she may tell you the same tiny opportunity here to implore my brothers, to be mindful around that. I think most of my colleagues are very wonderful about it. I have had experiences more so as a seminarian. I had several instructors who didn't take me seriously. I had one instructor that I struggled with and who I felt didn't see his female colleagues as equal to him. That was infuriating as a seminarian, and that was a lot of years ago now, but it's still out there. It's much better than it was, I think. Maybe that comes with a purple shirt. I don't know.

KLING: That makes me sad to hear, and angry too. Reflecting on my seminary experience, I guess I was blessed because most of the faculty at my seminary were women. I'm trying to think of the men that I had, and I can count them on one hand. I think I only had three men professors, with the rest being women.

CHALMERS: Well, how cool.

KLING: Yeah. I'm thinking. Most of the faculty that I had were women and they were all awesome. I doubt if any of them are reading this but the women professors in seminary were much better than the men.

CHALMERS: There you go. I hope they do read this.

KLING: The funny thing is one of them who I like, one of the male professors, is a Martin Luther scholar and a former Lutheran before he became Presbyterian and then started teaching. I took his class on the Holocaust, and I did a PowerPoint presentation on Martin Luther's essay, "On the Jews and their Lies." I spoke about how that essay fed the Nazi mindset and how the Nazis did everything that Luther advocated for. The professor was extremely uncomfortable. I did well, and 10 years later, this professor is the director of the Doctor of Ministry program. He takes our entire cohort out to dinner and the first thing he does when he sees me is bring up that PowerPoint presentation from 10 years prior.

CHALMERS: Well done, my brother.

KLING: Back to your original challenge, I'm really saddened by that, and I think some seminaries are probably just caught in that patriarchal mindset and they can't break free.

CHALMERS: Well, my colleague Theodore Feldmann likes to talk about, and I've heard other people say this, that we've got to stop putting new wine into old wineskins. I think a lot of my sister priests out there that I've spoken with have. The reason I'm bringing it up is because I want this voice to be a collective voice and not just my voice because I have this opportunity to speak about it. This is not just me, Cathy, saying, "Hey, I had a bad experience." This is a collective voice from my sister priests who are asking our brothers to be mindful of the old wineskin.

KLING: Yeah. Thank you for sharing that and being vulnerable and talking about it.

CHALMERS: I thank you for making space for that. I appreciate it. Yeah.

KLING: I would love to make more space. I have a hard time getting women to come on the podcast. I've asked women and I get this, "Well, no one wants to hear what I have to say." I'm like, "I want to hear what you have to say."

CHALMERS: My sisters, now it's our turn, we need to step up and be heard.

KLING: Yeah. Because people want to hear your stories. They're really cool and people want to hear them. Let's end on a positive note. What has been your greatest blessing in ministry?

CHALMERS: I kind of circled around it already, but I think it's the final product of the ingredients we've already put into the cauldron in this conversation. I think that is the great blessing of being a priest. There is enough sacramental justice in the world, in the ISM that I do get to be a priest, and I do get to follow my call, and I do get to be a chaplain that's legitimately credentialed because of the efforts of my dear colleague, Alan Kemp, that I do get to administer sacramental justice in seven forms or maybe well, six so far. That is a blessing beyond all measure to consecrate bread and wine and allow anyone who approaches with reverence, which is what Archbishop Richard Gundrey used to say before communion at his mass. Anyone who approaches the altar with reverence may partake. That's the ultimate welcome. It's what Jesus would do. He hung out with sinners and he fed the hungry and as we do to each other; we do to him. So, if you are to follow his command, then justice must be served and justice comes in a lot of flavors. So, in terms of the priesthood, that for me is the greatest blessing which is to be able to offer someone the Body and Blood of Christ as they understand it and let God do the rest.

KLING: Well, thank you so much for talking with me.

CHALMERS: I'm, I'm honored that you asked and I'm happy that we got a chance to get caught up with each other. I very much cherish you as a colleague.

Loving source, we are so grateful for this day, grateful for beautiful friends and colleagues and all of humanity in its foibles, and in its beauty. May we be blessed with discernment each day, and in each moment, may we be blessed with the wisdom to navigate these difficult times with grace, grace that can come only from you. May we be blessed with the humility that is born of self-confidence rather than self-aggrandizement or self-loathing, self-deprecation. Bring us your grace to be humble and strong and wise in these times in each moment and always henceforth, and it is in the Name of all that is Holy that we pray. Amen.
[Prayer by Bishop Cathy Chalmers]

Concluding Thoughts

Bishop Cathy's enthusiasm for the priesthood is contagious, and as I read her words, I think about the solemn privilege it is to stand at an altar and officiate at the holy sacrifice of the mass. It is a true blessing.

It saddens me to hear of the misogyny she has experienced within and outside of the Independent Sacramental Movement. Regarding the ordination of women by the Old Catholic Church in Europe, I discovered that the German Old Catholics started to ordain women in 1996 and then the Austrian, Swiss, and Dutch Old Catholics followed suit. The European Old Catholics were late to the table with the ordination of women. This is sad to me, but at least they eventually saw women as equals and worthy of the sacrament of holy orders.

Something else that causes me to pause and reflect is how she described the schism between the Catholic Apostolic Church of Antioch and the Ascension Alliance. I hold affiliate status with the Ascension Alliance and fully support their mission and vision of ministry. There is a lot of pain there because many within the Ascension Alliance were in the Church of Antioch and have history there with fond memories and the split was and remains painful.

I remember reading Gnosis Magazine in the late 80s and throughout the 1990s and in the back of each issue was an advertisement for Sophia Divinity School. While I have never been affiliated with the Church of Antioch, I have been familiar with it for a long time and it saddens me to see the schisms and splits within the Independent Sacramental Movement, even when they are necessary.

Within the Independent Sacramental Movement change is inevitable, it is a constant that is always occurring. Sometimes micro-denominations, or jurisdictions, morph into something else when leadership changes and has a new vision. I think about The New Order of Glastonbury, founded in 1983 (although one source showed they were formed in 1979) with Bishop Martha Schultz as their presiding bishop for most of the 1980s, 1990s, until her death in 2007. The New Order of Glastonbury changed its name and focus and is now the Open Catholic Church under the leadership of Bishop Nina Paul. They are doing splendid work now with their St. Teresa Open Catholic Seminary, but I miss knowing that the New Order of Glastonbury was out there, existing and being present in the world.

Since I started the podcast, *Sacramental Whine: An Independent Sacramental Movement Podcast*, I saw the creation of the Liberal Catholic Union by Bishop Bob McDonald. Bob McDonald left the LCU and ultimately, the Independent Sacramental Movement. The LCU disbanded and reformed as the Gnostic Catholic Union and after a couple of years imploded with the remaining members going their separate ways.

As the Buddhists proclaim, nothing is permanent. Change is a constant and sometimes change can be painful with a church schism or reorganization. Other times, change can be good, such as when a community recognizes misogynistic tendencies and works to do something about it.

For Reflection, Contemplation, and Prayer:

- Have you experienced discrimination based on your gender or sexual orientation? How did you handle how you were treated?

- What are your thoughts on sacramental justice? Have you ever been denied the Eucharist?

- In the Independent Sacramental Movement there is a lot of change. Jurisdictions split, disband, or morph into something else. What are some of your experiences with the changing nature of the Independent Sacramental Movement?

CHAPTER ELEVEN

— • —

"CHURCH PLANTING 101"

DEACON TAYLOR TRACY

"Pay careful attention to yourselves and to all the flock, in which the Holy Spirit has made you overseers, to care for the church of God, which he obtained with his own blood."
- Acts of the Apostles 20:28

He is a deacon within the Progressive Catholic Church and, after years of formation with many unexpected and exciting turns, he is slated to be ordained to the priesthood on Saturday, February 13, 2021. Deacon Taylor's love for ministry began at an early age when he began to sing in his church choir at the age of ten. By the time he was twelve, he was composing and conducting ensembles in his community, and by thirteen, he was hired as a church music director. Since that time fourteen years later, he has served as the director of music at churches ranging in size from 60 to 600. In addition to music ministry, he served as the director of divine worship and community at St. Paul University Parish, where weekly attendance grew from 600 to 2,000. His time at St. Paul's was a turning point; he got to see what "healthy" ministry really looks like; he led a staff of twelve and learned far more from them than they probably did from him. He continued his journey by serving as the executive director of a non-profit which served students in some of Wichita's most impoverished neighborhoods. He then moved to Kansas City with his fiancé, where he served in two United Methodist churches as director of music and youth and as the church administrator in another parish simultaneously.

He is currently on the Board of Directors for the North Kansas City Symphony Orchestra and has previously served with the National

Association of Pastoral Musicians' local chapter. He is also the founding artistic conductor of the sixty-voice chorus, United in Voice, a group composed of nine denominations and counting with an emphasis on celebrating traditional sacred music.

In addition to countless hours of church leadership and formation seminars, Deacon Taylor has studied at Wichita State University in music education, at Newman University in theology and philosophy, The Liturgical Institute, and the Sancta Sophia Academy for Clergy Formation in the Progressive Catholic Church, under the direction and mentorship of Bishops Robert Chung and Dr. Marc Morales Del Castillo.

Deacon Taylor Tracy is the founding pastor and lead planter for Christ the King Church in Kansas City, Missouri, an independent and affirming Catholic community. He is currently completing an 11-month planting process and will launch on Sunday, February 14, 2021, the day after his planned ordination to the priesthood.

His primary vocational interests include; church planting, parish ministry, church health, and evangelism.

[Note: On February 13, 2021 Deacon Taylor Tracy was ordained to the Holy Priesthood and Christ the King Church is thriving! He is now affiliated with The Society of Christ the King.]

KLING: What is your elevator speech? How would you describe the Independent Sacramental Movement to somebody who does not know what it is?

TRACY: I like what Bishop William Myers says, and he sums it up in one sentence. And it is, "We are a group comprised of validly ordained Catholic clergy, not under papal jurisdiction, serving the Church."

It seems to be good enough for everybody, and if they are curious and I get follow-up questions, I am more than happy to answer those, but I think that really hits the nail on the head. Most people are not concerned about apostolic succession and things like, but they are curious. I like to emphasize that we are in the Catholic, the universal Catholic church, the One Holy Catholic and Apostolic Church. I think people resonate with that.

KLING: I think many people will be interested in learning about the church planting process you are using in establishing Christ the King Parish. Can you talk about that process?

TRACY: Absolutely. It is worth noting that our church planting process has taken place entirely during a pandemic. Church planting is incredibly difficult and taxing during normal times, let alone during a pandemic, but I have had an absolute blast. It has been amazing to see what God is doing in Kansas and bringing this church community together. I have been excited about that and people have asked me, "If there's one book or leader that I've really based this process on?" I really can't say that there's anyone specific, but Daniel Im, who is a prominent church planting specialist, has a book titled, *"No Silver Bullets: Five Small Shifts That Will Transform Your Ministry."*

There is not one simple book or checklist, and you can plant a healthy church and off you go. I have been fortunate to have spent over half my life in parish ministry. Being able to spend one-on-one time with some truly phenomenal clergy that has helped me form as a clergy person. Myself now, I would pull them in and consider them part of that process.

KLING: If someone is interested in church planting, what is the first thing they should do?

TRACY: Pray. Absolutely, pray. Not everyone is called to church plant, and that's not a bad thing. We are not all called to be doctors, but the first important thing is you need to have experience. Practical experience. You need to go into a parish and serve. That might mean that you take off the collar and you serve in a non-clergy role. On-call, so to speak. You may have to humble yourself and serve under someone else for a while because that experience is invaluable. I have served in churches that have been in various phases of their congregational life cycle. That means that I have served in churches that have discussed closing, the final stages of their life and ministry, which is the beginning of something new. They are shifting to something different, but I've witnessed those things.

I have been the executive director of a nonprofit that I oversaw the end of, as the last executive director. It is unique to be the last, and you take a lot of notes of things. You learn from those things and then you can apply that knowledge.

Get into a church. If you have never served in a church before on staff or as a volunteer, you need to. You cannot just say, "I'm going to plant a church," because if you don't know what a healthy parish looks like, no amount of books or podcasts or anything like that is going to help you. I spent over 12 years in parish ministry before I even considered planting a church. I could not see myself doing what I'm doing now without that experience.

KLING: If the process starts with prayer, what are some things that are involved after that initial prayer is said?

TRACY: Before you even consider where you are going to meet, find people who are onboard with what you are trying to do, and you need to be organized. You need to have a plan and be strategic and intentional.

With Christ the King here in Kansas City, I emphasize that everything we do has to be intentional. We are not just throwing things out; we are not just trying to throw out as many posts out on Facebook as possible and hope that it sticks. Everything that we are doing is intentional and trying to deepen our relationships with our community, but we are focusing local. When you do that, then you establish your core. Your core team is the most important part. Before you even talk about a location because you must be able to cultivate the people, the church. You cannot just put a sign out in front of a building anymore and say, "Hey, I'm having mass at 10 o'clock," and hope you're going to grow a church. It doesn't work that way. That is why mainstream churches across the United States are in decline, because it just does not work. We call it stickiness. You must have stickiness in the church community. You must have a reason for people to come back and that is relationships. That is what it is all about.

People crave being connected. Think about people that are closest to you and be organized and intentional when you come to them. You need to say, "Hey, I feel God is calling me to do this. I think that I'm led to you to help me with this process."

Then at that point, they may say no, or they may say yes, but once you get these people, it's a long process. It takes a lot of work. I spend a lot of time with my core team. At least every week, I spend an hour with them. It is for multiple reasons. Number one, you want to build relationships with them. Number two, you want to encourage them and support them and educate them because you cannot expect them to know everything. The goal is to get them up to a point where they can do 80% of your job, because that's how churches grow.

Adam Hamilton is just down the street from us. He started in the basement of a mortuary here in Leawood, Kansas, which is 500 feet from my front door. They started in the basement of a mortuary and now they have 20,000 people that go through their doors before the pandemic. United Methodist Church of the Resurrection is the largest United Methodist church in the country. He did that in 20 years and that is because he was incredibly intentional about the process, and he made sure he didn't just have a great logo. He didn't just have a fancy website or fancy vestments; I don't even think he wears vestments. He developed his core team, which is so important.

The church planting world differs totally from parish leadership in an established church. You do not have an endowment with $2 million. You don't have an established building that you have to maintain. I think that is a blessing. That is a wonderful thing. I think there is true strength in being a parish plant. During the pandemic, because we are all on the same playing field, it does not matter if you have 20,000 people or if you have 10 people; we are all using the same tools and resources. It is up to us to use them strategically and wisely as possible.

Back to the core team. I am stressing this because is has been a thing that has come up throughout the 11-month process. In the beginning there is a lot of excitement, but folks are not entirely sure what they need to do because they have never planted a church before and that is why you have bi-monthly or bi-weekly meetings where you are meeting so that you are making sure make the entire team is up to par. Ensuring they have the tools and resources that they need.

I have also divided the team up. For example, I have a guy who has two master's degrees in music, obviously he is on the liturgy side of things. I have another person who is a phenomenal graphic designer. She does our communications because that speaks to her spiritually. Those are her gifts, and so she uses them. It is all about cultivating the core team, because if you can do that, and you have a solid core team, then you can do some wonderful things.

The Independent Sacramental Movement or Old Catholic, or however you want to describe yourself, we are already having to explain to people why we exist and what we do. So, we must make sure that everything that we do is polished and the whole word of the day is intention. Be intentional; you cannot just slap something together and call it good. You need to make sure that you have purpose and follow through, and that it is not just thrown out there. Those are things that we have discussed during this 11-month process.

When it comes time to look at spaces, I encourage people to think outside the box. My grandparents were United Methodist Church planters. My grandma's a graphic designer, and my grandpa was an engineer. I can remember them planting a church at an old auto shop. The garage became the sanctuary. This was in the late 1990s. Church buildings are not the end all be all. I encourage church plants to not to use church buildings for a couple of reasons. If there is already an existing church, the community already has that church's identity in their mind. It doesn't matter if you're already there. It could be a beautiful space and it may work, but I can tell you church plants that think outside the box and do things differently do better. Here's an example. We were looking at several beautiful church buildings with existing congregations. I told my core team, it's their house, their rules. It is nice to have a beautiful space, but at the same time, it's their house, their rules, it's their sign out front. They are paying the mortgage. One reason why we didn't use the space is because if they shut down during the pandemic, we will not be allowed to be in the building. I think it is much better to think outside the box and do something different.

Evangelicals do an amazing job of church planting. I encourage you to go and absorb what they have going on. They have tons of church planting podcasts, that are terrific. "Practical Church Planting" is another one that you can listen to and these guys who are real pros at church planting. We can adopt Catholic identity to it, but it's the model that they use, that is important. The most important thing is to talk to people. Vestments and furniture are all terrific, but don't spend your money on them initially. Don't focus on those things right away, because you are going to end up with a beautiful space, and you are going to have two people.

I think we have a wonderful opportunity within our Movement. A new age, so to speak, of Church and what it means to be the Church. I think we are going back to our roots. Churches at first, we did not have massive cathedrals. Where the Church is based on relationships, and you have to be a people person, and you have to know how to talk nice to people. If you want them to follow your lead.

KLING: In the Independent Sacramental Movement, there are a lot of bishops and a lot of egos. It seems like it really takes a servant leader to do church planting and it takes humility.

TRACY: 100%. I would imagine that our movement could have 80% fewer bishops and we would be better off.

KLING: I agree with that!

TRACY: And that's not to be mean, but it is like holy cow, put down the miter and stop doing those things. There's a time and a place for everything. It is part of our tradition. We all love good liturgy, but we offer something that nobody else is offering. That does not mean that you change the liturgy. The liturgy itself is beautiful. But we have to offer something that nobody else is offering.

Speaking of liturgy. Invest in and do as good of a job as possible. At Christ the King, you better believe we are going to be having run-throughs and we are going to be polished. Why? Because of stickiness. Why do people want to come back? They want to come back because there are relationships, but you also have to have a way to engage and connect with people. They say on average, if a visitor comes two times and they don't get connected, they're not going to come back. What are you going to do that is going to set you apart? One thing that I want to do with Christ the King is have visitor cards and we are going to have several charities at the bottom, and we will donate $5 to the charity of their choice. When they come in, they fill out their contact card and they turn it back in. It shows a couple of things. It shows that we are active in our community, this is called cross-pollination. That is what I like to call it. It is because we are supporting other communities. We are supporting other organizations within the community.

I have done a lot of surveys, and a lot of studying on what makes healthy churches tick. People love connections, they love relationships, but they also love community engagement and involvement. If we can show them within the first 10 seconds that we care, that is an amazing thing. That we care about our community and that we have boots on the ground. That we are organized, and that we have an amazing thing here that we are doing. We volunteer in the community as a requirement, and our core team serves in the community. Why? Because that's just who we are. Another beautiful thing about church planting is you don't have to worry about bad habits. When you tell your clergy friends you are planting a church, they will say, "Are you going to get more competition?" Believe me, we have tons. We have tons of fish that we need to go minister to, but I don't want people that are already in pews. I want people that don't have a church home, people who were rejected or who don't feel comfortable. Who don't feel engaged and who are tired. These are the people that I want to target. I don't want someone who is already going to a church. There are a couple of good things about this approach. It is because we are serving people and not that I am trying to be mean to existing church members. That's not it at all, but that's not my focus. I'm not trying to poach people from other churches. I want disciples. We don't have to worry about breaking bad habits, and I'm talking about disciples over consumers. We have a lot of consumerism in the pews.

It's a plague, and we have allowed that to happen, and that is why at Christ the King and with a new church plant, focusing on people who are not in established churches already, is a good practice. To say, "Look this is an important service and is an important aspect of who we are and our identity. We would love to have you as a member, and this is what we are requiring." I'm going to put less of an emphasis on weekly attendance and things like that, but that is emphasized since participation is key, but also giving back. It helps for a couple of reasons.

Number one, we are helping other nonprofits. We do Harvesters a lot, which is working to end hunger in the Kansas City community. It also builds a good reputation between Harvesters and Christ the King. They know us as the people that if they need anything, we will be there. These are the things that people get excited about. They like these things, and you want to reach out and network as much as possible. Find out who the people are in your community that are doing great things, and partner with them. You don't need to reinvent the wheel. You don't need to do all these new things. If God's calling you to do those things, that's terrific. You should do something that nobody else is doing, but as a church plant, you must be focused because if you try to do everything all the time, you are going to fail.

You will burn your people out because they are not paid, they are volunteers. You must be strategic about these kinds of things. I chose to focus on community outreach.

KLING: This is fascinating and good stuff. I have another question, but I want you to tie it in to church planting if you can. What is your take on evangelism and how can the various jurisdictions that make up the Independent Sacramental Movement do a better job of it? The reason I'm interested in you tying this into the church planting process is because you spend a lot of time talking about your core team. How do you develop core team when potentially nobody else in your town has heard of the Independent Sacramental Movement?

TRACY: I think that comes back to being polished. In church planting, go back to number one. You spellcheck, that is an important thing and everything that you do needs to be well thought out. I cannot emphasize enough the value of good graphics because we live in the social media age, and people can see things right away. Go to Canva (www.canva.com), it is wonderful. You can create all kinds of graphics, and they have templates for you to use. It is a terrific thing. You can upload your logo and you can use it. I mentioned that because evangelism, we are already fighting an uphill battle explaining who we are. You can have the best message and you can have the best elevator speech in the world, but if you don't have your social media ground game laid out and polished, it's really going to affect how people perceive you. "They say" church shoppers spend seven minutes on your website, then they will make the decision whether they want to continue reading or not. Most of the time, even if they do like it, they will not continue reading. They are going to check it out and then they are going to move on.

Think of it as this way: I only have seven seconds on a Facebook feed to get someone. I was blessed. One gentleman on our core team was a music director at the oratory down here in Kansas City, Old St. Patrick's for several years. Another one was a sacristan at the Roman Catholic Cathedral. I have these amazing people, but then I also have people that have done nothing with the church. They are so passionate about this process, so do not underestimate them because you don't know what God is calling them to do.

If they ultimately don't meet your "expectations," it is probably a failing on your part. It is a communication issue. It is a formation issue. You must be able to develop people, but then at the end of the day if they decide to stop, and then they decide, "Wow, this isn't anything that I expected," hopefully you have been open enough from the very beginning and developed enough to where you can explain the entire process to these folks so you don't have dropouts, but it may happen. Things happen, people move, people get sick, unfortunately. There are different factors.

All the things in this whole rant goes to if you develop your core team, then you can really do some great evangelization, because these are the people that are going to help carry you through into the community. What you're trying to do, and what Christ is calling you to do; but there is a couple of things here that I want to say on evangelists.

We have several folks that go into established churches and they say, "Oh we, we want to grow." Then you ask them, "When was the last time you invited someone to an event at the church?" And you don't get any conversation. Why is that so hard for people? You spend so much time stressing out about your church not growing, but then, when it comes down to it, you're not asking anyone. You're not talking to people. That's why I love community outreach as a tool for evangelism, because I'm not slamming down the Roman missal on a table. The first time I meet someone and saying, "Check this out," I'm just saying, "Hey, how are you? Let's pack some meals together." That is non-confrontational, and it's not intimidating. It is fun during normal times or even during COVID. When the weather's nice I might follow up and we will go out for a cup of coffee and chat and that is when we can get into the nitty-gritty and I can ask them questions and things like that, but you can't do it alone.

You develop the core team because the goal is to work yourself out of a job. To speak in terms of evangelism, in terms of liturgical formation, we must get people to focus on recruitment. I'm not worrying about picking the music, picking the hymns, I'm not worrying about. Why? Because we spent so much time developing the core team. I can focus on those other things. I'm aware and, of course, I'm there to support and help whenever it is needed, but for us to grow, you cannot do everything yourself. You must be able to communicate. It all starts with building relationships, but that is why you must be intentional. Like I said, the age of putting a sign out in front of the street and saying, "Hey, Mass at 10:00 AM," will not work, especially in our movement. It is not like a Roman Catholic Church or a United Methodist Church. Think about those churches that have had centuries of marketing in the community. People know who they are, even if they have never stepped foot in a building, and they have an idea of what it is like. For us we don't have that luxury.

It's all about relationships. I know I've said this a couple of times, but I can't stress enough the development of your core team taking the time to be intentional. I see folks with their hearts in the right place, and they get excited and then they throw something up and then they get upset because nobody participates. Did you have the ground game? Did you have the follow-through? You cannot create an event on Facebook and expect people to come. You have to talk to people, you have to do all these things, and you have to do the hard work. I do this full time. I was bi-vocational, and I worked as a banker. I was serving two parishes and going through the seminary formation program with the Progressive Catholic Church, and I said, "Something has to change." I have the luxury of being able to do this full time, but you don't have to do it full time. Work smarter, not harder.

KLING: You mentioned your family having a United Methodist background. That got me thinking about John Wesley and the foundation of the Methodist movement here in the United States on or right before the revolutionary war and how Methodism spread like wildfire. To where in the Midwest you can't throw a rock in any direction without hitting a Methodist church. Now, United Methodism is on the decline like everyone else. If you look back, what did Wesley do? He held people accountable. He had them work in small groups, and he was about building relationships and he wasn't afraid.

TRACY: He wasn't afraid to ask them, and he wasn't afraid to ask the big ask, "I need you to take this seriously, and with your whole heart." As opposed to, "I just need you to come to the meeting." It was a total transformation, and you are exactly right. That is another thing too. With our church planting here in Kansas City, we have designed it so that we are going to replicate, and we are going over to Lawrence, and we are in a multiplication mindset. We have a group of people. We have a group of 15 in Wichita that are on our target list. We are going to go in there and we are going to develop a community as soon as Christ the King is up and running. We are multiplying, so that we are going to go into other communities so we can establish more churches. Like I said, intentional so that we can replicate the process. It is a multiplication mindset. That is part of our core DNA, is that evangelism. A lot of cradle Roman Catholics are not exactly sure what that means, but if you have a beautiful message and if you let Jesus do the heavy lifting, you don't have to. You don't have to create the world's most interesting content because it has already been done. Your job is to share the message and to be a humble servant, to go where you are called. You are exactly right about the United Methodists. I think the goal was a church in every county and I think they got close.

KLING: Yeah, I think so too, but I think they lost what they had, and I don't think they operate in that same model anymore.

TRACY: No, and I have a perfect example for you. I think this is the sad part. A lot of churches overbuilt because they thought if we continue building, we will grow. I served in a church that was designed for 2000 members. They had 2000 active members. By the time I got there, they had 125. Think about that, they had a massive education wing and a gymnasium and all these things. Guess what happened the summer of 2014? The air conditioner went out, and it was $600,000 to fix, and insurance would not cover it. The endowments all went to fix the air conditioning system. It was so sad. If you are a church planter, you don't have to worry about selling the building. Plant light, so you can be agile. Our mindset is different, but you're exactly right. It is so easy to switch on autopilot. It is easy to change your mind if you are not careful to where you obsess over things that are distracting and not in the best interest of church growth. Some of that has to do with our formation. Don't think about how many Master of Divinity (M.Div) are out there. I'm going for an M.Div as well, and I think it is wonderful, but for the longest time they didn't teach church planting because it wasn't necessarily. To do church planting or knowing how to move your congregation out of a building. For the longest time, that was not in the conversation.

I am a proponent to reforming the way our seminary programs are operated. They are doing a great job of shifting to reflect the needs of the church today, and it's encouraging for me. I don't like to use the term that the Church Universal is in decline. I really don't like that because the message of Christ is not in decline. It is as powerful and as needed today as ever before. I'm not a doomsday'er. The church is changing, absolutely. I think that is for the best, because we were moving in a dangerous direction where we were becoming so consumed with ourselves and our own little communities and obsessing over our buildings. We lost touch with what it means to be a disciple of Jesus Christ. I'm not saying that there is not goodness and holiness, but I'm saying that I think our resources, our priorities are what it is. Luckily, now we are shifting. We're waking up to things and we're realizing we must be a church on the move. You can't just do it. You can't lock down on the foundation and call that good and say, "Hey, we made it," Pat ourselves on the back. That is not the end all be all. It is being out there in the community. Another thing that I think is important it is being on as many groups and committees as you can within reason. I'm a part of Toastmasters where I get to engage with people that I never would have met before and it's so fun. It's encouraging for me, and then I go in and shop the local groups. We are blessed that Christ the King is in the West Bottoms, which is in the Old Warehouse District in Kansas City, which is filled with "mom and pop" shops. We have a lot of local people.

What do I do every Saturday? I go and I get to meet them and it is a lot of fun and I tell them, "Hey, we're planting right down here. Can we exchange cards? I'd love to find a way that we can partner?" Then, when you have your t-shirt sale come up, you use them. You need flowers for the altar, or for the church space you use local as much as possible. Even in large cities, you have little pocket communities. Go find those pocket communities.

I would love to talk about space usage. We were lucky because we had 6,000 square feet on our floor. We intentionally designed it so that we would live within our means. We have it all grandfathered in, but right now we are only using a certain portion of that, and we are only paying rent on the certain portion. We can break down walls and expand into a larger space. I did not expect that we would launch in the space that we are launching in and that is one of the beautiful things of being quiet and listening and filling yourself with prayer throughout the entire planting process. God will move you and use you in ways that you didn't even think were possible. This is a good thing, because if you think you have it all figured out, you don't. No. Listen to what God is calling you to do. We moved into a neighborhood that differs from anything that we would have expected. We were planning on launching next to the college campus. Now we are in a cool up-and-coming warehouse district.

If you find yourself in a church space, use the space wisely. Many people think, "We'll have a soup supper and people will come and they will start coming to church or we will have a rummage sale, all these different things. You're not going to get anyone from this. You might get one or two if the soup is good. Use the space differently.

A Concert series is huge, I love to do concert series. Here is what I do with ours, as I bring in some great musicians and I say, "Hey, I'll give you 40% of whatever we make." It's a win-win because there is no cap on their compensation. They also have an incentive to mobilize. You are engaging with people, and you are using your space, and that is a great thing. Are you going to get people who are going to join the church? Probably not, but at the same time you are generating buzz and you are getting your name out there. At the end of the day, it's a win because I have had good things happen from that.

KLING: Two final questions. What has been your greatest challenge within ministry? I know planting a church is probably a challenge, but do you have a story of something personal that was a challenge for you?

TRACY: I was serving a church once. I have always had good experiences serving in churches, except for this one church. It was like a bad dating relationship. It was like the people themselves were good, but it was not a good fit. If I moved my music stand and I didn't inform anyone that I was moving my music stand, I'd get an email about it. There were a lot of wonderful people, but bad behavior. As a music director, as a professional, as somebody who's done this for years, if I need to move my music stance, then I need to move my music stand. It reached a point where it was so toxic that I would feel tension in my shoulders when I pulled up to the church. It is hard for me to get riled up and stressed, and I love ministry so much that I even enjoy the difficult parts.

Conflict happens. That is a part of the church. You might as well face it head on, but that was a church that was difficult for me. They are good people, but it was not a good fit. It was a challenge because I'm spending the entire year thinking, "Is it me? Am I doing something wrong?" It wasn't that we didn't try to fix things, but it was like I said, you have a church that has been doing something some way for 200 years, and then you have this young guy who comes in here and he does something different. You can't beat yourself up. Not everything is what God is calling you. That was a challenge for me, but I learned a lot. Which is important.

KLING: What has been your greatest blessing in ministry?

TRACY: Church planting has been my greatest blessing. That gets me up in the morning. That is why I stay up late at night and why I'm excited about it, and I must force myself to go to sleep because that is what I do.

It has been a blessing to humble myself. To submit myself to God and to follow his lead. It has been a blessing to break bad habits in myself. We have all had to break bad habits and realize that we are not in control over everything, and you can't do everything. So, taking stock of what is spiritually feeding our community the most.

KLING: In my work as a hospice chaplain, some of the greatest ministerial challenges have been my greatest blessings. For example, it was at midnight. I wasn't on call, but they called me because they couldn't find anybody to go to a particular nursing home and pray with a patient who had COVID-19. I had to put on a lot of PPE. A face shield, an N95 mask, a gown, gloves, and then go in there and just sit with her and pray for her. She died a few days later.

Knowing that, I brought her some comfort and then calling her power of attorney and letting her know at one o'clock in the morning and listen to her talk about how they couldn't go in and visit. This was a challenge. Some of my greatest blessings have been some of my most challenging cases.

Do you have any closing thoughts or comments? Any last words of wisdom?

TRACY: We are all in this together and we really must support each other.

"Christianity without discipleship is always Christianity without Christ."
- Dietrich Bonhoeffer

Concluding Thoughts

I was not raised within any religious tradition other than a secular version of Christianity that I call "cultural Christianity" because I was raised primarily in Ohio. Cultural Christianity reflects the local cultures religious sensibilities and in my part of Ohio that is primarily Protestant Christianity in a purely secular sense. A general belief in God, an acknowledgement that Jesus is important and a rudimentary knowledge of common myths such as "Adam and Eve," and "Noah and the whale." As a child, we celebrated Christmas, and I always received an Easter basket on Easter, but the resurrection or incarnation of Jesus was not something we discussed at my home growing up. I remember once my parents and I attended a Church of Christ, and at another time we went to a Pentecostal Church. These sojourns into sectarian Christianity were brief. I also remember when Mormon missionaries almost converted my father to Mormonism, but his apathy for religion finally took over and that experience was just a fad. As I grew older, I became envious of those people who were born and raised in highly cultural, religious traditions. Traditions such as Greek Orthodoxy, Orthodox Judaism, Islam, and eventually I would discover various forms of Paganism that reinforced a cultural paradigm.

Identity is important. I mentioned I was raised in Ohio; however, I was born in Japan because my father is a US Navy veteran and in 1970 my father was stationed in Japan. Being born outside of the United States, and not having been raised within any religious tradition, created an identity void for me. My ancestry is a mixture of German, Swedish, and British ancestors, but my cultural identity was "Midwestern Ohioan," which is not a strong identity marker. When I discovered religion in my late teens, I felt ignited, on fire, for something. This fire for God gave me a sense of purpose and it fueled my need for a sense of identity.

In reflecting on new church planting, I see a connection between starting a new church and building a sense of identity. The Independent Sacramental Movement is unique. I have mentioned before that the Movement is a spectrum of characteristics. Some within the Movement identify as Catholic and hold on to a strong sense of Catholic identity even without loyalty to the Papacy. The longer I am in the Movement, the less interested I am in feeling connected to Catholicism – even a Papal free Catholicism. I feel connected to all sacramental based forms of Christianity (Catholicism, Orthodoxy, and Anglicanism) through apostolic succession, but I also feel an urging and a pull from the Holy Spirit to foster something different. To manifest something new, which I call the 4th Way.

For Reflection, Contemplation, and Prayer:

- Relationship building is important in almost every endeavor we try to embark upon, especially new church planting. How do you nurture the relationships that you have built?

- Experience is important in planting a new church. This is another way of saying you need to be a good follower before you can be a good leader. In the Independent Sacramental Movement it is often thought that ordination makes a person a leader, but experience is essential to quality leadership. What has been your experience as a follower, as a core team member, and how does it influence who you are now?

- Good church planting requires good planning and intention. Every decision is intentional and done for a reason. It seems that many people go through life on cruise control and lack intention in their day to day actions. Living more intentionally can help us live a better life. What are some ways we can live intentional lives and become more mindful of the choices and decisions we make?

CHAPTER TWELVE

"INSTITUTION BUILDING"

SUBDEACON TIM OLIVIERI

"For the protection of wisdom is like the protection of money, and the advantage of knowledge is that wisdom preserves the life of him who has it."
- Ecclesiastes 7:12

What follows is a discussion with Reverend Subdeacon Tim Olivieri, where we talk about institution building. [Note: Father Tim was ordained to the diaconate in May of 2021 and to the priesthood in October of 2021. He was formerly with the Community of Saint George which is now the Ancient Apostolic Church of Alexandria].

KLING: Welcome back. Let's starting out by talking about institution building, to establish non-profit status and then evolving into filing for 501c3. Can you talk about this process? You have been instrumental in the Community of Saint George, which is the organization that we are both involved, and we are operating under the auspicious of the Young Rite. Can you start us off by addressing non-profit status?

OLIVIERI: Absolutely. I'm happy to talk about the work that we've done since I joined the Community of Saint George. The first administrative tasks I undertook was to incorporate us. We incorporated in the state of Ohio, and the first thing we needed was to establish a name. There was some discussion about that, because on the one hand we operate in the United States as the Community of Saint George, that is the organization that can be joined. But then we also have the Young Rite name. So, we settled on the Liberal Catholic Church - The Young Rite. That it is a Church, because the Young Rite has a unique and interesting history, it is not immediately apparent to someone that this is a Church.

I know when I first heard of the Young Rite; it sounded like it could be a campus Republican group, and we wanted to make sure that we conveyed it was a Church. The reason we incorporate is that we wanted to be established in a way that we could ensure continuity of the organization. One problem we see, especially in the Independent Sacramental Movement, is jurisdictions come and go. Sometimes, there is a falling out between members, and someone takes control of the Facebook group or the mailing list or the website, and then it all falls apart. What we wanted to do was to establish a permanent legal structure with bylaws and with succession planning so that nothing like that would happen to us. In the event it did, everything is owned by one corporation. The corporation has its officers, and nothing is owned by individuals. It is owned by the church collectively. This allows everyone to have ownership, not a legal ownership, but we all get to share in it. This is opposed to the idea of Bishop Oliver owns everything and he lets us use them. I think it helps establish us as; I don't want to say, a more legitimate church, but it helps us to establish us as a church that is built for long-term growth and development.

KLING: It turns everybody who's involved, who is a member of the Community of Saint George, into a stakeholder.

OLIVIERI: It does. I think it is important to know that whenever you are joining a group like this, any religious group, to know what is going on under the hood. If you give $5 to that church, is it going into one person's pocket or is it going into a corporate structure where there is oversight and accountability? That is how we built things. You don't need to be incorporated to file for nonprofit status, to file for exemption under 501c3. Churches are automatically exempt. Technically, we could have just said, "Okay, we're automatically exempt," and we could carry on, but we opted to file for 501c3 exemption. You can do that as an unincorporated entity; However, then you don't have the same protections as a corporation, in terms of succession planning and things like that, as well as liability protection.

KLING: There have been people who have been very critical of churches incorporating and doing the 501c3 filing because it is in some people's opinion that it gives the government control of your organization. It sounds like what you are saying is it is more about accountability and planning?

OLIVIERI: Yeah, and I can understand why some people might have a philosophical objection to more involvement with the government. For us, it does a few things. I'm not a lawyer, I work in the nonprofit space, and I have worked in the business world for several years, but I'm not a lawyer. You may need a lawyer and you should seek professional tax help and legal help as necessary. For us, I used to be a corporate risk manager, and one thing I look at is something as simple as liability, and an unincorporated entity does not have liability protection. If something happens, then individual bishops might be held responsible. Something like, you have a convocation, and somebody slips on the sidewalk.

It is a minimal intrusion to file for incorporation. We filled out a form. There is a template on the department of every state's Department of State, which typically handles incorporation. We filled out the forms from the Department of State in Ohio. We didn't need to go to Legal Zoom or any kind of service like that. There are detailed instructions. We filled it out. We filed the fee. I think it was $85 or something like that, and a few days later, we got the notice back that we were officially incorporated in the State of Ohio. Getting an employer identification number for tax purposes, basically what the IRS uses to identify corporations instead of a social security number like they use for individuals, that number was free. You get that online; you fill out a brief form and it populates the number within a few seconds. These are things we didn't have to pay for, but allowed us to do things like open up bank accounts and again, have the protection to open up corporate accounts that we can manage our web hosting and other expenses.

For the 501c3, churches are automatically exempt; however, for a lot of things, you need the actual 501c3 exemption letter from the IRS, which you do not get if you claim the automatic exemption. The automatic exemption is you saying, "I don't need to go to the IRS." If pressed, if ever there is a tax dispute, and if you want to become an endorsing organization through the Department of Defense or the Department of Veterans Affairs or the Bureau of Prisons, you need to have the 501c3 exemption. You need to have filed for it and received it to even apply for those statuses. We looked at those as they are services that enable our community to help support our members. A headache right now, and more filing fees, but it can help us with the people we have today, and with the people we will have years from now. We can grow and expand in our ministries without hitting a wall.

Our clergy may want government employment in the future, and we want to help facilitate their goals.

KLING: One of the important reasons for all the work that we have done with the non-profit status and the 501c3 is because we care about our people. An endorsement from the church is necessary for someone to get a job as a chaplain. If we are not incorporated, and we are just clergy working together, it is going to be hard to get that ecclesiastical endorsement recognized. If we have gone through all the processes of getting that non-profit status and the 501c3 filing, getting that endorser status recognized by the government is going to open opportunities for our people. That is what I think is important.

OLIVIERI: I agree, and speaking from a business continuity standpoint, it is a terrible thing and we've seen it happen in the Independent Sacramental Movement, time and time again, where someone decides they are going to leave the Movement or someone passes away, or someone for whatever reason unable to carry on with their duties as bishop and the group they had put together now suddenly falls apart because there is no mechanism in place for continuity. Websites, bank accounts, all these things cannot move on to the next person, and these are things you can do when you are incorporated, and when you have bylaws. You can go to the bank and say, "Here we are, our president is no longer with us, and this has the new president. Let's change the signatories on the account." I think that is important. It is important to the members, like you said, they may need this for work.

Beyond employment, many of us will not be employed in a place where we need to have ecclesiastical endorsement, but it provides us with stability. It provides everyone in the community with the knowledge that the organization will continue. Even if all the people who are in it right now are not here in ten years, and it is a whole new group of people, the organization can still live on and grow beyond us.

We are planting a seed rather than just building a castle.

KLING: After you plant a seed, you watch, and that is what we are doing. We are planting that seed. We planted the seed when the

Young Rite was formed in 2006 and then transplanted over here to the United States. Then in 2018, when the Community of Saint George was formed, the seeds that have been planted are continuing to grow as the Community of Saint George. [Note: and continues to grow with the Ancient Apostolic Church of Alexandria.]

OLIVIERI: I agree, and one thing that is important about planting a seed is that you cannot always control where the tree is going to grow. You have a general idea of what it is going to grow into, but it may take a different course. The branches may twist and wind in ways that you didn't expect, and if you are creating an organization, if you are creating a community through this organization, accept that there may be some twists and turns that you did not expect.

Unfortunately, it happens, not just in the Independent Sacramental Movement. Other religious organizations experience this too. People are not always trying to create a community. Some are trying to create a following and that is a different dynamic, but we want to have a community. We want to have bylaws that grant voting rights. Our process has transparency built into it. We want to create a community and I think we have done a great job.

KLING: Yeah, I think so, too. Since we are talking about institution building, let's talk now about institution building regarding education. I have talked about formation programs and such several times in the past because I believe that formation is essential in building lasting institutions. Let us talk about institution building in ways in which we, that is the Community of Saint George, under the auspicious of the Liberal Catholic Church - the Young Rite are working towards this goal of institution building regarding education and give some other folks out there in the Independent Sacramental Movement world some things to ponder for their own jurisdictions. You have done a lot of research on this topic.

Can you share some things that you discovered in your research?

OLIVIERI: Absolutely. One thing that I would highlight first is that within the Independent Sacramental Movement, it is easy to conflate the words education and formation. One can be a component of the other, but the words are not interchangeable. You see this in many denominations. You can get a Master of divinity at a seminary, and yet you are not ordained because there is a period of formation that may run concurrently to your degree, or it may follow afterwards.

We have talked about friends of ours in the United Methodist and Presbyterian Churches. They graduate with a Master of Divinity but are only one step in a long process that can take years. What follows from that is more formation than education. Their education provides them a foundation for pastoral formation that takes place in an actual church or parish. I want to get that distinction out of the way, because there is an educational component, but there is also the formation of the individual. Our education informs that, but there is more to it than just an educational component. As you have developed our program, we have learning modules for joining our community, for studying for the diaconate, for becoming a priest. This is an educational component, but there is a formation aspect too, because we are writing reflection papers, and we are discussing these papers with a course mentor. We are trying to bring about a change in ourselves, not just by learning things, but by trying to work our mind around what we are doing in this formation process.

We are not just working to get some credits to get a piece of paper, a degree or diploma. We are trying to become something. We are trying to become something else and take on an alternative path. That differs from going to college. With all those differences in mind, it leads us to an interesting place where I started doing some research. So, you studied with us and ideally you will get ordained, but what do we hand you at the end of it?

Do we say, "Well, that's the end of it now, ordination and that's it," this caused me to do some research, which was a massive rabbit hole, and is state specific. I can tell you what the outcome was for the states of Ohio and New York, where you live and where I live, respectively. In the state of Ohio, if you are a Bible College, a generic term that I confirmed with the state, it extends to synonyms of the same. You can have a Talmudic academy or an Islamic school, and not use the term Bible college, but if you have one of these schools and you say that you are only offering religious topics, and you are not offering, academic preparation, but only religious topics then you may award non-degree recognitions of completion is the way they put it. If you go through our course and our course does not purport to offer academic credit, you cannot offer a bachelor's degree, you cannot offer a master's degree, you cannot offer a doctorate unless you are willing to submit everything to the state and apply for recognition. There are a significant number of fees, and eventually you would have to pursue accreditation through an accreditor that is recognized by the US Department of Education. So, for our purposes, if you want to award a diploma or a certificate, or a *licentiate*, which is not an academic degree in the US system, it is a little easier. It is a similar situation in New York, but they are less comfortable with the *licentiate* because though they recognize it is not a degree and it is not a degree that the state of New York recognizes in or claims authority over and its laws and guidelines, they looked at it and said, "But some universities use that". So, not necessarily a no, but there are some additional questions.

What we learned from it is that first, you really need to check with your state and make sure that you are operating legally. Some states have very broad religious exemptions, and you can award any religious degree. As soon as you certify you are a religious institution, Florida, Virginia, Washington, Arkansas, Arizona, and several other states are all like that. If you are a religious institution. You can award doctorates, but for a good number of other states, not so much. Make sure you are following all the rules. This sparked some discussion on our part what we want to award. What is the utility of degrees? Is it good or is it bad to award a degree when we are not an educational institution offering the many services that educational institutions do? It was an interesting process.

KLING: You mentioned S.T.L., Licentiate in Sacred Theology. I did some research, and I found some interesting information online. Let me read some of it. The origin of the term *licentiate*. The term derives from the Latin word *licentia* which means freedom or to allow, which when applied to the phrase, *licentia docendi*, means permission to teach and *licentia ad practicandum*, signifying someone who holds a certificate of competence to practice a profession. In looking at this ecclesiastically, you could have a licentiate in sacred theology, but some of the other research I did was interesting. *Ijazah*, an Islamic term, is a license to teach Islamic doctrine and philosophy and was developed in the Islamic world in the 10th century. *Ijazah* seems to be the originating license to transmit *hadith* or sayings of the prophet. In the later 12th century, it appeared in the Latin west and a papal degree decree by Pope Alexander III. It was regulated by the pope as *licentia docendi*. There is some debate whether the *licentia* has its roots in the *ijazah*. One major issue is medieval Christendom was known for frequently taking knowledge from the Muslim world without attribution, leaving modern historians with eyebrow raising parallels, but sometimes there is no conclusive proof until further evidence is discovered. Nonetheless, the timeline matches up with the Latin translation.

It is possible that the origin of the licentiate in sacred theology, which is very popular within Catholicism, had its origins in the Islamic world. Fascinating stuff.

OLIVIERI: I had not read that far back. My experience, when I was in a Roman Catholic religious order, was that I encountered people who had licentiates in not just sacred theology, but also in Canon law. The J.C.L., or Licentiate in Canon Law, was common in priest circles as well. That is the only *licentiate* I have seen being awarded in the United States in Roman Catholic schools. There might be an S.T.L. floating around somewhere. It isn't a degree in our system, which makes it rare. We have associate's, bachelor's, master's, doctorate, with many types of doctorates. There are other degrees throughout the world that are not in our system. In Russia, for example, there is a qualification at the graduate level called candidate. To my understanding, it is just shy of a doctorate. We don't have it, but it's an actual qualification. You would put "Candidate of Engineering on your resume or CV. They exist outside of the US system.

This presents an interesting opportunity, because aside from the fact that they are not regulated as tightly, I like the idea. The way you are describing it, is that it is a license. It is allowing someone to do "this thing." It ties hand in hand with an ordination well.

KLING: As we are talking about this idea of the licentiate in sacred theology and ecclesiastical degrees, one thing I was thinking about is totally outside of the realm of both academia and any church ecclesiastical ties. That is the U S Navy. You and I are both US Navy veterans.

When I was stationed on the USS Dwight D. Eisenhower, my division officer was a warrant officer, and I was thinking about that as we are talking. I was a Photographer's Mate. They don't exist anymore, but they did back then during the First Gulf War when I served. If you look at the name, it is plural Photographer's Mate. This shows possession. The real photographer was the warrant officer. He was the Photographer, and we were all his Photographer's Mates that worked under his direction.

In looking at that system, you had all these people, Photographer's Mates, working under the leadership of the warrant officer. The warrant's designation is photographer. It is like how the S.T.L. , licentiate in sacred theology works. You have a person who is licensed by the ecclesiastical institution to propagate the faith in an educational setting, a license, if you will, to teach and to bring on the next generation. This is done in a way that is not regulated by accrediting institutions. It is regulated simply by the religious institution itself, and there is something appealing about that. I think it's an interesting parallel.

OLIVIERI: Warrant officers have their own interesting history and when I was in the Navy, I was a storekeeper, which is a supply clerk, which does not currently exist. I served during the invasion of Iraq, the invasion of Iraq that came after your invasion of Iraq. Photographer's Mates were still around before they merged them with journalists. It is an interesting thought, and you are right. In a Pontifical seminary, the minimum qualification to teach future priests is a licentiate in sacred theology. What you are saying is it is in those systems an academic degree, but historically, it functioned like a teaching certificate in a public school system. The qualification was more than a degree. It was not just something that you hung on your wall. It was permission to do something. It is permission to teach. I think there are some interesting parallels there, and it works well within the Independent Sacramental Movement because that is what most jurisdictions are saying. They are saying, "Listen, this is a person we have trained according to our theology, and according to the spiritual practice of our jurisdiction. They have our permission to teach these same things."

One thing I noticed when we get into these discussions about degrees is throughout the Independent Sacramental Movement, people latch onto certain ideas like, "We should all have a Master of Divinity." It is an odd thing because you can have a masters, a Master of Divinity from a Pentecostal seminary, and that is not really going to prepare you the same way as a handful of courses that don't end in a degree from a Catholic seminary. If you are in an Independent Sacramental Movement community, and if you have a Master of Divinity from a Baptist seminary, and you said, "I want to become a Catholic priest," you can't just walk in and they say, "Okay, Master of Divinity, check the box. You're good to go." You are going to need quite a bit of extra coursework, because that Baptist degree likely does not include sacramental theology, at least as understood by the Roman Catholic Church. There are a lot of things that you have not studied.

Sacred theology varies from group to group. You cannot always transfer it, and we have lost that with the idea of the Master of Divinity becoming the catch all degree. There is a lot of theological variation between groups.

Yes. I am pro-S.T.L. within our community. Look at the Ukrainian Orthodox Church in America. For years, their seminary in New Jersey has and is still unaccredited. I think they are pursuing accreditation now, but for decades they awarded a licentiate in sacred theology, which, as far as I'm aware, is the only Orthodox school in the United States that was awarding the S.T.L. They did that instead of awarding master's degrees because they were unaccredited. It did the job. So, it is not unprecedented. Here's an Orthodox Church that did it. As you pointed out, there is the Islamic tradition too. So, we can strike out our own traditions and our own histories. Independent Sacramental Movement jurisdictions develop. Even if someone did not do it exactly that way, our group or another group in the Independent Sacramental Movement can do that. They have that freedom. That is the fun part of independence.

KLING: I think that is part of our advantage over larger denominations. Change is hard for the larger organizations. Change in the United Methodist Church is next to impossible, but for us, we can decide, "Well, that didn't work. So, let's do this. We're going to do this starting now." I think that is helpful.

Recently, I was dialoguing with a fellow from a different jurisdiction, and he was telling me that their formation and preparation for the priesthood comprised reading 12 books and write a paper on each in, and poof you will be a priest. I was thinking about this, and I thought, "No." Then, after reflecting on our program, the entire complete program from start to finish comprises 60 modules. That seems like a lot, but some modules, if I offered them in a traditional seminary setting, would be three modules adding up to create one three credit hour course. I would put our education right up there with my Master of Divinity and say that our program is going to be better suited for doing the work that we are called to do than I was when I finished my masters at an accredited seminary.

OLIVIERI: I think there are a lot of groups that unfortunately have brief programs like that. I think you hit it on the head, and yet, if you were to look at a Catholic seminary, and at a Catholic priest, a Roman Catholic priest, who earned a Master of Divinity, they had full-time formation going on concurrently to their M.Div. A recent M.Div graduate from a Roman Catholic seminary might be in a very different place than a recent graduate from a seminary affiliated with the United Church of Christ or with the United Methodist Church, etc. One of those things where we should embrace opportunities to form and to grow. We need to be okay with not having the same letters as other people.

We have our own tradition. We have our own need as clergy and as people who are growing in a way that is different from a lot of the big box denominations. It is an excellent opportunity for us to take a step back and realize that we do not need the post nominal letters as much as we need learning and the experience to grow. To learn with other people and to grow as a community.

KLING: Do you have any closing comments you'd like to share?

OLIVIERI: Since we started talking about formation and degrees, it is very easy to feel that you are less than other clergy down the street because they have a church and because they have a degree. Within the Independent Sacramental Movement, we need to embrace who we are as individuals. Who we are as jurisdictions, and we need to respect and love ourselves enough to go forth and do the work without feeling insecure about some of these things that are going on around us? There is never any degree that is going to make Rome accept the Holy Orders of your jurisdiction. There is never any degree that is going to guarantee that people are going to come and worship at your church. With prayer, with faith, we can move forward stronger. If we can let go of these worldly notions that hold us back in the Independent Sacramental Movement, we will be stronger.

"Compassionate and Loving God, sometimes we your children feel we are not good enough. Sometimes we reject who we are. Sometimes we are insecure. Help us, O Lord, to embrace who we are and to respect and love ourselves as you love us. Help us to reject worldly notions that hold us back and to become what you have called us to be. Guide us and give us the peace that only you can provide. In the name of the Father, and the Son, and the Holy Spirit we pray. Amen."
[Prayer by Bishop David Oliver Kling]

Concluding Thoughts

Subdeacon Tim's comment about accepting who we are gave me an opportunity for reflection. These words are so important. Let me share a story. I graduated from a United Methodist Seminary back in 2012 and then completed a clinical pastoral education residency in 2013 and then secured a job as a hospice chaplain that I have been at since December of 2013, eight years now as I write this – almost 9 years. Since I went to a United Methodist Seminary, I have a lot of United Methodist friends. Five years ago, a friend of mine announced he was being appointed a district superintendent of a United Methodist Conference. My seminary specialization is in Black Church and African Diaspora Studies, and he thought I would be an excellent pastor at one parish in the district he was going to oversee. He asked me if I would consider serving in his district. I thought about it and talked to my wife about it and we thought it would be a marvelous opportunity.

I would have had to endure the United Methodist Ordination process but that really didn't bother me because I was already ordained so I saw that as a formality. I could still serve as a pastor in the Methodist system while working through that process.

I told my friend that I would welcome the opportunity to serve.

He had to put me in touch with another district superintendent who had to interview me and get me into their system. I spoke to this other district superintendent a few times over the phone. The conference was in another state, so phone was the best means of communication. During the last conversation with him he searched my name on Google and my connection to the Independent Sacramental Movement came up, and the Theosophical and esoteric connections within the Liberal Catholic Church tradition and the Young Rite came up. My friend, who was slated to become a district superintendent, knew my history well and there were no secrets between us. But this superintendent did not know me, nor did he understand the Independent Sacramental Movement, Theosophy, or an esoteric understanding of Christianity (which can be Orthodox).

The last communication I had with this superintendent was a voice mail thanking me for considering their conference but suggesting I look elsewhere. The takeaway from that experience and being able to reflect upon it is accepting who I am. Embrace the quirks and blessings alike within the Independent Sacramental Movement. And love it for what it is, a beautiful thing. A Gift from God.

Don't let anyone tear you down or make you feel less than. A Master of Divinity doesn't make the priest. I had one from a United Methodist seminary. What makes you a good priest, or deacon or bishop is your character, what is inside your heart with what is in your head, but knowledge will not make you a good priest. The demons of the world have all the knowledge the world can offer. What makes you a good priest is your character. Your intentions and your actions will write about your legacy. Formation builds character.

For Reflection, Contemplation, and Prayer:

- What are your views and thoughts on the difference between theological education and spiritual formation? Is it better to have both at the same time or education first and then formation?

- The purpose of formation is to help the would be priest function as a priest in a well rounded manner and developing from a spiritual center. Formation should be life changing, but should authenticity be sacrificed at the altar of formation or should formation and authenticity work together? What are your thoughts on this challenging subject?

- The Independent Sacramental Movement is fluid, and constantly changing. Incorporation and 501c3 status provides some stability to a very fluid Movement. What is your experience with the fluidity of the movement and what do you see as the future of institution building within the Movement?

CHAPTER THIRTEEN

WHAT IS A CHAPLAIN?

CHAPLAIN DAVID OLIVER KLING

"The greatest among you will be your servant."
- Matthew 23:11

A chaplain is a professional who represents a specific faith tradition operating often within a secular environment intending to provide spiritual and emotional support to individuals within the environment's context, such as a healthcare setting, correctional institute, the military, and others.

Good advice for anyone interested in chaplaincy would be to suspend your sectarianism. Institutional settings that have chaplains need their chaplains dedicated to interfaith ministry. Chaplains need to be of service to those within their institutional setting. Suspending your sectarianism does not mean sacrificing who you are as a person of faith. It means being open to diversity and being able to embrace that diversity to be of service to others where you find them. This means being strong in your own religious conviction. Your identity as a chaplain should flow from your theology and that theology should be expansive enough to embrace the needs of others, both within and outside of your tradition. Suspending your sectarianism means your agenda is one of service and compassion; and the person with whom the Chaplain serves sets the agenda.

Here are some examples:

Occasionally, someone will ask me, "What faith are you?" When they asked that question, they are trying to vet me as a chaplain. They want to see, "Do I have the right to be there with them? Or if my faith is compatible with theirs, or they are just anxious?" I usually respond with, "I've been a chaplain for several years." And I often add, "I went to a United Methodist seminary down in Delaware, Ohio." That usually ends it, but sometimes I will add that I took courses at Trinity Lutheran Seminary in Columbus, Ohio and/or the Pontifical College Josephinum, the Catholic seminary near Columbus. That is usually sufficient. Ultimately, they are not really wanting to know what my faith tradition is; instead, they just want to make sure they can trust me. No one has ever said, "You didn't answer my question! What faith background are you?" I never go into a long elevator speech about being a bishop in the Independent Sacramental Movement. Occasionally, I have said, "My denomination is like Greek Orthodox and the Episcopal Church." No one has ever asked me to go into more detail, which is good because my time with them is not about me but is about them and what they are going through at the time of my visit.

I had a patient who was Roman Catholic. I conducted the initial assessment on Good Friday and the next day was Holy Saturday. The family called in and requested a chaplain, they were requesting me, but I wasn't on call. The on-call chaplain was busy doing something else, so they called the chaplain supervisor. He ended up calling me because I only lived five minutes away from the patient. He asked me if I could take care of it. I showed up at the house and I talked to them, and I said, "Do you want me to get a hold of your priest?" I knew the patient was Roman Catholic, but they responded, "No, please don't." They had felt slighted by their parish priest. The patient had lived out-of-state until a couple of months prior to her coming on hospice and when she moved back to be close to family, they did not want their priest because they had issues with how he treated their father when he died. The patient's husband was cremated and because he was cremated, the priest would not allow them to have his funeral service in the church. They had to use a chapel down the basement, and this angered them and even though it happened in the 1990s, they were still angry. After I arrived at the patient's home, they asked me to anoint her, to officiate the sacrament of the sick. I anointed her, and she died later that day. Normally, Roman Catholic patients will ask for a Roman Catholic priest and they will accept no substitute. This family wanted their mom anointed and had no issue with me doing the anointing, and I was happy to honor their request.

Another patient I had was Serbian Orthodox. The social worker came up to me and said, "They want the patient anointed. Can you get someone?" I thought, "Wait a minute, the face sheet claims she is a Christian, but did not specifically she was Catholic and she never mentioned to me she was Catholic." A little confused, I went and spoke with the family, and I discovered that the patient had been Serbian Orthodox, after she was married. When she got divorced, she started going to a Disciples of Christ church. All the children were raised Serbian Orthodox. I asked the eldest son, "Do you want me to call your priest," and they were adamant, "Oh, please don't do that. He'll charge $500 just to walk in the door." I don't know if that's true or not, but that's what they told me. So, I responded to him, "I can, and I would be happy to anoint your mother." And I did, and they felt better. I trust it was helpful for the patient too, sacramentally, I'm sure it was.

I had a patient who was a 96-year-old woman; she was in the hospital and her daughter, and her grandson arrived. The daughter was in her 70s and the grandson was in his 50s. They were about losing it. The patient's chart shows she is Baptist. The family insisted that I anoint her. Baptists do not celebrate the sacrament of the sick, anointing. I asked the family some questions. I discovered that the 96-year-old patient had never been baptized. She must not have been a very good Baptist if she couldn't find the time in 96 years to get baptized. When I found out that someone had not baptized her, I said, "I can anoint her, but I have to baptize her first." I will not anoint someone who is not baptized. I ask the family, "Is this something that she would have wanted," and they responded, "She'd always wanted to be baptized, but she never got around to it." I took them for the word, and I baptized her in the hospital bed. Of course, I did not do full immersion, and they did not question the baptism. They must not have been Baptists either. After the baptism I anointed her, which theologically was unnecessary after a baptism. The anxiety level amongst the family went down, and I moved onto the next patient visit.

Another example, I was on-call and was called out to visit with an African American family, and the patient and his wife were Baptist. His daughter was wearing a hijab, and it was during the month of Ramadan, it was right around nightfall. I noticed she was the only one eating, and she really seemed to enjoy her food, you could tell. She had likely been fasting the whole day. I visited with the patient or her father for about an hour. Towards the end of the visit, I asked if I could pray. They responded, "Of course, please." I put together a prayer in my head, and I said that prayer in such a way that it would be meaningful to the patient and his wife, but also his daughter. After spending an hour with the patient, I got to know him a little. I also wanted the prayer to be meaningful to the daughter, who was obviously a Muslim. Right before I started praying, she walked into the room. After the prayer ended and as I was leaving, the daughter came up to me and said, "That was a lovely prayer, and it was meaningful to me." She told me she was a Muslim. It turned into a very meaningful visit for everyone. I did not end the prayer on a sectarian note that could have alienated the daughter; instead, I said a prayer that would be meaningful to everyone. These are some examples of what I mean by suspending one's sectarianism. You must be of service to everyone. Sometimes it is difficult. Sometimes I have had patients who were aggressively atheist, but I still must provide care for them. I do not try to convert them. I do not try to change their views. I must be with them where they are because they set the agenda.

Does being a Chaplain mean I'll have to do things I don't want to do? If you have no tolerance for the spiritual beliefs of others, then you might be out of your comfort zone as a Chaplain; however, being a Chaplain doesn't mean being someone you are not. If someone asks you for something you do not feel comfortable doing, decline in such a way that protects their dignity and your own. For example, if you're a Muslim or a Unitarian Universalist and a hospital Chaplain and a Christian patient asks for communion you don't have to hold Mass in their room, but you could politely refer the request to another Chaplain or someone in the community. It is how you handle the request that is important. A Chaplain should be able to recognize what is going on inside them emotionally and spiritually and act professionally.

Here are some examples:

When I was in my chaplain residency, we worked different shifts to experience what it is like during different times within the hospital. I was working the evening shift. The other chaplain I worked with was a staff chaplain, and he had been there for many years, and was a Quaker. There was a request from a United Methodist patient at the hospital for communion. The staff chaplain came to me and said, "You went to a Methodist seminary. I need you to go handle this request." I was common for chaplain residents to get the visits the staff chaplains did not want to handle. Off to visit with the United Methodist patient, I went. I arrived at the patient's room, and I spoke with her. The woman said, "I haven't had communion in a long time, and I really feel the need to go to Communion. Can you help me with that?" I said to her, "I can get ahold of your pastor, and he or she can come in and handle that for you." Her response was, "Can you please not do that? Can you do it?" I thought about the request, and I said, "Sure, I can do it." I went and got a United Methodist hymnal that we had in our Clinical Pastoral Education library, went back to her room after having stopped by a few places to get the elements to say mass in her hospital room. I used her tray table as a makeshift altar. I did not use the full liturgy; I use a truncated version. I said mass in her in her room, and she received communion. Later that week, my CPE supervisor asked me why I did it. I said to him, "It felt right, and I wanted to do it." His response was, "Okay, just making sure." The Quaker chaplain turned this over to me because Quakers do not do communion. In my tradition, being an Independent Catholic, I do communion; however, I did it in such a way that was familiar and meaningful to her. I had to change how I would normally do things because I am High Church. The setting, in her hospital room, certainly was not highly liturgical, but it was meaningful. It was within a range of my comfort zone that I fine with doing it, but it was not in the comfort zone of the Quaker chaplain.

Another example, I used to do a communion service and worship service at a nursing home. We did not always have communion, but sometimes I would celebrate mass and we would have communion. On every occasion, I would preach, and we would sing hymns. The nursing home residents always wanted me to sing "Old Rugged Cross." Honestly, before I started doing the service there, I had never heard the hymn. I knew the name of the hymn, but I never actually heard it. I learned to sing this hymn, acappella, and I made it through. I could have declined the request, but it was in my comfort zone, just barely. I did the best I could, and the residents seemed pleased with my efforts.

One drawback of being an early riser is that I usually arrive early to the office. Because I get there early, I am often asked to go do things because there are no other chaplains around. On one such occasion, I was asked to go to a house and try to resolve a conflict. The 97-year-old patient, who had heart disease, had passed away in the home. The patient's son was adamant that he wanted to know the cause of death. The family was angry. They wanted a corner to perform an autopsy. They were not blaming us, the hospice company for her death, because she had only been on hospice service for a couple of days. They wanted to get to the root of the matter of what caused their mom to die. I was asked to resolve the issue and was advised that it would be uncomfortable. I followed my training. I figured out who was the main decision maker within the family. The patient's spouse was not. I could tell he was not the one who would decide and the patient's son, while being very emotional, I discovered he was not the decision maker either. I waited for his sister. Finally, she arrived, and what I did was follow the emotions. I listened as their anger turned to sadness. I affirmed their anger. We talked about how they were feeling overwhelmed, and their fears. Now that she was gone, there was a void in their life. What were they going to do? Who would lead their family? By validating their feelings, and talking to them about their feelings, I eventually arrived at a point where I shared with them, "You can request a coroner case, but you're going to have to pay a lot of money for it and that is only if you find a coroner who will do it." The coroner would perform an autopsy on a 97-year-old with heart disease who was on hospice. Her death was not a corner case, so the coroner would charge for an autopsy. After I explained this, I added, "Or we can start laying your mother by getting a funeral director here to get her." The patient had been dead for several hours now. At that point, I pulled out of my pocket some funeral home choices to suggest to them, and they picked one. By this time, they had calmed, after the opportunity to express their emotions and share their feelings. They had started processing their feelings. At first, it was so overwhelming that all they wanted to do was figure out what caused her death and try to make sense out of it. Visits like this one are not something that I normally do, resolving conflict. It was in my comfort zone, and I could resolve the conflict. Sometimes as a chaplain you will be asked to do things that are a out of the norm for you.

The hospice that I work at, we have a policy where we don't want anybody to die alone. Sometimes I will be sent to a nursing home to sit with a patient who has no family or whose family is not there. I just sit vigil until either I'm relieved or the patient passes away, often in the middle of the night. As a chaplain, they will ask you to do a lot of things. Sitting with a dying patient is easy, resolving conflict might be challenging, and singing Old Rugged Cross acappella in front of a group of people might seem impossible; but you learn to stretch your comfort zone as a chaplain.

Chaplaincy brings up all of our personal issues and creates its own anxieties. As a chaplain, you will encounter many people in diverse situations and, in providing care to them, a lot of your own personal issues will rise to the surface. A Chaplain needs to regulate their own anxiety and provide a non-anxious presence to others. Chaplaincy is less about rational knowledge and more about emotional health. It's about entering into someone else's spiritual distress without getting pulled into it and allowing it to take over. It's about being able to function in multiple settings as a leader, being the person who can journey with someone else and helping them in their life journey.

Here are some examples:

When I was in my chaplain residency, I was called to an ICU room. They had a patient who they were taking off all the machines that were keeping her alive and they expected that when she was off of everything that she would quickly pass away. I show up and there was family present. There was the patient's daughter, her husband, and their adult son. The patient's daughter, son-in-law, and grandson. After I arrived, they ignored me. I'm standing at the foot of the bed, three feet from the bed, when the patient's daughter turns to her family and says, "Let's pray for mom." The patient's daughter prays, and I'm thinking, "Okay, why am I here?" Shortly after she ended her prayer, the nurse comes in and removes all the equipment that was keeping the patient alive, and then the nurse leaves. The four of us stood there for about twenty minutes. During that time, it was uncomfortable. Silence can be uncomfortable for a couple of minutes, but twenty minutes seemed like an eternity. While I was standing there, I thought, "They don't need me. Why am I here? This is a waste of my time. It is two o'clock in the morning. I'm tired…" But I weathered through it, I just stood there and said nothing. After twenty minutes, the grandson turns to me, and he has tears in his eyes. He talks and I listen. I shared with him the emotions that I heard him expressing. His sadness, his feeling overwhelmed, and we talked about his grief. Then the patient's daughter turns to me, and I have a similar conversation with her. During the period of awkward silence, I could have said, "If you guys need me, please call for a chaplain, and I can come back." I did not say that I waited until they needed me. I could have waited an hour, and that could have been a waste of my time, maybe. But it took twenty minutes before they realized they could not do this alone. They needed somebody to help them, they needed a chaplain. I was there because I had successfully wrestled with my anxiety in dealing with twenty minutes of awkward silence.

Here's another example was when I was down in West Virginia, during my chaplain residency. I kept telling my mother, "You need to come visit West Virginia. It's a beautiful state, you'll love it. Come visit!" She finally decided she would come and visit. She and my aunt arrived at 6:00 PM. We started watching a movie and we could hear the wind outside was picking up speed. The power went out around 7:00 PM. We go outside to investigate, and we look around. It is a windstorm. We are from Ohio. Going outside and looking around is what we do when the power goes out and we are caught in a windstorm. We are not afraid of a little wind! We are outside looking around. I am talking to the neighbor, and my mother is standing on the porch. Suddenly, a tree falls on my mother. Boom! It was "only" a branch of a tree, but it was the branch of a hundred-year-old tree and was at least a foot and a half thick. It was the size of a tree, and it had fallen on top of my mother. Her pelvis was fractured in two spots. She had a broken arm. She was damaged, but fortunately, there was no head trauma. The experience put her in the ICU, and while she was in the ICU, I went to see her and discovered that she was intubated. Intubation is when a tube goes through the nose to the lungs to help a person breathe. My first thought was the memory of my father, who had been on a ventilator. He had passed away and, in my mind, as soon as they put him on the ventilator, he stopped walking. He lost the ability to ambulate, and my first thought was, "That's going to happen to my mom, and that tube needs taken out because I don't want her to have the same fate as my father." I had to talk myself down mentally because I recognized the two were not the same. Just because my mother was intubated did not mean that she would get too weak to walk and ultimately die in the hospital. She was not my father on a ventilator. His medical condition differed greatly from her condition. I realized that being able to recognize this would help me provide care to others. Sometimes I have been with a physician and a nurse when they tell a family the status of the patient. The status of their loved one and their options such as, "You might want to remove them from the ventilator, but they probably won't make it. It's the only thing keeping him alive." Often, there is that one person in the room that says, "Don't kill my dad!" My own experiences and anxieties can help inform my spiritual care. Recognizing the emotions that get stirred up is important in providing spiritual care to others.

Here is another example of what I'm talking about when dealing with anxieties and your own personal issues. When I was a chaplain resident, I used to talk about how easy it was for me to build rapport with a veteran, because I am a veteran. I was in the Persian Gulf War and the United States Navy. Whenever I encountered a veteran patient, it was so easy to develop a good relationship with them, because we would start talking about our military experience, and we would just go back and forth like we were playing tennis. The patient would tell stories, I would tell a story, and we would go back and forth, and we would become buddies. When I shared this with some of the chaplains that I worked with, one of them said to me, "Well, why don't you see if you can provide pastoral care to a veteran without sharing your own veteran status?" I thought about his words to me, and the next veteran patient that I encountered, I did not mention that I too, was a veteran. Instead, I used my experience as a veteran to inform my pastoral care. The result turned out to be a pleasant visit, because the visit focused on the patient and not on me. It is important to recognize within yourself your quirks. To use those quirks to make you a better chaplain and learn about your own anxieties. Learn how to regulate them to prove good spiritual care.

Do Chaplains reject academic insight and knowledge? Chaplaincy is about the balance between the intellect and the heart. It is not simply an intellectual exercise that one can do simply by reading a book or taking a class. Chaplains will commonly find themselves surrounded by complex emotional states in dealing with people in intense grief, anger, denial, etc. A chaplain needs to handle complex emotional states, and this requires the chaplain to have a degree of emotional intelligence while also possessing a thorough knowledge of their own spiritual tradition. The chaplain will draw from their own emotional experiences to be of service to others and this requires the chaplain to wrestle with their own emotions, so they can understand themselves and identify their own emotional states to help identify the emotional states of others. A chaplain should be able to go deep into the emotional and spiritual pain of another because they have gone deeply into their own emotional and spiritual pain. It is difficult attaining this self-awareness strictly through rational study and discourse.

Here are some examples:

You never say to a family or a patient, "Oh, I know how you feel." It is a best practice to not say you know how someone feels. There was a time when I visited with a family member of a patient who had lewy body dementia, which resulted from his Parkinson's disease. He could not talk anymore, and his wife would say, "He doesn't even know I'm here." My response to her was, "But his soul knows that you're here." Once, I was talking to her, and we were talking for an hour, and I had talked to her several times before this conversation. This time, she was talking about her feelings about her husband. She was mourning him. She was mourning his absence from her life, because even though his heart was still beating, he was not there for her like he used to be and she was filled with grief over how her husband was gone. As she talked, I thought about my father, and his death, and how I felt. I caught myself, because I was thinking, "Oh, I know how you feel." The emotions I heard her expressing were the same emotions I felt when my father died. I caught myself from saying, "Oh, I know how you feel." What I said to her was, "When my father passed away, I felt overwhelmed, I was angry, and I felt powerless. And it was hard for me." After I said that, she looked at me, and her eyes lit up. She said to me, "That's exactly how I feel. You understand, you know how I'm feeling." This is an example of how I used my pain to inform the spiritual care I provided to her. I had been talking to her and communicating with her about her husband for at least a year. So, we had many conversations. This may not have been something that I would have said to someone who I met for the first time, but it was someone that I felt I could share a little about my spiritual pain to help her understand her own spiritual pain. Sometimes you can relay personal experiences to help build connection, and sometimes it is better not to do so. Experience will be your guide. Think back to the example that I gave about veteran status. Sometimes it is helpful to mention that connection and sometimes it is best to hold back that information. A chaplain needs to distinguish when it is appropriate and when it's not.

I had a patient who was gay, and he had declined a chaplain. I found out that a volunteer was going to see him, and I said to the social worker, "Why does he have a volunteer but declined chaplain, that makes little sense?" She responded, "He's an atheist." I asked the social worker, "Can you get me in there?" She said she would try and eventually she succeeded, and the patient agreed to allow me to make visits with the social worker. The first visit with this patient seemed like a test to me. He tested me by frequently dropping the "F bomb." He went into detail about how he was raped by his father, and then by his parish priest, and that was why he was an atheist. He did not shock me. I kept returning each month with the social worker. Eventually, after six months of visiting him, he said, "Can you come back next week? Just you?" So, I did, and I met with him every week, with just him and I. In the time that I spent with him, by the end of our time together, he recognized that he was not an atheist. A lot of people had hurt him, and he took that out on God. He changed his perspective, but it took a long time. When dealing with his powerful emotions, I had to not take anything he said personally. I knew early on he was testing me. I said to him once, "You would not have allowed me to continue visiting you if I had not accepted you, right?" He responded, "You're right. You're okay, but if you had not accepted me, I would not have had you back." I said to him, "What would a God look like that accepts you for who you are, just as I have done?" He responded, "I have always just assumed that God hated me."

You can read about spiritual care in a book, but you really must practice it. Spiritual care is an art. Just like visual art, you can study it, but to truly become adept at any form of artwork, you must practice it, to master your craft! It is hard to learn how to deal with strong emotions with only some book knowledge. This why I firmly state that chaplaincy is about the balance between the intellect and the heart. Chaplaincy with no heart is cold and chaplaincy without intellect, without some study behind it, can make for many mistakes. You need both head and heart.

A Chaplain is someone who reflects theologically and who uses their theological reflection to inform and empower their care for others. This sets chaplains apart from other caring professions. A chaplain is someone who can assess the spiritual pain of another. Being able to perform an assessment requires the ability to engage in theological reflection. A chaplain is self-aware and can deeply reflect upon their own pain to journey within the distress of others.

Here are some examples:

I already mentioned how you use your own self-knowledge to inform your care. I have mentioned that when talking about anxiety, but now I will share some examples of what I'm talking about here with reflecting theologically. I had a patient who declined a chaplain. The social worker kept talking about how cool this patient was, and I said to her, "Can you get me in there?" She responded, "He doesn't believe in God." I responded, "So what, get me in there if you can." The social worker and the nurse talked to the patient and told him, "You might benefit from some male companionship. Your entire care team are women. Having a man to talk to might be beneficial." The patient agreed to see me, understanding that I don't pray or be too religious. During my first visit to his home, he was sitting in his recliner and was watching TV. In the corner, there was a curio cabinet, and inside was a model of the Starship Enterprise from Star Trek. He also had a model of the Millennium Falcon, from Star Wars. My first thought was, "This is my people!" The movie that he was watching was the movie "Dune," from the early 1980s. I said to him, "Is this Dune?" And he responded, "Yeah, I watch it almost every day." He was getting his spirituality from the movie Dune and other popular movies and programs. If you peel back the layers of much of popular culture, there are themes embedded within the stories that people gravitate towards and where they will find spiritual meaning.

When I was in seminary, I took a course in "Theology and Film," and we had to watch films and write papers on them while reflecting theologically. I took this course back in 2010, and some films we watched were "Sling Blade," and "My Big Fat Greek Wedding." We watched the film, wrote a paper, and discussed the film and our papers. Even before the course, I was already of the mindset that pop culture can feed people spiritually. The course was helpful. When I had the patient who watched "Dune" every day I could talk to him about the film, how it was meaningful to him while reflecting theologically on the film myself and using my reflection to inform my spiritual care in a way that was not "preachy." I realized that the spiritual pain that he struggled with was his connection to his family. He did not want to burden them with his cancer diagnosis; therefore, many in his family did not even know he was on hospice. He was a private person. He enjoyed living alone. He had been living alone for a long time, but deep down, he wanted his family to know how he was feeling, but he could not express his feelings to them. He and I talked about that towards the end of his life, and in the end his family was present. They visited him and he had a good death.

Another example, I had a patient who was at the hospital, and I went to see her. It is common for patients to externalize their feelings. It is hard for people to wrestle with their emotions. It is a challenge for people to say, "I'm dying of cancer, and I'm scared." Often what they do is externalize how they are feeling. When I started talking to her, this was several years ago when Barack Obama was president. The patient went on a diatribe about how terrible the president was and talked about her political views for an hour. I listened to her and affirmed her values and viewpoints. When there was an opportunity to switch gears, I took the opportunity, and we started talking about her cancer diagnosis and how she felt about it. We discussed how it was troubling to her, and I actively listened to her talk about the cancer and listening to her externalize her feeling through her long discussion on politics helped gain her trust. So, for an hour, she externalized her feelings, but the actual issue was the cancer that would eventually take her life. After I prayed for her and was leaving the room, she said to me, "Chaplain, more people need to believe like us." I smiled in response. The funny side of the story is that I did not share her politics at all. I disagreed with everything she had to say, but she did not know I found her politics repulsive. My political views did not come through because it was not about me. It was about her, and eventually we could discuss the actual issue. She was scared.

How does a Chaplain do an assessment? The emotional and spiritual state of a person can get caught up in spiritual pain that takes one or more different forms. Spiritual pain often surrounds issues of meaning and purpose, hope and hopelessness, forgiveness, and intimacy and connectedness. A Chaplain will have sufficiently reflected on these areas within their own life to be a compassionate caregiver to another. Theological reflection is the means by which a chaplain navigates through the pain of another, and their own pain, and helps to give this pain a context to be better understood.

Here are some examples:

I had a patient who had ten children and was married, but he told me once that he was not a good father. He also shared that he was not a good husband. He cheated on his wife, and he confessed he was not a good father or husband. On hospice and dying, he had time to reflect on his life and did not like who he was and felt he had run out of time to correct the wrongs in his life. He said to me, "I don't think God can ever forgive me for the things that I have done." Of course, God's mercy and forgiveness is infinite; however, in his mind he wanted to continue to punish himself for what his past behavior. Usually when someone says, "God can never forgive me," it is code for "I cannot forgive myself" and they are stuck in the spiritual pain of forgiveness. This patient knew his grandchildren were stealing his narcotics, but he felt he needed to be in pain. He felt he needed to suffer, to atone for his sins. As a chaplain, your task is to help them navigate through their pain and hope that you can get them to a point where they can forgive themselves.

I had another patient, a woman who was in her 70s. When I met her, she did not have long to live. She died a couple of days after I initially talked to her and prior to coming onto hospice; she was cooking three meals a day for her husband and her fifty-year-old son who still lived at home. She talked about how the previous week she was up on a chair trying to change a light bulb. When I met her, the cancer was finally taking over, and she had to be hospitalized. She was on the verge of dying. Her life had no more meaning for her because she knew she could not provide for her family anymore. Her sense of meaning and purpose came from being of service to her family.

One of my professors in seminary, Dr. Linda Mercadante, used to say, "Bad theology kills." I got to realize "bad theology" when I was visiting with a patient at the hospital during my chaplain residency, he was a cancer patient. I had visited with him several times on the oncology unit. One thing that he used to say to me was how he wished his wife could visit with him, but they were both in their 50s, and she had to work. They lived at least an hour away from the hospital and she could not make the drive during the week. It was on a weekend, and I was called to oncology. The patient requested my presence and when I walked into the room, I saw a woman there and he introduced her as his wife. I thought to myself, "Oh, that's great. She could come visit with him during one of his treatments." Then he said to me, "The doctor come in said I only have two weeks left to live." As we were talking, I presented the dilemma and I said, "What are you going to? What are you going to do in these two weeks?" Immediately, his wife said, "We're going to pray for a miracle." I could see the look on his face change. The last two weeks of his life would be filled with her praying for a miracle, and all he wanted to do was spend time with her and not with his cancer. I presented the dilemma again, and she proclaimed the same response, "We're going to pray for a miracle."

At that point, their local pastor came arrived. I decided not to compete with him. When he came into the room, I shook his hand and I introduced myself and I told them, "You all are in excellent hands." As I was washing my hands, I could hear them tell their pastor the news of what the doctor had said and I overheard their pastor said, "Well, that's what the doctor says, but what does Jesus have to say about this? Let's pray for a miracle." The pastor's words made me sad because I knew that miracle would not happen. I left I but was called back down forty-five minutes later. I assumed their pastor was gone. When I entered the room again, I discovered their pastor was still present. The family said that the doctor came back and recommended hospice. The patient's prognosis was still two weeks, but now the suggestion of hospice reinforced the patient's inevitable death. As we were talking, I brought up the dilemma again and said, "What are you going to do with these two weeks?" Both the patient's wife and the pastor almost simultaneously said, "We're going to pray for a miracle." I knew that there was nothing I could do, and I felt powerless. I could see the patient was heartbroken. His spiritual pain was one of intimacy and connection. All he wanted to do was spend quality time with his family before he died and not spend two weeks focused on his cancer.

One thing chaplains do is assess spiritual pain. I did not have time to work with this patient. I felt powerless and Dr. Linda Mercadante was correct. Bad theology kills. When I pray for patients on hospice, I never pray for them to recover because that seems cruel. They are on hospice for a reason. I pray for peace and harmony. I pray for comfort. I pray for understanding.

A Chaplain needs to be both a generalist and a specialist. A chaplain will often be called upon to do "minister things." An institutional Chaplain could be asked to lead an interfaith worship service, or preach at a memorial, lead others in prayer, or facilitate a support group. A chaplain needs to have some knowledge of interfaith community liturgy, preaching, and education to function confidently in an institutional setting, regardless of their religious tradition. Therefore, chaplains train in seminaries and not in schools of psychology or social work; because a chaplain needs to be a generalist in "ministry skills." A chaplain, regardless of their faith background, will be asked by those with whom they serve, to perform basic "minister stuff," and the professional chaplain will comply with these requests.

Here are some examples:

When I was at the hospital as a chaplain resident, I had to go to the Behavioral Health Unit and conduct an interfaith spiritual discussion group. They decided they did not want to do a worship service because of some the logistics but wanted the chaplains to lead a discussion group that was interfaith. The discussion was intended to accommodate any religion or no religion, but focus on spiritual values and talk about an individual's spirituality. Years later, in my hospice work, I have been asked to conduct Bible studies, lead worship and communion services, and conduct countless funeral and memorial services. When I preach at a funeral, I do not have an "altar call," trying to bring people to Jesus; instead, I focus on acknowledging the grief of those present and create a service that is meaningful without being "preachy."

In my hospice work, I recently had the honor of conducting a marriage ceremony for a patient and his fiancé of sixteen years. She finally agreed to a date, and I married them in their bedroom because the patient could not get out of bed. He died two days later, and his widow said she was sad that he was gone, but that it filled her with joy that they finally got married and she could grant his last wish. As a chaplain, I have baptized patients, brought them communion, anointed the sick and the dying, and perform basic ministry skills daily.

I someone asked me, "Can you preach today?" I could. If I didn't have a Bible with me, I would ask for one and a couple of minutes to prepare, and I can get up and preach a sermon just off the top of my head based on the training that I have received. Chaplains need to do that with confidence. Chaplains are specialists in spiritual care but should also be generalists in basic ministry skills.

Do Christian Chaplains need to embrace concepts foreign to their community? Every profession has its own jargon and culture, and chaplaincy is no exception. Being an institutional chaplain often means functioning in a multi-faith environment. The terms that are commonly used within chaplaincy reflect the general norms of Pastoral Care Departments within the various settings that use chaplains; therefore, it is up to the individual chaplain to translate these norms into their own contextual usage. For example, when you hear the word "preaching" or "preacher" you might translate that into "sermon" and "homily." Likewise, when you hear the term "pastoral care," you might prefer to think of the term "spiritual care" instead. To function professionally in a multi-faith setting, the chaplain needs to be flexible and willing and able to translate practices into their own theological and spiritual context.

Here are some examples:

A chaplain needs to be flexible and willing and able to translate practices into their own theological and spiritual context. When I was in West Virginia, people would refer to a chaplain as pastor. When I heard them call me pastor, I did not respond with, "I'm not a pastor.

I'm a chaplain." I just ran with it because in their mind, the two words were synonymous. Do not get hung up on your own jargon, instead be flexible. I have known chaplains who only do funerals according to the Anglican Book of Common Prayer; however, when I do a funeral, I use a template that I customize for each family. Would it be appropriate to have a requiem mass for every one of my patients that requested a funeral? Probably not, although I could if they requested one. Flexibility is important when working within an interreligious context. As a chaplain, remember that flexibility means adaptability, and a chaplain needs to adapt to their surrounds and function professionally.

A Chaplain needs to be a mirror. A chaplain is a specialist in pastoral and spiritual care. When someone is undergoing intense emotions, it is often necessary for them to process their emotions to achieve emotional balance and harmony. A chaplain is not afraid of grief or emotional distress and will enter another's emotional pain and help them through reflective listening. A chaplain will effectively be a mirror by reflecting back to a person how they are feeling and what is going on within them emotionally and spiritually. A chaplain will mirror back to a person their emotional state in a way that helps them process their feelings. Without effective emotional processing, people get "stuck," and chaplains help people from getting caught in emotional loops that often feel hopeless. When the time is right, the chaplain will help them go deeper into their pain to help them find a way out.

Here are some examples:

I was when I was in my chaplain residency, I was called to the emergency room. The ER nurse said to me, "There's a guy on suicide watch who doesn't want to be here. Can you see what you can do to calm him down?" I walked into the room and his father and stepmother were there so I asked if I could speak with their son alone. They were happy to comply because they seemed frustrated with the patient. I pulled up a chair and introduced myself as a chaplain. He was in his mid-20s, and he looked at me and said, "You and God can go and f*#k yourself." I nodded slightly and responded, "Sounds like you've had a bad day. Tell me about it." He explained how he woke up that morning and his fiancé, who was laying next to him was dead. She had overdosed, but he lived on. During the time I had with him I listened to what he was telling me, and I would paraphrase his words such as, "When you saw she wasn't breathing you must have been filled with dread and overwhelmed with emotion." I did not share any "me too" moments, but focused on his story and pointing out the emotions that were encoded in his words. We talked about his fear of never seeing her son, a boy that he was not the biological father but who he loved as his own. He was angry that he survived, and she died. He was angry that his family did not listen to him, but carted him off to suicide watch at the hospital because he said to his father, "I don't know if I can live without her." After spending an hour and a half with him, he seemed calmer. He was processing his grief. I told the ER nurse I did not think he was suicidal. He was grieving and had had no one sit down and listen to him. Eventually, the people from psych arrived and did an official suicide risk assessment and agreed with my assessment. He was grieving the sudden loss of his fiancé and was flooded with emotions he was trying to simultaneously process.

People can get stuck emotionally and spiritualty when they do not have words to describe how they are feeling. Point out what you notice and if you are wrong, they will correct you, and that is a good thing. If I say to a patient, "You're angry..." and she responds, "I'm not angry, I'm disappointed," it is no reflection of poor spiritual care, you just use this new information to inform the spiritual care you are providing.

As I have mentioned previously, people externalize their emotions and talk about other things like politics, the weather, sports teams, and anything else other than the real issue. Through active listening and mirroring back their story, you can peel back the layers and hopefully discover the real issue and reveal their spiritual pain. Do not look for problems where there are none, but most people have something that they are struggling with and can benefit from spiritual care.

A chaplain is a professional and an integral part of an interdisciplinary team regardless of the setting. That setting could be a hospital, a prison, or a hospice. Prayer is a tool that the chaplain can use to help provide quality spiritual care, but prayer is not the only task of the chaplain. The chaplain knows when it is appropriate to pray and when to listen. Chaplains come from many faith traditions and use their own experiences to inform the care they give to others by being mindful of their own feelings and emotions while continuously reflecting theologically on the spiritual tasks they encounter. A chaplain is guided by compassion and inspired by faith.

Here are some examples:

I work with a nurse who jokingly says that I am the chaplain who does not pray. Of course, I pray for my patients, but when we made visits together, sometimes I did not pray. This was usually during an initial assessment with the nurse, social worker, and me. There was a lot going on and I view prayer as an intimate and personal thing and the nurse needs to do her assessment, and there are often several family members present. I do not see prayer as always essential during a visit. I use my pastoral judgment. This is how I earned the nickname, "The chaplain who does not pray."

Prayer is something in a chaplain's spiritual tool kit. Once, I arrived at an assisted living facility and walked into a patient's suite to conduct an initial assessment. In the living room was a nurse and a nursing assistant from the hospice company where I worked. We exchanged some small talk, and she said, "The patient is in bed. She's alert and will talk to you." I walked into the patient's room, and she greeted me, and we talked for several minutes as I was getting to know her better. At one point she said, "I need to use the bathroom." I fetched the nurse and nursing assistant, who had to help the patient into the bathroom. While they were helping her, I got a phone call. A nurse at another facility asked if I could visit a patient and her family who was actively dying. When the patient was back in bed, I went back into her room and said, "I'm sorry but I have an emergency I need to attend to, I promise I will be back in a couple of hours to finish our visit." She was amicable to that and as I turned to leave, I paused, turned around and said, "Can I pray for you before I go?" She said she would like that, so I prayed for comfort and peace. Then I said my goodbyes to the nurse and nursing assistant in the living room and headed to the other facility. Before I left the parking lot, I received a phone call and the patient who I just prayed for had passed away. She likely took her last breath as I said, "Amen," and turned to leave. I shared this story with the nurse who had called me, the nurse who used to refer to me as the chaplain who did not pray. I told her, "When it comes to prayer, I rely on my pastoral judgment, and the whispering of the Holy Spirit."

I have had several experiences of patients dying seconds after I pray for them. A chaplain has tools in their spiritual care tool kit. Prayer, active listening, and being comfortable with awkward silence are but a few examples of these tools. Chaplains are professionals and need to work well with other professionals as part of an interdisciplinary team, regardless of their setting. In summary, remember these points:

• Chaplains need to be dedicated to interfaith and provide spiritual care to all faiths and those with no faith.

• Chaplains need to be aware of their own triggers and anxieties.

• Chaplaincy is a balance between rational knowledge and knowledge of the heart, or emotional intelligence.

• Chaplains reflect theologically and should understand various types of spiritual pain.

• Chaplains are specialists in spiritual care but also ministry generalists.

• Chaplains should be flexible and able to adapt to unique situations.

• Chaplains should be a mirror through active and reflective listening.

• Chaplains are professionals and work well with others.

Chaplaincy is important to me. Back in 2004 when my father died the hospital did not have a budget that allowed for chaplains. My mother and I had to wrestle with our grief alone. I understand what it is like to suffer through grief alone, and it is my hope to help others navigate loss and grief. I hope you find these words on chaplaincy helpful.

"Christian tradition is ongoing, and the truth it reflects never stands still. Neither do persons or the church, which participate in it."
- Mary Elizabeth Moore

Concluding Thoughts

I find myself in a unique position service as a hospice chaplain and as a chaplain (lieutenant) within the Ohio Naval Militia, an all-volunteer component of the Ohio National Guard. I have been doing end-of-life chaplaincy for almost nine years and it has been a good breath of fresh air being able to do ministry among the living. Lately, I do more "general ministry" functions like preaching and leading worship both within my sojourn with the Ohio Navy but also in my hospice work doing worship services at nursing homes for the residents, mostly who are not on hospice service. When I wrote, chaplains need to be generalists in ministry skills that hold true. I have worked with hospice chaplains who are not ordained with much experience in ministry, often with no seminary education and only with a unit of clinical pastoral education. Their greatest challenge is basic ministry functions, such as preaching or leading worship. Their background is in pastoral care but not the other skills a minister/priest is supposed to have competency.

The general ministry skills are contextual. I will preach a different sermon to the sailors of the Ohio Navy than I would at a nursing home because each community has different needs, and I must be mindful of the needs of each. I have told sailors, "If you want to accept Jesus, then you should go to church the three weeks each month you are not at drill." While preaching to the sailors, I view my role as supporting the mission of the command and not only supporting that mission but also building up morale. Likewise, when I'm preaching at a nursing home, I must consider the context and situation that the residents find themselves. It would fall on deaf ears if I preached about issues pertinent to a young couple just starting a new family, so knowing your audience is important to the preacher. I preach a sermon that addresses the concerns of someone retired living in an assisted living facility with five to ten years of life left.

When all I do in a week is visit patients with Alzheimer's disease, patients who cannot talk and who are often sleeping or unable to communicate then my week is often unfulfilling. I recognize that my prayers for these patients have value, but those visits do little to energize me. Although, I have had great visits with family of Alzheimer's patients. My point? Chaplaincy can be a rewarding calling and a wonderful experience and when, as a chaplain, I am able to utilize all my ministry skills then I become more fulfilled as a chaplain. The work I do as a hospice chaplain and as a volunteer Naval chaplain feeds me in different, yet complimentary, ways and for that opportunity I am truly grateful.

For Reflection, Contemplation, and Prayer:

• Spiritual care has been referred to as "an art." What makes spiritual care an "art form" and not just another skill set?

• Chaplaincy is an unregulated profession, and some people serving as chaplains have not received any training in chaplaincy. What has your experience been with chaplains? Was the experience good or bad?

• Chaplains serve in many different types of settings. The common denominator within chaplaincy is the ability of the chaplain to listen. When talking with others do you find yourself focusing on listening or on the next thing you want to say? How can you become a better listener?

Chapter Fourteen

Introducing The 4th Way

By Bishop David Oliver Kling

"See, I am doing a new thing! Now it springs up; do you not perceive it? I am making a way in the wilderness and streams in the wasteland."
- Isaiah 43:19

What follows is a sermon I preached for a Doctor of Ministry course, Preaching for Change, where I preached on Isaiah 43:19 by introducing the 4th Way. In this Sermon I introduced the concept of the 4th Way and the dissolution of the Community of Saint George and the foundation of the Ancient Apostolic Church of Alexandria. I have been asked by several people, "Have you embraced the work of George Gurdjieff and his philosophical system that he called "The 4th Way?" The short answer is no. Our 4th Way is not the same as the 4th Way promoted by George Gurdjieff; however, the two are no inimical. They could easily be combined.

Fear not, have hope, because we are going to successfully find our way in the wilderness and drink deeply in the desert. This passage, and many others within the Book of Isaiah, stresses deliverance from the clutches of Babylon upon the people of Israel. It represents a contrast between an oppressed people and the oppressive nature of Babylon and the captivity that Babylon forced upon the tribe of Judah.

In our modern times, the use of the term Babylon is attributed to that which causes oppression and holds us back from our true potential. Babylon represents the powers that keep us subjugated and from reaching our true potential. This oppression can be physical, such as someone physically preventing you from success; but it is often the inner-Babylon that is the vilest. The attitude and cultures in place that keep us bound, fettered, and captive.

This setting of deliverance from Babylon is a metaphor for where we, as members of both the Community of Saint George and The Young Rite within the United States, rest existentially with the Independent Sacramental Movement. Yes, we are about to embark on a new thing. We are making a way in the wilderness and finding hydration in arid land. I will hand you the map that will show you the way, a 4th Way.

Ironically, our story goes back to the plight of a foundational figure in our movement, Bishop Dominique Marie Varlet. I mention this is ironic because Bishop Varlet, shortly after his consecration to the episcopacy in 1719 was appointed by the Vatican as Bishop of Babylon, a small diocese centered around the city of Baghdad in what is now Iraq. Varlet never made it to Baghdad, to his diocese of Babylon. Instead, he roamed around Europe, getting into conflicts with Rome, and ultimately ending up in Utrecht in the Netherlands and establishing a schism by consecrating bishops for the infant Old Catholic Church of Utrecht, who themselves wanted to be free from Roman interference.

Bishop Dominique Marie Varlet paved the way for us today. He established a line of apostolic succession that made it possible for many of us in the so-called Independent Sacramental Movement to hold the ancient and apostolic priesthood. But Varlet also passed something else onto us, like how some might view original sin – a taint passed on from bishop to priest, not in the laying on of hands, but in the passing on of a culture of oppression. Varlet passed on the essence of Babylon, an attitude that is oppressive, at times a subtle oppression, but oppression none-the-less.

The phrase, Independent Sacramental Movement was used once, and it stuck. It is the most common phrase to describe the movement that tells the story of who we are as a people of faith, as a spiritual movement; but it represents part of the essence of Babylon. Independent, what does that mean.

For many within the movement, independent represents what Erich Fromm would describe as negative freedom or freedom from something. In this sense Independent Sacramental Movement means free from Roman Catholic influence. Bishop Dominique Marie Varlet became free from Vatican oversight, and he helped the Catholics of Utrecht become free from Roman Catholic oppression and interference too; however, most importantly, and often not stressed enough, is positive freedom, which is having freedom to do something, something else, something different, something new. We, in the Independent Sacramental Movement, have the positive freedom to do a new thing, to make a way in the wilderness, and drink freely in the wasteland. We will find a way, and as I mentioned, this way, for us, is the 4th Way.

To understand the 4th Way, I'll describe Ways 1 through 3.

In the Occidental, or Western World, the 1st way is the Roman Catholic Church and is the main current within our movement. The 1st Way includes Old Catholics, Independent Catholics, Inclusive Catholics, and especially traditionalist Roman Catholics. The 1st Way tends to be a spirituality centered on Good Friday and the cross, and even those who embrace the reforms of the Second Vatican Council still have the vestiges of a Good Friday spirituality that is imbedded in their spiritual DNA, a Good Friday spirituality all year long, even if subtle. Those of the 1st Way must always carry their cross and remain mindful of the ultimate sacrifice of Jesus.

The 2nd Way is the Eastern and Oriental Orthodox Churches, from the Coptic Church to the Russian and Greek Churches. Theirs is a spirituality of Pascha, of the Resurrection. The doctrine of original sin is not realized within the Orthodox world, instead of being born into sin the Orthodox teach that we are born into mortality and therefore suffer the same penalty afforded to Adam and Eve, that of death, but the idea of a tainted soul smudged with sin is absent. Humanity is condemned to die, but that death is resolved through the resurrection of Jesus and an understanding that the most important event, to those of the 2nd Way is the resurrection.

The 3rd Way is the Church of England, the Anglican Communion, and their spiritual descendants within our movement. They directly spring from the 1st Way, going back to their separation from Rome in 1532. Theirs is a spirituality of Good Friday, of the cross, combined with a Protestant Spirit where they, as a distinct movement, have waffled between high church, low church, and latitudinarian sensibilities of the broad church. The Protestant spirit is one of reform, of moving away from tradition and then sliding back towards it. Iconoclasts one day and showering in images the next. One day closing all the monasteries and centuries later embracing new monasticism, spiritual direction, and Lectio Divina for everyone. Seven sacraments or two sacraments? A spirituality of protest, of reform, and certainly with a colorful history.

The 1st, 2nd, and 3rd Way all have aspects of sublime beauty, and like most old and venerable institutions they also have troubling aspects. No institution, religious or otherwise, can succeed without enduring some blemishes. There are aspects and characteristics of these three ways that I personally revere, respect, and honor. While the 4th Way has its own challenges it is the 4th Way that has possession of my heart, of my soul, and of my being.

The 4th Way. Something happened in 1913. Let me share with you a story. Our story.

Let's back up a little. In 1908, former Roman Catholic and Anglican priest, Father Arnold Harris Mathew was consecrated a bishop on April 28, by Old Catholic Archbishop Gerardus Gul, with Bishops Johannes van Thiel, Nicolaus Spit, and Johannes Demmel at the Cathedral of St Gertrude in Utrecht the Netherlands, establishing Mathew as the "Regionary Bishop of the Old Catholic Church in the British Isles."

In December of 1910, Bishop Mathew issued a "Pastoral Letter" indicating he was independent and autonomous from Utrecht. Bishop Mathew established the Old Roman Catholic Church of Great Britain and installed himself as the Metropolitan and Old Catholic Archbishop of London.

Returning to 1913. The year 1913 saw a steady stream of people into Archbishop Arnold Harris Mathew's local congregation and on July 22nd, 1913, James Ingall Wedgwood was ordained to the priesthood.

Wedgwood and the people he brought into the Old Roman Catholic Church of Great Britain were fervent Theosophists. The Theosophical Society was founded in 1875 by Helena Petrovna Blavatsky. Julian Rees describes the Theosophical phenomenon as,

"Theosophy, broadly speaking, advances the view that there is a deeper spiritual reality which can be accessed through intuition, meditation or some other state transcending human consciousness, and that human beings are sparks of the divine trapped in the material world who desire to return to their spiritual home."

The tenants of Theosophy include the establishment of a universal and inclusive brotherhood of humanity that explores all religions and philosophies. The Theosophical Society connection is important because Father James Ingall Wedgwood and several members of Archbishop Mathew's local congregation were avid Theosophists.

- Initially, Mathew seemed sympathetic to the ideals of the Theosophical Society and spoke fondly of Annie Besant, who was president of the Theosophical Society from 1907 – 1933.
- On August 6, 1915 Archbishop Mathew issued another pastoral letter to all of his clergy forbidding them from holding membership in the Theosophical Society.
- James Ingall Wedgwood is consecrated bishop by Bishops Frederick Willoughby, Robert King and Rupert Gauntlett on February 13, 1916.
- The small group of clergy and members in London, practically all theosophists, now came under Bishop Wedgwood's leadership. The "birthday" of the Liberal Catholic Church is usually counted as from this date. Bishop Wedgwood being the first presiding bishop of the fledgling Liberal Catholic Church.

The Liberal Catholic Church, and the tradition that followed it represents a convergence of Catholic, Old Catholic, Anglican, and Theosophical ideas all brought together to create a new path – what I would call the foundation of what would become the 4th Way. The Liberal Catholic Church tradition has struggled with its connection to esoteric practices, such as the connection to Theosophy. Since its foundation there have been numerous schism and groups using the Liberal Catholic moniker. Some groups have faded away, some remain. Here are some of the various micro-denominations within the Liberal Catholic tradition that I am aware:

- The Liberal Catholic Church – London Synod
- The Grail Community
- Life in the Spirit Monastery
- Liberal Catholic Church - Theosophia Synod
- Holy Celtic Church International with the Mar Thoma Liberal Catholic Church
- The Liberal Catholic Church - "Progressive" or "Warnon" Synod
- The Liberal Catholic Church International
- The Young Rite

- The Open Episcopal Church
- The Order of St Thomas
- Mission Episcopate of St Lucy
- United Liberal Catholic Church International
- Ancient Liberal Catholic Church
- United Liberal Catholic Church International
- The Metropolitan Liberal Catholic Church

Some of these micro-denominations hold onto the esoteric and theosophical roots advocated by Bishop Wedgwood, and some do not, whereas some have made divergent ideas optional. What remains is a constant effort to figure out what it means to be a part of the Liberal Catholic tradition; and I believe some of these bodies just like the name, Liberal Catholic.

Our connection to the Liberal Catholic Church tradition is through The Young Rite. On the Feast of Whitsunday, June 4th, 2006, Markus van Alphen, a priest in the Liberal Catholic Church, is consecrated to the episcopacy by Bishop Johannes van Alphen, his father, who had been the 8th Presiding Bishop of the Liberal Catholic Church. It is this date in 2006 that inaugurated the Young Rite.

Markus van Alphen was born June 27th, 1960, in Pretoria, South Africa into a Theosophical and Liberal Catholic family. The Young Rite held onto the esoteric principles of the Liberal Catholic Church and brought a freshness into the movement by ordaining women, and by advocating for a free priesthood where anyone who sought ordination as a priest could enjoy the sacrament of holy orders without extensive formation for the private celebration of the Eucharist within their home.

The free priesthood characteristic of the Young Rite did not translate well into the culture of the United States. People were being ordained simplex priests, with faculties to say mass only in private, and then leaving the Young Rite to pursue public ministry elsewhere. This caused the formation of the Community of Saint George, a Young Rite jurisdiction of clergy celebrants who valued formation and education. This was a theological-work-around the Young Rite's mandate to ordain anyone who asked for it.

The Young Rite has been active in the United States for at least twelve years and I, Bishop David Oliver Kling, have been active as a bishop within the Young Rite since 2014 and a bishop on the governing Council of Three since 2016; however, the Council of Three has not convened to discuss business since 2017 and the three bishops charged with leading the Young Rite have little contact with one another and are separated by thousands of miles. The Young Rite has been very active in the United States, but my European sources have informed me that activity in Europe and outside of the United States has been negligible at best.

"See, we are doing a new thing! Now it springs up; do you not perceive it?" It is time for change. We have listened to the Holy Spirit, and we will travel a new way, a 4th Way.

The oppression of Babylon that I mentioned previously is the spiritual baggage inherent in the Independent Sacramental Movement, especially within those micro-denominations claiming a link to the Liberal Catholic Church tradition. Some of which I have already elaborated upon, but let me continue to break it down:

- Constant emphasis on "freedom from," and the refrain of "Independent Catholic," reinforcing freedom from something.
- The lack of stability of Bishop Dominique Marie Varlet, spiritually passed down onto his spiritual progeny.
- The dysfunctionality, poor leadership, and spiritual blemishes of Archbishop Arnold Harris Mathew, like Varlet, passed down onto his spiritual progeny because the same dysfunctionality can be seen today.
- The lack of formation and education of the clergy, seen and promoted by the irresponsible "vision" of the Young Rite.

So, what is the 4th Way?

The 4th Way is a new vision of the Liberal Catholic Church tradition founded by Bishop James Ingall Wedgwood and further built upon by Bishop Charles Leadbeater. By a new vision I mean to interject a "what if," and that is "what if" Wedgwood and Leadbeater would have founded the Liberal Catholic Church today, and not in 1916. What sort of spiritual currents would converge to create this new church?

The 4th Way is a spirituality of Transfiguration. We do not ignore Jesus on the cross, nor do we ignore the risen Christ; however, our spirituality is a spirituality of right now and one of personal transformation. We seek the transfigured light of Mount Tabor, right here and right now.

The 4th Way is a convergence of sacramental Christianity, holding in trust seven sacraments: baptism, confirmation, Eucharist, confession, marriage, holy orders, and anointing of the sick. It is a convergence of

Theosophical values and ideas that may seem foreign to Christianity but have roots within the tradition, such as reincarnation which also exists within strands of Orthodox Judaism. Of Universal Salvation that was taught in the theological schools of ancient Alexandria. The 4th Way is a convergence of animistic ideas that promote the sacredness of creation and the blessings bestowed upon us by creation itself; rejecting the notion that creation is inherently evil but instead good, and that humanity while condemned to eventually die, is not stained by sin but by sacredness inherent in creation, resulting in a type of Christian animism. The 4th Way is the intersection of sacramental Christianity, Theosophy, Hermeticism, and a Creation affirming spirituality.

The 4th Way holds three concepts in tension: Tradition, Innovation, and Culture.

The 4th Way has a sacred obligation to be stewards of the Liberal Catholic Church tradition. It is essential to maintain a strong connection to our spiritual heritage and as such remain custodians of the rich theological and cultural heritage that is the Liberal Catholic Church Tradition and in general the Christian traditions of the 1st and 2nd Ways that have converged upon the Liberal Catholic Tradition over time.

Our reverence for tradition gives us insights that allow for a greater depth in understanding that tradition considering change through expressions of innovation. We do not dwell in the past. We are rooted in the success of previous generations with an eye to the future. Looking towards the future allows us to tread new paths and explore new territory that expresses our affection for Liberal Catholic tradition and what it means to be a person of faith today.

Likewise, the Independent Sacramental Movement is a rich theological and spiritual phenomenon, but the spirit of Babylon has prevailed over the years creating a culture that is problematic in many ways. Since culture is a type of learned behavior, it is our hope to help shape and mold a functional culture that breaks the oppressive hold that the culture has had upon the community since the time of Archbishop Arnold Harris Mathew.

"We will make a way in the wilderness and the streams in the wasteland will provide us with drink."

As Bishop Markus van Alphen walked away from the Young Rite and retired back in 2016 it is time for the rest of us in the United States to retire from the Young Rite and lay it to rest. Bishop Markus had always stated that the Young Rite will exist for as long as it needs to, and he did not feel it needed to exist forever. May the Young Rite rest in peace. As an institution, it has served its purpose. As we walk away from the Young Rite and all that it was, the Community of Saint George remains, but remains only to be transfigured. The time for change is upon us.

"See, I am doing a new thing! Now it springs up; do you not perceive it? I am making a way in the wilderness and streams in the wasteland."

The Community of Saint George served its purpose as a jurisdiction under the Young Rite umbrella, but the time for change is upon us and the Community of Saint George shall be transformed. Its mission is complete, and its purpose fulfilled.

As we bow our heads in respect to the work of the Community of Saint George and whisper, *requiescat in pace*, we welcome the Ancient Apostolic Church of Alexandria. The time for the 4th Way is here and it shall be represented by those micro-denominations that fully embrace the Liberal Catholic tradition inaugurated by Bishops Wedgwood and Leadbeater and especially by the Ancient Apostolic Church of Alexandria, founded upon the foundation forged by the Community of Saint George.

Let me break down the name, Ancient and Apostolic in honor of several things including, the priesthood started by Jesus Christ in the laying on of hands and the passing of apostolic succession from the original apostles, to succeeding bishops throughout history within the 1st, 2nd, and 3rd Ways. Ancient in embracing a wealth of philosophy from the ancient world, honored as it be honored since Christian theology owes a debt to Greek Philosophy. Apostolic in not only holding onto apostolic succession but also the seven sacraments also instituted by Jesus Christ. An unwavering sacramental character.

Why Alexandria? The Coptic Orthodox Church is the physical heirs of the See of Alexandria, it is not our will to usurp that claim. By Alexandria, we mean a spiritual Alexandria. In the ancient world Alexandria was the center of learning, a true epicenter of spiritual creativity and genius. Cosmopolitan at its core, Alexandria, as a center of learning, was home to a Great Library, and many scholars, theologians, and philosophers studied in the great city.

- Philosophers such as Euclid and Plotinus, studied and lived in the city.
- Hypatia, a Neoplatonist scholar and mathematician made her home in Alexandria.

- The Septuagint, the Greek translation of the Hebrew Bible, was translated and transcribed in Alexandria.
- St. Mark, author of the Gospel of Mark, is believed to have preached in Alexandria.
- Several of the early Christian theologians were either from Alexandria or studied there including, Origen, St. Athanasius the Great, Arius, Gregory of Nazianzus, St. Clement of Alexandria, Saint Pantaenus the Philosopher, and St. Gregory the Miracle-Worker, to name a few.
- Alexandria was home to the Alexandrian School, a system of philosophy, science, and medicine that represented the intellect of Jewish and Hellenic thought in syncretistic harmony over two thousand years ago.
- Alexandria was home to the Catechetical School of Alexandria, a center of theological scholarship in the early church that resulted in the development of much of what is considered Orthodox theology today.

At various times in the history of Alexandria the Christians and Pagan scholars did not get along, but we envision a spiritual Alexandria that embraces theological and philosophical harmony. That can peacefully deconstruct the Christian tradition and reinterpret aspects of the tradition in innovative ways while respecting and honoring the past. Creating a fusion, a syncretism, a convergence of various strands of philosophical and theological thought into a cogent reality that embraces sacramental Christianity, Theosophical ideas as taught by Wedgwood and Leadbeater and contemporary ideas and practices, along with Christian animism, and a reverence for creation and original blessing.

"See, I am doing a new thing! Now it springs up; do you not perceive it? I am making a way in the wilderness and streams in the wasteland."

We honor our past and abandon the oppressive cultural machinations of the worst characteristics of the Independent Sacramental Movement.

We are Free to be and become. We embrace stability and structure; we strive for dynamic leadership, and professional functionality; and we value and honor scholarship, education, and priestly formation.

The Ancient Apostolic Church of Alexandria is the 4th Way, a new and yet, a venerable way of being a Christian in today's world, of being a person of faith in today's work, of being free.

Wise and Loving God, you are the sacred source, the eternal flame burning within us, we honor you this day and always. As we embark on a new thing, help us to make our way in the wilderness, help us to drink deeply from the sacred well of creation, guide us in our journey, and bless us as we honor you, O Wise and Loving God. We pray, in the Name of the Father, and of the Son, and of the Holy Spirit. Mother of us all, Amen.
[Prayer by Bishop David Oliver Kling]

Concluding Thoughts

I have been enrolled in a Doctor of Ministry program since the summer of 2019. Since I started the program, I have been laser focused on what I want to dedicate my research on for my final project. I established my research question early in the program with, "How can we leverage the Community of Saint George for long-term sustainability and viability?" I have tried to focus every course I have taken in the program to help feed this research question. Recently, I took the course "Preaching for Change," and used this course as the impetus for the sermon "Introduction to the 4th Way." My Doctor of Ministry cohort consists of parish pastors who are dealing with ministerial issues very different from my own. In truth, we are building a denominational structure and while we are small, we are working with strategic planning, marketing, and what seems more like business planning than in the trenches ministry. My focus for my final project in the program differs greatly from the ministry I do day-to-day as a hospice chaplain, or during drill weekend as a chaplain with the Ohio Navy. The varied experiences I have within the different ministry settings I serve do help, but also spread me thin.

The sermon, *Introduction to the 4th Way*, is designed as an internal sermon to promote change. I founded The Community of Saint George as part of the Young Rite, a movement that attempted to breathe new life into the Liberal Catholic Church proper and the Liberal Catholic Church tradition. The Liberal Catholic Church was founded in 1916 as a synthesis of Old Catholicism and Theosophical ideas by Bishop James Wedgwood. One characteristic of the Young Rite is the ordination of anyone who requests ordination to the priesthood. That has been problematic for us in the USA because people would seek ordination to offer mass privately but instead joining another micro-denomination shortly after ordination and then becoming a public celebrant within the new jurisdiction with no formal training or formation. The Community of Saint George was founded as a work-around this founding philosophy of the Young Rite. The Community of Saint George being a community, a fraternity of sorts, of clergy celebrants. A celebrant is a cleric within the Young Rite that has formation and training, and the Community of Saint George only accepts celebrants and would-be celebrants; therefore, the work-round the founding philosophy of the Young Rite, to ordain anyone who asks for it, is abrogated by the Community being for celebrants only. In the sermon I addressed how we, as a Community, are not only disassociating from the Young Rite but also transforming the Community of Saint George into a new micro-denomination, the Ancient Apostolic Church of Alexandria.

One of our members, said he was uncomfortable with how I spoke about the Young Rite. Overall, his impression of the sermon was favorable and how he felt inspired; however, he was worried about how some within the Independent Sacramental Movement might perceive us and our treatment of the Young Rite. In the sermon I referred to the founding philosophy of ordaining anyone who asked for it as an irresponsible practice and pointed out that Bishop Markus van Alphen "just walked away," and how we are walking away from the Young Rite but not the Liberal Catholic Church tradition that we have been part of since our inception. In our discussion I asked, "is anything I said in the sermon untrue?" He responded with, "No." I said that I was pleased at his feeling uncomfortable in one sense but ultimately inspired because sermons shouldn't always be "warm and fuzzy," and when promoting transformational change, there should be some discomfort.

In reflecting on my sermon and my project's research question, the best way to promote long-term sustainability and vitality for the Community of Saint George is through transformational change itself. The Community was founded, in part because of an identity crisis. We wanted to separate ourselves from the reputation of "we ordain anyone," or "If you want ordination fast, go to the Young Rite and then figure out where you want to end up." What developed since 2018 is a mixed sense of identity. The Young Rite on one side and the Community of Saint George on the other, it was an eschewed sense of identity because even though we claimed "no free ordination" we still attracted folks who did not want to do the work we required for ordination. To leverage the Community of Saint George for long-term sustainability, we needed to transform the Community and work on those factors of our identity that were impeding building a solid sense of identity not only as a community but as individuals. In working on writing the sermon, and then recording the audio, and finally of putting the video together, I focused on the transformation process. The sermon is persuasive, and the intention is to convince the listener that what we are doing is good and right for us.

The sermon itself has stirred up some fears within me that acknowledging and reflecting upon is important. The Young Rite has always maintained an "esoteric" approach to Christianity, in valuing the mystical parts of the tradition. Likewise, the Theosophical influence upon the Liberal Catholic Tradition is something we want to not only maintain but expand upon. My fear rests in being judged and looked upon suspiciously by those I work with in hospice chaplaincy and within the State of Ohio Defense Force. In the Community of Saint George, we could "kind of" hide our esotericism and focus on an exoteric approach to Christianity. In producing the sermon, and putting our identity into words, I laid all our cards on the table. In articulating "what is the 4th Way," I was making public our unique sense of identity. This is both liberating and scary at the same time because authenticity is something I value, but I also value respect and I know there are quarters within the Independent Sacramental Movement that will reject us completely and others may more fully embrace us. However, a part of me wants to be valued and respected by everyone, but I must acknowledge that there is a cost to authenticity and working on the final sermon has helped me navigate, emotionally, this truth.

For Reflection, Contemplation, and Prayer:

- Authenticity is important, what are ways in which you live your most authentic life?

- There are places within Christianity that has significance to the tradition. Places such as Rome, Antioch, Alexandria, and many others. What are some of the places that have become important to you and why?

- Change can often be essential to growth. What are some examples, in your life, that you have had to change in order to grow?

CHAPTER FIFTEEN

MY FRIEND JOE

BY VERY REVEREND DOCTOR PETER PREBLE

"Perfume and incense bring joy to the heart, and the pleasantness of a friend springs from their heartfelt advice."
- Proverbs 27:9

I am not the type of man that has many friends. It is not easy for me to let people into my life, so I tend to keep most people at arm's length. But every so often, someone special crosses your path, and you just know that this guy, this person is a true friend. For me, that person is Joe.

I first met Joe virtually before that was even a thing. I had only been ordained a few years, and I was finding my progressive theological voice, and I stumbled upon this guy from Scranton who taught me about living the Gospel in everyday life. Joe cares deeply for everyone that he encounters. Joe lives the Gospel of Jesus Christ and his command to love your neighbor without condition. Joe is a strong advocate for everything that he believes in and fights hard for those beliefs.

Although I met Joe about 13 or 14 years ago, it was not until 2018 that we met in person. Joe had helped me find my progressive theological voice, and I had moved on from the denomination that ordained me and was serving in another, more progressive denomination. Joe had been ordained a priest in the Independent Old Catholic Church, one of the churches affiliated with Utrecht in Holland. Old Catholic Priests have valid orders but are not under the authority of Rome. I asked Joe if there was room for an ex-Orthodox priest now serving in the United Church of Christ, and he paved the way for me to join. Joe was standing beside me when I knelt at the altar in the War Memorial Chapel at the Washington National Cathedral as I was welcomed into the fold.

Joe is a dreamer and a planner, and we talked for hours on the phone and on Zoom about the Church and how we were going to make it a place that welcomed everyone regardless of their background or any of the other things that keep people out of Church. We wanted a different Church, not one hung up on buildings and material wealth, but that worked to make lives better for not just a chosen few, but for everyone. Yes, I know it is a lofty dream, but Joe made it sound possible. Joe so desperately wants to spread the love of God to everyone.

Last fall, Joe was elected Auxiliary Bishop of the Diocese of the Eastern United States of the Independent Old Catholic Church. At the same time, I was elevated to Monsignor, and I saw Joe's fingerprints all over that honor that was bestowed on me. I had the honor of being the Master of Ceremonies for his consecration, and what will be one of the greatest joy of my life, I celebrated the Eucharist with him at the High Altar at Washington National Cathedral. That holy ground where so many theological giants have stood and that place from which the message of love rings forth each and every day.

Joe did not know this, but I had decided that my gift to him was to create his Bishop's Staff, his crozier, the symbol of his Episcopal Office that he would carry with him for the rest of his life. I crudely fashioned it out of wood as a reminder to Joe of the wood of the Cross of Jesus the Cross that we must bear each day in ministry. It was not perfect, and there were some rough spots, just like in our spiritual lives, but over time, with use, those places would become smooth. I had the privilege of presenting my gift to him at his consecration.

Joe was there for me when my mother died, and he was there again, two years later when my father died. Joe was one of the first people I told about my wife and me expecting our daughter. And Joe was one of the first I told when she was born this past April. Joe shared my moments of great joy and great sorrow. Joe is my mentor and my confessor.

On Wednesday, February 24, 2021 my friend Joe died, and his death has left a large hole in my heart.

I think I can honestly say that Joe was more than my friend, Joe was my brother, and I loved him. Joe will be missed by so many, but I have to smile thinking about Joe sitting with Jesus, arguing some fine point of theology.

My friend, I never told you how much you mean to me, and I am sorry for that; I hope I brought a little humor into your life. Joe and I used to Facebook Message each other these funny little MEMEs and other things that we might not want to post on Facebook. The day before he died was the feast of the Chair of St. Peter. I took a picture of my chair, the very chair I am sitting in to write these words, and I sent it to him and wished him a happy feast day. He responded with a heart, and that was the last communication I had with my friend.

Joe, you will always be in my heart. Thank you for all that you taught me. Thank you for giving me the courage to preach God's message without apology. I hope I make you proud.

Love you brother!

———————

"There is nothing on this earth more to be prized than true friendship."
- St. Thomas Aquinas

———————

Concluding Thoughts

Like Peter I do not have many close friends. I know a lot of people and have many associates and people who know me and with whom I talk to on a regular basis, but the number of people I call close friends is small. When one of those close friends is gone, it leaves a real void in your life. Your soul hurts.

I did not know Joseph Grieboski well. I had interviewed him for the podcast, *Sacramental Whine: An Independent Sacramental Movement Podcast*, and he and I talked a couple of times and then he died. Since I started the podcast I have had the honor of talking with a lot of people and having them on the podcast as guests. Some people I hear from a lot, and some want to be recurring guests on the podcast and then they move on and I don't hear from them anymore. It would seem that some folks simply wanted to use the podcast as an opportunity and then move onto something else, and this has always saddened me. The podcast and their association with it was just a means to their own ministerial ends. I mention this because people come into your life, and leave it for various reasons. Joe was different.

I have cultivated some solid friendships based upon the work I have done in ministry. My work in hospice has generated great friendships with nurses and other chaplains; my work in the Ohio Military Reserve and the Ohio Naval Militia has garnered me some great friendships; and, hosting a podcast on the Independent Sacramental Movement has helped me cultivate great friendships too. I mentioned that Joe was different. I felt a connection to him and his work and a friendship was starting that was based on reciprocity. We could help each other and enrich each other's lives, but he was taken from us and that too saddens me. I imagine Joe, now part of the Church Triumphant, looking in on us, those of us who counted him as a friend, from time to time and continuing to influence our good works through his prayers and intercessions.

For Reflection, Contemplation, and Prayer:

- What is your theology of friendship? What is a friend and how do you cultivate and nurture your friendships?

- How do you live the Gospel message to love your neighbors?

- Do you have a mentor, a confessor? How does this person enrich your life and how do you enrich theirs?

AFTERWORD

BY BISHOP CATHERINE CHALMERS

Thanks Be to God for this collection of prophets and priests, renegades, and rejects, we who will not be silent. In this third volume of Sacramental Whine: Chronicling the Independent Sacramental Movement, and like its preceding volumes, Bishop David Oliver Kling and his Independent Sacramental kin have spoken truth to power, opened their hearts, told their stories, and woven our his/her/story.

In these podcasts there is a richness and a diversity beyond prior imagining: a diversity of thought, and spirit, and calling, a richness that can only serve to enlighten and empower all those who have heard the whisperings of that Still, Small Voice, and who are called to reach beyond the artificial or edificial bounds and binds of traditions which no longer resonate. This said, we are not merely "Former Romans" (or wannabes) but insightful theological practitioners who transcend being labeled by what we are not; rather, we are reaching for a sacramental truth unbound by institutional and dogmatic shackles, be we woman, or queer, or theologically inclusive, or simply not called to celibacy.

Some of us have already drawn upon not just mainstream Western ideas and liturgies but are cultivating and demonstrating a depth of reverence and respect for the Eastern Churches and the oldest roots of tradition, alongside other ancient traditions such as the Mozarabic, Celtic, Coptic, and more; alongside mystical insights from Judaism, Christianity, and Islam; alongside the esotericism of Leadbeater, Blavatsky, Besant, Steiner, and more; alongside insights and influences from Taoism, Vedanta, Buddhism, Indigenous, Nature based, and syncretic traditions, New Thought, and more. Purists may shudder, but as we recognize and reverence Wisdom in its many iterations aren't we simply being Universal — Catholic — in our celebrations??

Bishop Oliver has curated an amazing collection of voices, including his own — powerful and didactic — and he is a committed and generous steward of the ISM's many human resources, a passionate collector of stories and ideas. His offerings here are informational and thoughtful, and he has a wonderful way of drawing his interlocutors into conversation about this multifaceted gem that we are.

My own hope and vision for this collection of people that we call the Independent Catholics or Independent Sacramental Movement is not just as a harbor for "non-Romans" but is as "deep and wide" as the Love of God described in the old bluegrass hymn.

May it be so and continue to be so. Amen.

Most Reverend Catherine Chalmers, MDiv, DD, BCC
Bishop, The Ascension Alliance, and Community of Ascensionists
Ordinariate of the Divine Presence
Director of Chaplaincy
Vice-Rector, Ascension Theological College

Made in the USA
Monee, IL
17 May 2022

96553294R00125